Rowing Forward
Looking Back

To Dick + Phoebe
Thank you very much
for all your help + insights
over the years.

Best Wishes

Sandy Mayfh

2002

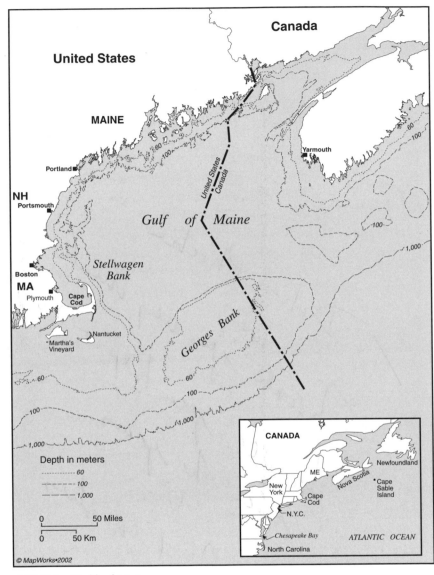

MAP 1 *Gulf of Maine*

Rowing Forward Looking Back

Shellfish and the Tides of Change
At the Elbow of Cape Cod

Sandy Macfarlane

Copyright © 2002   Sandra L. Macfarlane

All rights reserved

First Edition, 2002

ISBN   0-9723278-0-0

Published by the Friends of Pleasant Bay
         P.O. Box 845
         So. Orleans, MA 02662

Printed by Paraclete Press, Brewster, MA

Cover Photos by Barry Donahue
Cover Design by Clint Kanaga, Paraclete Press
Book design by Sr. Martina Albro, Paraclete Press

Aerial Photographs of Pleasant Bay courtesy of Kelsey-Kennard Photographers
         Box 736
         Chatham, MA 02633

Aerial Photograph of Town Cove courtesy of Cape Cod National Seashore

Satellite Image of Cape Cod courtesy of Cape Cod National Seashore

Scallop illustrations by Karen Ripka

Maps by Mapworks, Norwell, MA

*In memory of Bruce, a master
at practical applications of ideas,
who taught me many things.
Among them, he taught me to love
this place in different ways than I
already did, enriching my life
immeasurably in the process.*

Acknowledgements

This book would not have been possible without the generosity and foresight of the Friends of Pleasant Bay. For asking me to write it and supporting the endeavor, I am very grateful.

Lending his expertise as a career journalist, Jeff McLaughlin had the vision, experience and technical skills necessary as my personal editor to elicit creativity from me in a truly joint project. His dedication in time, patience and understanding, as he taught me some of his skills and how to find my own voice, were incredible gifts. His belief in me is something I shall treasure.

I am especially indebted to Linda Deegan and Henry Lind who reviewed the manuscript and added valuable comments that helped me stay on track.

I am very grateful to the Town of Orleans, beginning with the Selectmen of 1974 who saw a need and filled that need. Gardy Munsey, my first supervisor, was incredibly supportive of my efforts. He taught me and I taught him and together we made a formidable team.

To the people I worked with over the years, especially my faithful secretary and friend, Nancy Hurley, various administrations, department managers, staff, committees, volunteers, and the citizens of Orleans who supported my work throughout my career, I am truly thankful.

I am immensely grateful to the many, many researchers at institutions across the country, and in Canada, especially those on the East Coast, who gave freely of their time and expertise whenever asked, thus helping me address issues in Orleans. There are so many of you I'm fearful of forgetting someone, so let me say to all that I hope you know how truly grateful I am.

To the other resource managers on the Cape, I say a special thank you. You understand, more than anyone else, the pressures exerted from every direction in your efforts to protect the Cape Cod of the 21st century.

To Fred Taylor, writing professor at Antioch New England Graduate School, who taught me to take a risk and to put me in my writing, a new challenge, I am immensely grateful.

Lastly, I give a hearty thank-you to my friends who gave moral support to me in this effort. I am indeed very fortunate to know such great people. You all will continue to be in my heart.

Foreword

Back in July 1999, the town of Orleans' former Shellfish Biologist and Conservation Administrator, Sandra Macfarlane, was the keynote speaker at the Annual Meeting of the *Friends of Pleasant Bay*. Sandy, as she is known locally, had just retired from the position she held for 25 years; and the *Friends* were eager to hear her thoughts on the status of Pleasant Bay.

Her talk struck a chord with many of us. Sandy spoke with love and familiarity, as one who had spent her days probing the Bay's bottom and traveling its shallow waters in order to broach its biological secrets. However, most striking was the way Sandy's professional life story chronicled the three decades during which development began to silently wreak havoc with the Bay's fragile ecosystems.

Upon the conclusion of her lecture, several members of the Friends compared notes and quickly agreed, "Sandy needs to write a book!" And thus a natural alliance was formed, resulting in this wonderful chronology of one woman's life's work to study and understand the delicate interrelationship between humans and the waters they cherish. Sandy has captured the essence of this interrelationship in her vivid descriptions: local shellfishermen striving to make a living out on the bay; the awkwardness she felt when first she dragged a bullrake over the Bay's floor; the sudden, startling dawn when she first grasped the connection between prolific building taking place on shore and the decline of shellfish in the Bay.

These experiences, as well as Sandy's career-long efforts to balance human interests with conservation of the Bay's natural resources, provide a rich background for today's continuing debate:

How can we make use of and enjoy Pleasant Bay and similar estuaries without destroying them? Sandy's book affords us no easy answers, but it does take us on a journey that dramatically increases our understanding as to why seeking those answers is of vital concern to us all.

Patricia Anthony
President, *Friends of Pleasant Bay*

Table of Contents

Table of Maps xiii
Table of Photographs xiv

Chapter 1   A Sense of Place 1
Chapter 2   "The Bare and Bended Arm" 8
Chapter 3   All I Knew Was That I Loved the Salt Water 22
Chapter 4   Long Raking in the Bay 30
Chapter 5   Bountiful Harvest 37
Chapter 6   Opportunity Knocks 46
Chapter 7   Where Did All the Quahaugs Go? 48
Chapter 8   Foot by Foot 52
Chapter 9   Half Moon 73
Chapter 10   Replenishing 79
Chapter 11   Hypothetical Problem? 91
Chapter 12   Beautiful Blue Mussels 95
Chapter 13   Hunter-Gatherers 100
Chapter 14   Farming the Sea 105
Chapter 15   Hand-me-downs 112
Chapter 16   Raising the Stakes 115
Chapter 17   Blood Red and Tropical Green 121
Chapter 18   Simulated Systems 130
Chapter 19   "Send Sandy to China" 141

Chapter 20   A Most Remarkable Year 154

Chapter 21   Shifting Gears 164

Chapter 22   Lost Opportunity 169

Chapter 23   Sand Worship 177

Chapter 24   Solid Ground 196

Chapter 25   Private Rights? 207

Chapter 26   Succulent Morsels .224

Chapter 27   Gunning Camps to Mansions 235

Chapter 28   Drop of Rain 248

Chapter 29   Insidious Silent Partner 253

Chapter 30   The People Speak 264

Chapter 31   Resolving Issues 278

Chapter 32   A New Day, New Hope 286

Rowing On 294

Table of Maps

Map 1 Gulf of Maine . . . . .Frontispiece

Map 2 Cape Cod 9

Map 3 "Elbow" of Cape Cod 12

Map 4 Pleasant Bay 16

Map 5 Nauset Estuary 25

Map 6 Watersheds of Orleans and Zoning Districts 261

Table of Photographs

Satellite Image of Cape Cod and the Islands 10
Important Shellfish Species 45
Scalloping in Town Cove 67
Aerial view of Pleasant Bay, Pre-1987 68
Quahaug propagation boxes in Town Cove 77
Planting quahaug seed in bottom frames 80
Floating sand-box quahaug raft 80
Gardy and author planting quahaug seed on raft 81
Shellfish lab and town launching ramp
    adjacent to Jeremiah's Gutter 85
Author checking clams planted in rows on Cape Cod Bay flats 86
"Clambulance" at Shellfish Lab 113
Stormwater flowing down launching ramp 127
Stormwater drainage pipe 129
"Spawning" quahaugs 131
Upweller silos 134
Nauset Spit with dunes 179
Nauset Spit after storm with dunes flattened 180
"Fighting Chance" rock surrounded by water — pre-dune washover 181
Erecting piping plover nest exclosures .187
Park Superintendent, Paul Fulcher, planting beach grass 189
Aerial view of Pleasant Bay with Chatham breakthrough 198
Coastal bank after the "Perfect Storm"—Stair posts in mid-air 206
Sand and grass plantings on coastal bank 213
Boulders and equipment on beach for revetment construction 218
Gabions and grass plantings 219
Seaweed mats 256
Thermal imagery of Town Cove showing groundwater flow 259
Docks along shore scoured by prop dredging 268

Chapter 1

A Sense of Place

Both the brackish pond and short, narrow, salt river that drained it were completely still aside from the current of the incoming tide. The only sounds were the gentle swish of water dripping from the oars on each stroke and the metal-on-metal ping as the brass shank of the oarlock hit the sides of the round brass fitting. The pond and river, both protected by what passes for high land on the outwash plain of Cape Cod, often show scant evidence of winds that might be roiling the waters out in the bay. The small river empties to a larger one, most often called simply The River. Once in its tidal current I could get more of a sense of conditions out in the bay. When I got to The River the trees on its banks were still as the boat moved swiftly past the buoys to Namequoit Point, the entrance to the bay.

A few strokes beyond the buoys, I stopped rowing and looked around. The glassy calm water reflected the clouds in the early morning sky, and the landforms bordering the water. The colors, muted tones of grays and dark greens, served as a reminder that the day had not yet fully awakened. Patches of blue sky were reflected as more of a dull green but every detail was mirrored. The small boat, slicing through the water, made ripples as it moved, the con-trails of a human-powered craft, extending out and away from the boat in long lines. The bubbles created from the oars closed in and merged into one line behind the boat. Water dripping off the oars made a swishing sound at the end of the stroke as I pulled them back into position for another "catch" that would pry the skiff forward again. The sounds of the oars and soft swish of the bow cutting through the water were the only sounds in the stillness of the bay.

Colors brightened all around as the sun rose higher. Clouds added a cottony texture in the sky above and in the reflected image on the water. The water was a bluish reflection of the sky, and the surrounding land was reflected as the dark green of summer's end. The season of growth was over and fall's colors had not yet emerged. The mirror image was my companion for more than an hour as the small boat glided around the bay in time with the rhythmic ca-chunk of the leather-sheathed oars in the brass oarlocks.

The high tide allowed travel in the shallow waters around Sipson's Island that are often unnavigable. Looking at the surface of this part of the bay, one would not suspect that less than a foot of water covers these sands at lower tides. As the boat coasted past Little Sipson's Meadow, a salt marsh out in the center of the bay, a great blue heron kept a watchful eye on me, the intruder in its space. Near Little Sipson's Island, a small hummock of land about 15 feet above the water level at its highest point, a second heron glanced warily at the passing boat. They appeared as sentinels guarding the narrow channel that separates the island from the grassy meadow, one facing north, the other southwest. At the edge of the island, a group of cormorants stood to dry off, their wings spread wide.

When I'm rowing, I see where I've been, not where I am going, and so I heard the sound of splashing water before I saw anything. The sound was similar to cormorants taking flight when they paddle four or five strokes before they have enough steam to get airborne. But this sound was not of cormorants. Turning the boat around, I was dumbfounded to see great splashing in this shallow water, the unmistakable sight of fish "breaking water," large fish chasing smaller fish. I stopped rowing so as not to disturb the fish, hoping to actually see them. Soon, a school of dozens of small striped bass passed under the boat, clearly visible in these shallows. "Small" means 12-18 inches; bass can grow to well over 3 feet, 50-pound whoppers or more. These fish appeared to be oblivious to me, swimming instinctively toward some unknown foodsource. I wondered how often they feed amongst these shoals that seem to leave them little room to move. The splashing sound of fish breaking water in the early morning stillness always catches me by surprise. What a thrill to actually see these impressive gamefish, verifying fish stories I had heard but did not quite believe.

As I resumed rowing, the oars almost hit a purple jellyfish, a sight uncommon in the bay. Soon there was another and another until I saw about 50 altogether. They had bumps on the convex upper portion of their body, with long tentacles drifting down in the water. Larger and with tentacles longer than their skin-toned common cousin typically found here, they looked somewhat ominous. Instinct told me not to pick one up with an ungloved hand. Later, I found that they were stinging nettles, found generally in Chesapeake Bay, hundreds of miles south of Pleasant Bay, and probably had been unwitting passengers in the tumultuous, surging waters created by three hurricanes that had passed by recently.

Among the jellyfish, I noticed an odd shape. When examined closely, it was made of individual transparent, gelatinous egg sacs positioned in such a way that they looked like a small ladder. Each egg sac had a sperm-shaped animal within. Soon there were more, of different sizes. Then there were hundreds and the boat was in the midst of these floating ladders in every direction. I wondered, what unknown creature starts its life in this manner? I realized that someday I'd have to go to the library at Woods Hole to find a reference on marine egg masses.

I glanced down again at the bottom, so clearly visible in the placid water. On a day like this, the whole undersea realm opens up to any air-breathing creature that chooses to glimpse its inner workings. I saw holes in the sand where clams, razor clams and worms had found a home. Single clam and scallop shells littered the bottom, evidence that they had probably provided sustenance to the bay's other inhabitants. I saw hermit crabs scuttling along the bottom in a borrowed periwinkle shell and small fish darting through the water. Ripples showed where tidal action had moved the bottom sand in unceasing but varied rhythms.

I'd been rowing for a couple of hours now. I looked at the eelgrass swaying under water to determine whether the tide had changed. The direction of the grass blades is a sure indicator. Dismayed, I saw the tide had turned and realized that rowing against the current in Hog Island Channel would be difficult.

A great blue heron flew overhead, issuing its call, a guttural "quuu-ark". It is a primordial, almost unearthly sound that I've heard only when the birds are in flight. It was a stark contrast to the silence of the herons on guard near Little Sipson's Island. Gulls and terns were also flying and cormorants as well. But only the terns and herons announced their presence.

As I rowed along the edges of Little Sipson's Meadow, I noticed that the flower heads of the marsh grass, *Spartina alterniflora,* had turned a tawny color, giving the meadow a shimmering, golden hue. Glancing east. I saw the color of the dune grass out on the barrier beach was beginning to change to a golden green too, the first step toward the tan of fall and winter. The golds and golden-greens told me to treasure this magnificent late-summer day on Cape Cod, because the ocean would soon be cooling fast, and the Bay's weather would be coming down from the frozen north, not the humid south. I looked northeast from the marsh, toward the barrier beach and the North Atlantic beyond, and imagined a cold, wet, 40-knot January storm.

Sand dunes, nature's first line of defense, protect the bay from the onslaught of the sea in a fury. Storms may rip at their oceanside faces, devouring sand and pulling it out to sea. Storms create the narrow "winter beach" and attack the barrier further by clawing at the dune grass that stabilizes the sand with its 15-foot-deep roots. But the sand of winter's storms does not go far offshore and is re-deposited each spring to form the broad expanse of the "summer beach." It's the summer that has made this barrier famous as Nauset Beach in Orleans, part of the Cape Cod National Seashore. The beach grass rhizomes recover from the winter storms, sending out new shoots all summer. As I rowed at summer's end, the evidence of last winter's assault was but a memory as the dunes had become fully vegetated. The cycle would soon begin again. These dunes and the great Nauset barrier beach are undeveloped, in sharp contrast to such ecosystems in so many other coastal areas from Massachusetts to Georgia. Shaped by wind and waves, the beach that protects Pleasant Bay moves and changes in a seemingly seamless fluidity as it has done for thousands of years.

My boat and I had cleared the east side of Little Sipson's Meadow and I was out in what's called Crooked Channel. The water was still high enough to go almost anywhere and I lazily headed north toward Hog Island Creek. As I glanced west, toward the mainland, I saw the hill above Little Bay where Quanset Sailing

Camp used to be. Although the nearly treeless hill was covered now with large expensive homes, their motor boats moored nearby in the bay, I saw only the big green lawn of the old camp, and sailing boats at the moorings, waiting for the fresh-faced kids to take them out for a race against one of the other sailing camps around the bay.

Twenty years ago, there were four camps along the Orleans shores of Pleasant Bay. Each had a fleet of shallow-draft sailing boats, perfect for sailing the shoal waters of the bay. The boats were wide and sturdy with large sails to catch the southwest winds that predominate in summer. Southwesterlies perk up as the day goes along. They can be quite challenging after lunchtime. Afternoon races and instruction were reserved for the older, more experienced sailors. What a glorious sight to see the boats jockeying for position and hearing the laughter of the kids as they learned the skills necessary to sail. Quanset Sailing Camp was specifically for girls while Namequoit and Viking were boy's camps and Pleasant Bay Camp was a co-ed day camp. There was plenty of competition for the budding sailors.

I never attended the camps but they were etched into memories of my early days on the bay. My boat was built as a sailing skiff that could also be used for rowing and it was always a joy to be on the bay with fleets of sailboats all around.

None of the camps is still functioning; today, only the Viking property has some open land left. All the others succumbed to the pressures of development. Camps, operating for 8-10 weeks each year, could no longer pay their way. The sale of the camps helped to fuel the race to develop every acre left in the towns that border the Bay and especially those lots right on the water, the camp land. Camp Quanset became a subdivision known as East Egg. When it was first developed, one of the roads was named Easy Street. It has since been changed to Little Bay Road, much more in keeping with the area, but I wonder if the new residents have a clue about the land's past.

Rowing is meditative, but the current was against me and I realized I had to bend to the oars. Refusing to be saddened by thoughts of the costs of real estate development on that glorious day, I continued on my journey to Hog Island.

My reverie of what was, but is no more, was further jolted by the roar of a man-made machine. A boat, large for this bay, had rounded the corner and was in full view, loaded with recreational fishing gear. There was no apparent muffler on its engine and as I continued on my journey, the deafening noise could be heard for 10-15 minutes as it traversed the bay in the opposite direction. It had whizzed by at five or six times my top speed, and I wondered what the fishermen could see at that rate. I wondered too what developers could see at their frenetic pace.

Presently, Hog Island Creek appeared. Once in the channel between Hog Island and Sampson Island, I realized that the tide was running at a pretty good clip and it would take some strong strokes to maneuver the little boat through the twisting channel against the current. Osprey nests, built on wooden platforms atop posts, which conservationists erected in the island marshes to encourage re-population of these magnificent fishers, were empty. The season was past for nurturing the young and the ospreys had flown south as their relatives have done for centuries.

Other birds had not migrated yet. Some flying by me were so small and so fast that I couldn't identify them. Others sat in trees, resting on journeys that had begun far to the Cape's north and would end far to the south. Great egrets, large graceful white birds with long slender necks, looked like they should be in the tropics, not here on Cape Cod.

The islands on both sides, Hog on the south and Sampson to the north, are uninhabited and protected in perpetuity from development. On these islands, wildlife abounds and I was a guest. The islands have all the biomes of a coastal environment, from sand flats and shallow water creeks to extensive salt marshes and wooded uplands. I have often seen deer prancing through the thick underbrush of Hog Island, but I spied none now as the sun was climbing high in the sky. In the creek, none of the evidence of the developed shoreline was visible. I didn't mind that it took me longer than usual to go through the channel.

As I exited the creek, I saw and heard more boats in the main channel across the bay and realized that the morning solitude had been broken. The weekend warriors had staked their claim on the bay that means so much to so many. Each in their own way must enjoy what the bay has to offer. I enjoy most what it has always been, a part of nature, and enjoy least what it is in danger of becoming, centerpiece of a pretty view.

Finally my journey had nearly ended. I felt a slight breeze and the glassy water gave way to small ripples, the cat's paws of a wind out of the south. The breeze pushed me up the rivers and back to the pond, where, with the boat secured, I would launch another day.

The row had rejuvenated me, reminded me of the beauty and logic of nature I saw as a girl and young woman, when I first decided I would spend my life trying to understand how the marine environment works.

The row had made me realize too how fragile were the conditions for natural beauty and ecological order. My 25 years as a shellfish biologist and conservation administrator had shown me that loving the bay's beauty is not enough to protect its logic. Everyone who sees this bay falls in love with it. That's the problem, here and in the other beautiful estuaries of Cape Cod: We are loving them to death.

Chapter 2

"The Bare and Bended Arm"

The peninsula of Cape Cod, Massachusetts, is really not much more than a large sandbar. Created by retreating glaciers about 15,000 years ago and composed of glacial till, the Cape in a satellite image resembles a flexed arm sticking out about 40 miles east off the mainland (Map 2). Like a sandbar, it is an ephemeral, fragile piece of land that is part of a geologically evolving chain of events. It is timeless change here; Cape Cod will be gone in the geologic blink of an eye. Daily, it is disappearing, as the forces of nature rework the sediment at its margins, building here but depleting there, the depletion happening faster than the accretion.

Natural sea level rise is taking some land at the barely perceptible rate of two or three feet a year in most places, but global warming is speeding up the process. It is estimated that at the current rate, the sea will rise about a foot over the next century although some scientists recently projected that the rate could double long before the year 2100. Some climatologists believe the severity of storms lately is a visible result of the greenhouse effect; and while sea-level rise is the main engine over the long haul, violent storms can take the greatest toll in the disappearance of the landform we know as Cape Cod.

The Cape's crenulated shoreline attests to its coastal diversity. Long expanses of sandy beach are broken here and there, revealing inlets that lead to coves, bays, marshes, protected harbors, salt ponds, salt rivers, coastal banks, and other physical features that add miles of shorefront to each of the fifteen towns that represent the social/political divisions of the peninsula. These physical features are known as estuaries, a term denoting those areas where the land

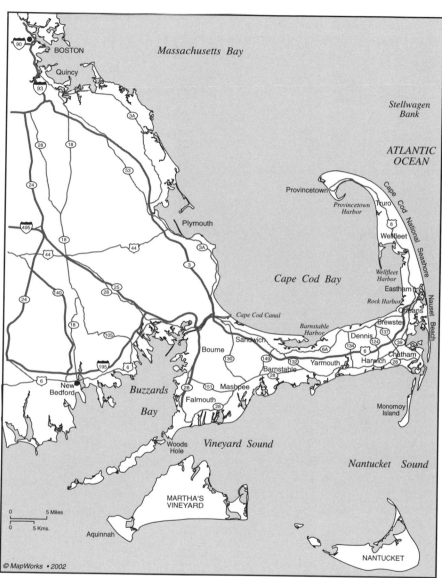

MAP 2 *Cape Cod*

meets the sea and where the salinity (the level of salt in the water) is higher than fresh water and less than the open sea. Arms of sand and vegetated dunes called barrier beaches jut out from the land to protect the calmer waters of the bays and coves from the onslaught of the sea and its fury. An inlet through the beach provides the link from the open ocean to the bays.

Cape towns are remarkably similar and dissimilar at the same time. Each town has bays, coves, rivers, inlets, beaches and other natural coastal features, and often the dividing line between towns is drawn through a body of water. Each town has political dominion over its territory, each separate governing body setting different rules and regulations concerning almost all manner of life. Municipalities are strong political entities and in many respects are rather provincial in their regard for town boundaries, especially in their approach to natural resources, even though nature knows no such boundaries. The people who dwell within each town have historically been zealous in guarding the qualities they felt truly defined the town. But in the last century, change came so fast in some towns that defining the town's character became a challenge.

The town of Orleans is located in the "elbow" of the Cape. It is a small town of 21 square miles, but only 14 square miles is land, including islands and marsh, while the remaining seven square miles, or one-third of the town, is salt water. It is blessed to have major parts of three separate estuaries, all formed by retreating glaciers, within its boundaries: Cape Cod Bay, Nauset Estuary and Pleasant Bay (Map 3). In what were to become the smaller estuaries, Nauset and Pleasant Bay, the glaciers had left depressions called kettle holes. These low areas eventually filled with seawater from the rising sea level, forming a series of rivers and ponds that still connect to the sea through inlets in the sandy barrier beaches.

Fresh water is as important a resource on the Cape as the salt water. The fresh water ponds are valuable ecosystems, supplying food for wildlife, and aesthetic and recreational sustenance for humans, just to name a few attributes. They are vital to the overall health of the landscape. Cape Cod is dotted with hundreds of such fresh water ponds. They are not only important ecosystems in their own right, but also provide a window to the water that lies beneath our feet. The connection between fresh and salt water is an essential ingredient in the life of the estuaries, and the integrity of the water is essential for life on the Cape.

The rainfall soaking into the ground, called aptly enough groundwater and stored underground in the space between the sand grains, is the Cape's only source of drinking water. The Environmental Protection Agency accordingly designated all of Cape Cod as a "sole-source aquifer" in the 1970s. After about ten years, the term sole-source aquifer reached the vernacular of the public, but there was a time lag between knowing what a sole-source aquifer is and relating that concept to true understanding and hence protective action.

Conceptually it is difficult to understand that the Cape we know above ground is not sitting on a solid bedrock foundation but rather on top of sand and debris left by the glaciers. The glacial legacy is huge: Bedrock is 400 feet down in some places. In that amalgam of sediment under the Cape and above the bedrock, some of the sand is saturated with water. To complicate matters, the groundwater does not remain stationary under the surface. It flows with gravity from higher land to the sea. It reaches the bays and coves first. There, the

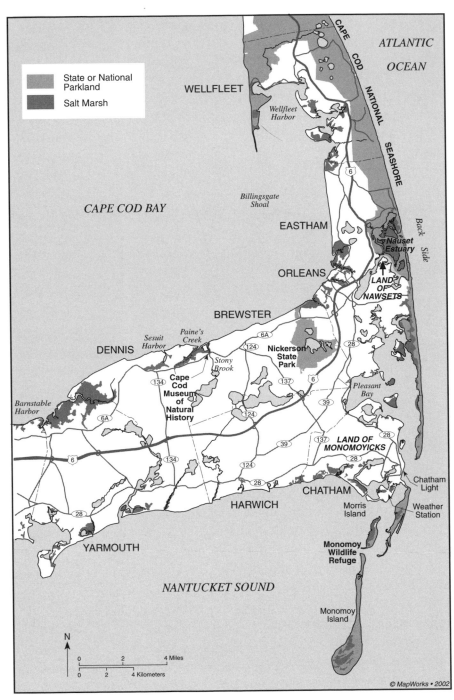

MAP 3 *"Elbow" of Cape Cod*

fresh water dilutes the saltier seawater and creates the magnificently productive estuaries that proliferate along the Cape's shoreline.

The groundwater movement also means that any contaminant affects not only the drinking water supply but may also affect the estuaries and the marine life of the estuaries that form a delicately balanced ecosystem. Other communities around the nation may rely on a fenced-in and carefully guarded reservoir of water that is piped to service the community's fresh water needs, and there, people can easily appreciate that protection of the reservoir is of utmost importance. It is a bit different when the drinking water is below your feet and unseen. Here any potential contaminant originating from any land use above-ground can trickle down to contaminate the Cape's drinking water supply.

To paraphrase Rachel Carson in her landmark book, *Silent Spring*, it is not possible to contaminate anywhere without threatening the purity of water everywhere. Today's concern with water quality was not even a remote thought when few individuals peopled this land.

Long before the Pilgrims or other Europeans arrived on the Cape, Native Americans lived on the land. Small bands of Indians formed separate units, but all the tribes spoke languages of the eastern Algonquian family, which encompassed the area from the Canadian Maritime Provinces to North Carolina in the south and extended west to the St. Lawrence, Hudson and Susquehanna Rivers and the Appalachian Mountain range. Separate bands such as Monomoyicks and Nawsets occupied most of Cape Cod, but all belonged to the largest group, the Wampanoags.

The Europeans and the diseases they brought with them decimated the Cape tribes. The Wampanoags of Mashpee on Cape Cod and Martha's Vineyard are the last remaining members of these great tribes.

Pleasant Bay was the dividing line between the Nawsets to the north and Monomoyicks to the south (Map 3); evidence of their encampments near the shores show that both groups relied on the bay's bounty for food. The deep purple of the old quahaug shells were also made into beads and used for adornments and for a form of barter. They called it wampum. Today wampum jewelry is still made locally on the Cape and on the nearby island of Martha's Vineyard where a tribe of Wampanoags still lives in the town of Aquinnah.

Vikings are said to have sailed these shores a thousand years ago, and when the European explorers arrived in the early 1600s, they used the Cape for food (Gosnold in 1602) or shelter in storms (Champlain, who entered what is now Nauset Harbor in 1604). Gosnold named the place Cape Cod, impressed by codfish so plentiful that he said you could almost walk on their backs.

The Pilgrims who eventually settled in Plymouth, Massachusetts, first landed in Provincetown at the tip of Cape Cod. It was there that they signed the Mayflower Compact, the first governing document for the new colony. The Mayflower was actually bound for Jamestown in Virginia and sailed as far south as Pollock Rip south of Chatham. But when their small ship encountered rough seas the Pilgrims turned north again and landed in Provincetown. A few weeks later, concerned about fresh water supplies at the tip of the Cape, they sailed west across Cape Cod Bay to the mainland to establish their settlement.

Once the Pilgrims had learned how to survive — in large measure by following advice from Wampanoags — it wasn't long before some members of the group left Plymouth and arrived back on the Cape. That was the beginning of the settlement process that continues today. One of the first to arrive was William Nickerson in what is known today as Chatham. One of his 20th century heirs, W. Sears Nickerson, painstakingly researched his family history as well as the history of the area. Another descendant, Joshua Atkins Nickerson, wrote essays reflecting on his own lengthy life in the town. In both cases, Pleasant Bay figured prominently (Map 4). W. Sears Nickerson wrote in his book, *The Bay As I See It*,

"The Bay itself lies like a great blue patch on the ragged elbow of Cape Cod. Of all the bays, coves, creeks and salt water ponds which fray the weather-beaten shoreline of the Cape, the waters of Pleasant Bay and those of Nawset Harbor are the only ones emptying directly into the Atlantic. Around and outside it all shimmers the lace-like tracery of breakers on the Back Side forever and ever weaving new patterns of white...."

"I believe The Bay must look today much as it did thousands of years ago ... It undoubtedly lay a little more open to the sea in that far day, before the Outer Beach had had time to make down from Pochet and close it in. The sea-worn headlands and boulder strewn shores of the Islands, which even now practically barricade its eastern side, offer ample testimony to their ancient battle with the open ocean. The Inlet, which even within historical time opened directly into The Bay opposite my Nick-Shack, has been pushed hither and yon at the caprice of storm and tide, but the great Bay itself undoubtedly remains essentially as the melting ice pack left it."

Read a Nickerson book or talk to an "old timer" and you will soon discover that the Cape of the latter half of the 20th century in no way resembles that of the first half of the century. In fact, more changes have taken place in the past 50 years than in the first 300-plus years since the Nickersons' ancestors arrived.

Gone are the meadows and open fields, replaced first by cedar trees, in turn succeeded by pines and oaks and beeches. Gone are the dairy farms and orchards. Gone are the vegetable farms that grew staples like white turnips and asparagus, now considered delicacies. Gone are the fish shanties along the shore where people who made their living from the sea kept their gear. Gone are the last visible images of salt works, vast drying vats that produced salt from evaporating seawater. Gone is the railroad, a transportation network to move passengers and freight about, replaced by paved bicycle paths and a road system that makes the automobile indispensable.

Gone is a way of life that depended on the land and the sea for its very existence. Gone is the necessity to develop the skills needed to depend on the land and sea, skills needed to hunt, to trap, to fish. Rare now is the sound of a gun, once commonplace, when the duck or goose or deer provided meat and protein for the family and "market gunning" provided money for other staples. The clam hoe and quahaug scratcher once were as essential pieces of equipment in nearly every household as hammer and ax. The fishing pole once was used here to get fish as food for the table. Every fish that was

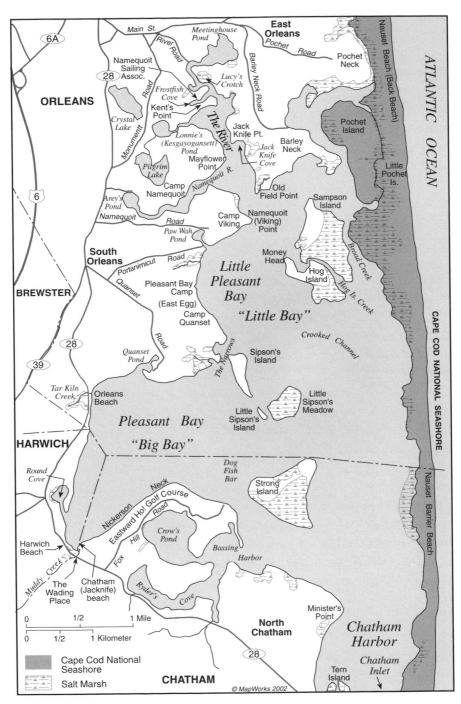

MAP 4 *Pleasant Bay*

edible was harvested when it came into the bay. There was sport in fishing, but fishing was not merely for sport.

Almost gone now, relegated to a corner of society because of their dwindling numbers, are the people proud to call themselves "Cape Codders," people who were born here and lived their lives here as had generations of their families. These were people who exemplified true Yankee traditions: frugal, principled, cunning, expert barterers, cagey, terse, and resilient. These were people for whom the land meant everything.

This Cape Cod land was sandy but hard. Henry Thoreau talked about its harshness when he walked the Lower Cape in the mid-1800s. It had been denuded the century before and had not recovered. Topsoil had blown away after the hardwood trees were cut, leaving the sand where little would grow. Without the trees, the winds howled over the landscape. When the land would not support much, the people had no real choice but to leave or turn to the sea. Many left. The population decreased when there was no alternative but the sea.

Those who stayed behind had to fight Nauset and Chatham inlets in sailing craft to get to the open Atlantic or to sail into Cape Cod Bay. The nearshore areas produced clams and quahaugs too and if they were forced to stay ashore, they still might be able to scratch some shellfish on the low tide.

Cash money might have been hard to come by, but these were people who knew that at least they would never starve because there would always be enough clams and quahaugs around and in good years, maybe some scallops.

As the second half of the 20th century began, the country had been through the Great Depression and two world wars. People who were not in the armed services often left the Cape during World War II to work in factories off-Cape to help the war effort. Then they returned, eking out a living the best way they could. Talk to these people, now in their 70s and 80s and it's not uncommon to hear flat statements like, "We had no money," especially during the leanest years of the Depression and war. Yet, when reading books or newspaper columns about growing up in the 1930s, '40s or '50s by local raconteur Dana Eldridge or other writers, one can't help but get a sense that while the people may have had little money, they did not feel particularly poor. They knew they lived in a very special place where they could dig a mess of clams or scratch some quahaugs or net a cod or flounder or go shoot a few ducks or geese for the table. But often as not, they breathed in sustenance too by simply standing on the shore with the birds, surrounded by the quiet beauty of the flats and bays.

Off-Cape, the 1950s brought a sense of prosperity. Gasoline was no longer rationed as it had been in the war and people could travel more. The population centers of New York and Boston were within a day's drive and the Cape became a popular destination. Those towns closest to the bridge — Bourne, Falmouth, Barnstable, Yarmouth and Dennis — developed first, with cottage colonies and motels lining the roadways. Waterfront property, especially along Nantucket Sound, was quickly snatched up.

As Joshua Nickerson noted in his book, *Days to Remember*, the Cape was becoming an affordable and appealing vacation spot for a huge number of people. Accessible, with plenty of cabins for rent and sparkling beaches everywhere, the Cape towns were a natural draw for city-dwellers within a day's drive. Many vacationers got a taste of the Cape and dreamed of someday living here. Highways were built to accommodate the increased traffic and the driving time from Boston shrank from 3½ -4 hours to 1½ -2 hours, making the place even easier to get to and more crowded as more people found out. Off-Cape money spent on-Cape meant more for everyone living year-round here. The growth explosion was beginning.

Some people were only too happy to accommodate the influx of new people by selling them their precious land, obtaining wealth in the process and fueling the drive to further develop the Cape. Others could not hold onto their land for the next generation and "making it through" for them meant selling their land to "people from away" just to make ends meet. The division of land meant an infusion of much-needed capital to give the Cape an economic boost it could not have gained from traditional farming or fishing.

Many Cape Codders learned to live two lives: a "seasonal" one when they tried to make enough money to make it through the winter, and the rest of the time, when they played "catch-up," hoping they could pay their bills until the "summerfolk" returned to get the economy pumped up again. Local folks developed a love/hate relationship with those two lives. On the one hand, the more people flocked to the Cape as tourists in the summer, the more the land was eaten up for development and the more un-Cape-like the place became. On the other hand, the more tourists who came in the summer, the more jobs there were.

"Native" Cape Codders continue to make their livelihood as a result of this two-season economy but resentment for it still simmers just beneath the surface.

When John F. Kennedy took the presidential oath of office in 1961, most of the Cape tourists sported license plates from MA, CT, NY, NJ and PA. But Kennedy spent his own vacation time in Hyannisport and the televised images put Cape Cod on the national map. People from all over began flocking to the Cape. There were mind-numbing implications if popularity continued to soar.

Some Massachusetts visionaries, including then Senator Kennedy, picking up ideas that originated on Cape Cod, saw vast open areas in the Lower Cape region from Chatham to Provincetown and could visualize what the area would be like with unrestricted development. They lobbied for a National Seashore to be established in the National Park System of the Department of the Interior. President Kennedy then signed into law an act that froze development along a 40-mile swath and established the Cape Cod National Seashore. Unlike other national parks in the west and south, which were created out of land that had no development, the Seashore boundary encompassed parts of six existing communities, all 150 or more years old.

Everything about the move to create the park was contentious and hotly debated at the time on the Lower Cape, from setting exact boundaries to seeking ways for the feds and towns to agree on working relationships. When the boundary in Eastham was being discussed, for example, Fort Hill, overlooking Nauset Marsh, had development stakes on it where house lots were already laid out in case it was not made part of the Seashore. It was. Today, it is one of the most popular public areas with its magnificent vista of Nauset Marsh, Nauset Harbor, the barrier beach and the ocean beyond. Little or none of that panorama would be possible to see if the land had been privately developed.

The flip side is exemplified by Morris Island in Chatham, across the channel from Monomoy National Wildlife Refuge, located on two islands south of Nauset Beach. Morris Island was left outside the boundary and is now filled with luxurious homes.

Many on the Lower Cape saw the Seashore legislation as ensuring disintegration of local control. The Seashore's mission, many felt, would lead to inevitable conflict between national interests, where the Seashore would represent what appeared to be in the best interest of all the people of all the states, and local interests, where the towns would stand up for what they deemed best for their inhabitants. To try to resolve differences, the Seashore established an advisory council with representation from all the towns within the Seashore boundary, but balancing Seashore needs with the wishes of the towns continues to be challenging to this day. Today, the Seashore ranks in the top 10 for National Park visits with over 5 million visitors annually.

Large private tracts of land still remained around Pleasant Bay too, in the 1960s and '70s, some owned by families that were among the earliest settlers, and some that had been purchased and set up as summer camps. For over 90 years, most of the 20th century, seven camps operated on the Bay. Two were relatively short lived, lasting for a decade or two, but five became a welcome long-term presence on the bay, four in Orleans and one in Chatham. Thousands of kids came to the camps over the years. It was an era when, as Marcia Monbleau said in her 1999 book *Pleasant Bay, Stories from a Cape Cod Place*, "a lot of kids were in a lot of boats, having a lot of fun." It wasn't unusual to see more than a hundred boats out on the Bay filled with laughing kids learning to sail. Large sections of waterfront were still undisturbed as recently as the late 1970s. Now, almost all the land around Pleasant Bay is developed.

Aside from dealing with the division of land, the Cape Cod people of the latter half of the 20th century and the dawn of the 21st have been forced to adhere to rules and regulations unthinkable earlier. Towns are required to administer regulations adopted by state and federal agencies that cover almost every facet of life. Towns also may adopt regulations of their own, wetland bylaws or zoning regulations for example, which are intended to protect a resource or prevent a hodge-podge of development, although some see such restrictions as intruding on personal freedoms.

But most significant for the story that follows, the towns, long ago empowered by the state to enact local laws to manage shellfish resources under broad state guidelines, never surrendered their authority. It is one of the few states with a system of municipal shellfish jurisdiction.

That was where I would fit in. I would become, in 1974, the first shellfish biologist ever hired by a Massachusetts town. And later I would become the town's first Conservation Administrator. But I'm getting ahead of myself.

Chapter 3

All I Knew Was That
I Loved the Salt Water

All I knew was that I loved the salt water. Spending my childhood summers of the 1950s at the Cape in a small cottage on Route 6 in Eastham, just over the town line from Orleans, gave me an inkling of the wonders of an estuary — the Town Cove, part of the Nauset system — though at the time, I didn't know what an estuary was.

I grew up in a peninsula of Quincy, a city just south of Boston. I could watch from my bedroom window as oil tankers docked across the river, low in the water when they arrived and much larger and higher when they left, leaving their cargo in the giant fuel tanks adjacent to a Boston Edison electric plant and a Proctor and Gamble plant. Behind them loomed the vast Fore River Shipyard, one of the primary ship-building facilities on the East Coast — it built the first US aircraft carrier — and a major employer for the city.

Further up the river and around the corner of the peninsula, there was a little cove and a small beach where many of the neighborhood kids spent their summers. There was a lot of green slimy seaweed on the mucky ground at low tide and the place smelled bad twice a day. I went there a few times but I didn't like the beach much. I knew what a good beach was like and I was extremely lucky that I had a better beach to go to during the summers.

My father's sister had rented a small cottage on the Cape for years and after my father died when I was very young, my aunt continued to rent the cottage for my mother and her three kids for the whole summer. My aunt came on weekends. We did not have a car and relied on my aunt to take us to our little cottage the day school ended and return us home the day after Labor Day, one day before school started again.

The cottage, named Breeze Cottage, was tiny. The kitchen had a chest-type refrigerator, the likes of which I've never seen again. There was a dry-sink cabinet and a sink, a small table for a wash bowl, a small white metal cabinet, and a two-burner hot plate. The living room was also the bunkroom. It had two bunk beds and an armless flat couch that could be used for a bed, leaving just enough room for a cot for my sister, who had to give up her regular bed on the enclosed porch when my aunt came. The cottage had no running water but there was a hand pump outside and an outhouse attached to a very old barn. The cottage is still there, relegated to a storage shed now, and it looks even smaller to my adult eyes.

The property was owned by Charlie Smith, who, with his daughter and son in-law, Helen and Roscoe Gibson, lived in the 200-plus-year-old farmhouse that was very close to the road. Roscoe had retired from the railroad and he and Helen lived with Mr. Smith during the summers in the big white house on the highway. The old farmhouse had rooms to rent plus two apartments that were also rented. Most of the people who rented the apartments were child-less and so my sisters and I amused ourselves playing croquet (I got rather good at it over the years) and horseshoes, or by walking down the road to Log Cabin Farm to pick blueberries.

Mr. Smith, a very kindly old man, who eventually passed away at about age 93, owned a small piece of beachfront across Route 6, the main highway that runs from the Cape Cod Canal to Provincetown. The beachfront was on the shores of the Town Cove and when Mr. Smith died, a bench was put on the bank with a sign that said "Charlie's Rest". Adjacent to the Smith property was Collins Landing (Map 5), a town landing with a paved driveway that ended with four or five parking spaces and a shell/gravel launching ramp. Beyond the high-tide line toward the water, the ground became progressively more soft and muddy with eelgrass and shells. I was forever bringing back scallop shells to the cottage to paint or just to have around the house. From the vantage point at the landing, the Town Cove looked like a big oval salt water lake, but in reality it was connected by a narrow channel to Nauset Harbor and Nauset Marsh further east.

The adjacent property on the right of the town landing belonged to the Collins family. There was a one-story building on the water called Collins' Fish and Fiddle Club where small boats, maybe 14-feet in length with 4hp engines, were rented for fishing. The Collinses also owned a few cottages on a small knoll that were rented to the same people year after year. At the base of the knoll, beyond the Fish and Fiddle Club, there was a beach, and a dock with a float to swim and dive off, or to tie a boat.

Unfortunately, we were not allowed to go beyond the town landing because somebody said that somebody was having a feud with somebody else — a Collins vs. a Smith/Gibson and we were to cause no trouble. I was thrilled when, in junior high school, I met a girl in my Quincy school whose aunt rented one of the Collins cottages for her family. That friendship — it was miraculous to me — meant I was finally able to go to the beach across the street from my cottage.

Nauset Harbor was a beautiful area with marshes and tide flats and huge sand dunes at the far eastern margin, dunes that faced the Atlantic Ocean. The dunes were part of the great Nauset Beach with its crashing surf and frigid water.

My aunt's best friend owned a house overlooking Nauset Harbor, a house where my parents had spent their honeymoon. Once in a while, their youngest son, who was at least five years older than my oldest sister, Janet, took us for a boat ride out into the harbor. We played on the sand flats or in the cold clear water where he taught me how to swim. The inlet to and from the ocean brought in that cold water, and was clearly visible near what was then known as "the Bluff," now commonly known as Nauset Heights.

Terns used the flats for nesting in the summer, dive-bombing anyone who got too close, and we were always amused when our navigator, who was the tallest of our group by far, was dive-bombed repeatedly by the squawking terns when we got too close to a nest on the flats.

My sisters and I played at the edge of the water at Collins Landing and occasionally braved the eelgrass and mud and actually went in the water. But most times we waited all week for my aunt, who would take us all to Skaket Beach.

Skaket Beach is the only beach on the Cape Cod Bay side of Orleans and is well-known as a safe beach for little kids. When the

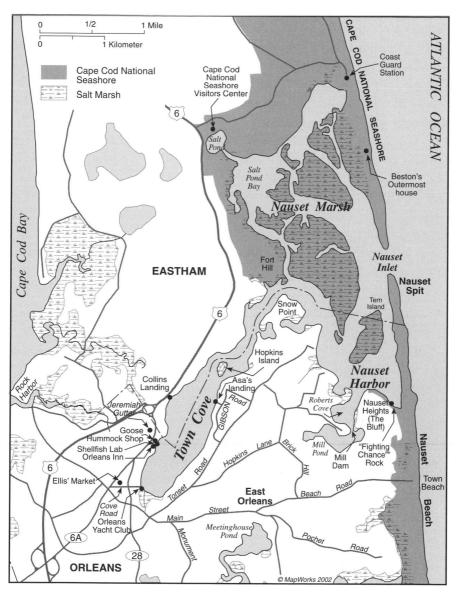

MAP 5 *Nauset Estuary*

tide goes out, sand flats stretch for a mile and a half offshore with a few tide pools interspersed among long and large ridges of sand. Exploring these flats can entertain anyone, let alone a little kid, for hours. When we were lucky enough to go, however, I seemed to have given my mother fits, or so she told me later. She bought us brightly colored bathing caps to try to keep track of us in the water and would count one, two... Where is she? I was under water more than on top and I was in the water every minute available.

The requisite hour spent on the beach after lunch was interminable.

As we got older and families with kids and cars rented the apartments in Charlie Smith's farmhouse, we got to go to Nauset Beach on the ocean side. It was a much more dangerous beach for children because of the cold water, surf and undertow, and sometimes riptides, and my mother was always fearful when we were there. But I loved it, especially either side of low tide when I could play in the waves for hours.

When we couldn't get to the beach, Roscoe would take us to the "boat shop" where he was the manager. The boat shop, owned by a dentist named "Doc" Raddin, was a small shingled shack about a quarter mile further up the Town Cove from Collins Landing, and also provided small boats to rent for fishing. The shop sold bait and outboard oil and gas and serviced boats that were kept in the Cove. My sisters and I hung around in the afternoon, irritating the older teenage boys who worked there. While Janet (six years older than I) was able to run the engines, my other sister, Susan, and I were only allowed to row the boats close to shore. Our main "job" was to bail the boats after a rainstorm, a task the boys were only too happy to let us do. Every now and then we went flounder fishing by ourselves without supervision and although I don't remember bringing home many flounders, we did have a great time.

But the best part of those flounder-fishing trips was sometimes having the chance to climb into a boat on the Town Cove and going all the way to Nauset Harbor. I loved those days. The boat shop was torn down many years ago, replaced by a big (100 feet long or so) blue steel building belonging to the Goose Hummock Shop, an early visible commercial change for what had been a quaint stretch of Cape shoreline.

Sundays in summer held a special magic for me because the Orleans Yacht Club held their weekly sailboat races in the Town

Cove. Often the races were held close to the Yacht Club at the head of the Cove, but if the wind was right, the boats came further up the cove where I could watch them from Collins Landing. They were so beautiful, gliding on the water pushed by the wind alone. The races are still held every summer Sunday and I have not lost my love of watching them parade up and down the Cove.

I'm not sure how the interest in marine biology began but I knew I loved the water and everything to do with the water but it had to be salt water. I was fascinated by small creatures I saw in salt water. I always thought that lakes were only good for washing off the salt and that done quickly.

The Jacques Cousteau specials that aired on television during some of my most impressionable childhood years were particularly meaningful. When I mentioned the specials as being influential to my choice of career at a scientific meeting, the response was that probably everyone at the conference in our age group could trace their reason for going into marine science to Cousteau. That's quite a legacy.

When I was in college, at the University of Massachusetts in Amherst, my advisor asked me one day what I wanted to do with my education. I said I wanted to work with natural resources in some capacity on the Cape. He said my choices were limited and I said I knew that. In my case, it was not so much a matter of what I wanted to do as where I wanted to do it because since childhood, I knew that I was going to live in Orleans as soon as possible. He suggested that I take more courses in ecology and courses dealing with other resources such as forestry and wildlife management because of the limited job market on the Cape. I did and really found my niche with those additional courses. I graduated in 1971 and immediately moved to Orleans.

I had the naïve temerity to believe that once I graduated, I would be able to find a job in my field even though jobs were few. I thought that I might be able to work for the Cape Cod National Seashore or Nickerson State Park or the Cape Cod Museum of Natural History but all three locations would only accept volunteers; none was willing to hire me. I was sure something would turn up. But nothing did.

So I worked as a waitress at a couple of different restaurants and then as a clerk at Ellis' Market, a small family-owned grocery store renowned for its excellent meat and its policy of allowing a customer to run a charge. The store was a community institution where everybody knew everybody else and customer service was important. I liked working there even though I was disheartened that I didn't have a job in natural resources. But I tried to keep abreast of anything that might lead to a job and I was still fascinated with what was going on around the shore.

I learned a lot in those early years after I moved to the Cape. I gravitated naturally toward people who also loved the water and opportunities increased for me to be on and near the water. Friends I had met had boats and I went fishing in Cape Cod Bay, shellfishing in the Cove, sailing and fishing in Pleasant Bay.

Early on, I didn't know much about Pleasant Bay. I had spent most of my summers around the Town Cove, Nauset Harbor and at Skaket Beach, and really only knew Pleasant Bay as a beautiful place that you could see from Route 28 on the way to Chatham. I was glad to finally be learning something about this other magnificent body of water. Every minute I could spend on the water was a blessing and I never tired of it.

I still didn't know much about motor boats though. Other people always ran the boats. Eventually, somebody would tell me to take the helm or teach me how to start the engine and something about the mechanics.

My friend Bruce, who later became my husband, brought home a sailboat one day and said it was for me. I couldn't believe it. What a treasured gift!

I had borrowed a Sunfish a couple of times but didn't really know how to sail. Being told how to sail is a lot different from being shown how to sail. My new boat was a 14-foot fiberglass Cape Dory with classic lines. It carried a strange split mast known as a Gunter rig, designed, I think, to make the boat's use flexible because it could be taken down with relative ease. The design made the boat more trailerable, because the mast and boom could fit neatly inside the boat and not hang over the edge for overland transit, but it was not quite flexible enough to stash the mast, boom and sail inside the boat while rowing.

I rowed the boat several times and it was a good rowing skiff too but I sailed it most of the time back then. I loved being out there. It's only been in the past five or so years that I switched. Now, the Cape Dory is primarily a rowboat, the boat I use to explore both the Nauset and Pleasant Bay estuaries.

But I've gotten ahead of myself again.

Chapter 4

Long Raking in the Bay

From the road to Chatham (Map 4), you could watch men in their boats using long-handled rakes to harvest quahaugs (sometimes spelled quohog or quahog) but I knew nothing about the shellfish, much less the implement or how to use the long-handled things. I later learned that the men were called bullrakers and the implement was a bullrake. When I asked why that term was used, I was told that it took a guy with bull strength to use the rake but I didn't know just how appropriate the term was. And I also didn't know that it would be those quahaugs that would get me the job I had been hoping would come my way.

Warren S. Darling described bullraking in his booklet, *Quahoging out of Rock Harbor, 1890-1930*. Privately printed in 1984, this gem does a great job of capturing an era that is long gone. Darling described the bullrake as "three feet wide, rectangular iron rakes [that] had four semi-circular hoops and were fitted with as many as 25 4-inch dagger-shaped teeth positioned along the front lip. They weighed at least 20 pounds and more than doubled that when hauled up from the bottom of the bay."

Darling described not only the implement but the method of fishing in exquisite detail. The men raked

"an area of the sea bottom roughly the length of the boat and as wide as possible without missing any strips or raking the same area twice. The first few passes were made by 'running the rode' that is, putting the rake, teeth up, on the rode and sliding it down the line with a rapid hand-over-hand motion. When the tee [at the top of the wooden handle] came to hand it was used to twist the pole and flip the rake off the rode. With the rake's teeth set into the sea bottom he moved them through the top layer by a continuing rhythmic series of short, hard, backward-downward jerks of the tee end of the pole."

It got trickier, as Darling explained:

"While doing this he was also inching backwards at the very edge of the boat until he reached the stern. In this stage the bend in the pole was critical. The tide pressing on the submerged, arched pole held the rake into the bottom so that it 'fished' properly. Finally, after reaching the stern, he walked forward until the pole was vertical, hauled the net full of quahaugs and 'shack' up and dumped it on the culling board. Now his son had the task of sorting out the net's contents, throwing overboard the stones, old shells, snails and seaweed and saving the few quahogs while the quahoger repeated the operation. He ran the rode for several more passes and then threw the rake out to the left and right of the rode to cover new territory."

Cape Cod Bay is rarely peaceful and yet these men balanced themselves along the gunwale, literally scratching quahaugs for a living. The good fishermen could make between $10 and $30 a day on the days they could fish, which was excellent money for Cape Cod, but more often than not, weather or some gear calamity kept them ashore.

The bullrakers of Pleasant Bay that I saw were working on a set of quahaugs that showed up in the bay in the late 1950s and were being fished throughout the 1960s. The set wasn't just in Orleans. Chatham and Harwich had their share of bullrakers too. But "set" can be a confusing term. Most species of shellfish occur in groups or "beds." Quahaugs are the exception.

Quahaugs are often found spaced apart and not clumped one on top of the other. But when there are a lot of them in a general area it's known as a good "set" of quahaugs. A good set results either from one particular year producing a bountiful crop of juveniles that lived to be harvested, or from a succession of years of good survivability.

This set was incredible. Portions of the bay were packed with quahaugs and people were able to keep fishing in the same area for two decades with good results.

Quahaugs, known everywhere else but Cape Cod and Rhode Island as hard clams, are particularly flavorful morsels with a very distinctive taste, and are often served raw "on the half shell." But they are a versatile food product that also can be used in chowders, or as clams casino or baked stuffed or clam fritters or in numerous other ways. They can also grow to be quite large, about four inches across the shell, and as they grow, the vernacular name changes, from littleneck to cherrystone (or "cherrys") to chowders. The most valuable in the marketplace, however, is the littleneck, the smallest allowed by law to be harvested, because those are the ones served raw as appetizers and are in highest demand by restaurants and bars.

Those quahaugs in the bay were certainly well known in the marketplace through the '60s and into the '70s. They were littlenecks. They had a distinctive shape and a great "shelf life" (the amount of time they could be refrigerated and keep their quality). They had so many ridges on their shells that they were rough to the touch, and instead of being broad across the shell, they were deep, so that their shells were sort of cupped or heart shaped when viewed on edge.

Usually, each raised ridge on the shell indicates a single year of growth and so they are called growth rings, although sometimes ridges may be added within a single year when the quahaug is disturbed in the sediment. For the quahaugs of Pleasant Bay's great set, if each of the rings truly represented a year of growth, they were fairly old (on the order of 20 or more years old) and yet they were still called littlenecks. It's more likely though that with so many guys fishing out there, individual quahaugs could have been raked out, brought up to the culling board, thrown back overboard to dig in again and be dug out again several times throughout a year. So disturbed, their growth rings might not be "accurate."

It would be sort of like they were on an elevator. Dug up by the rake, up to the culling board, measured and thrown back, up and down, up and down, up and down. Until they finally grew to legal size, they could be disturbed many times given the number of shellfishermen out there every day.

To me, watching the guys in their boats, long before I read Darling, they were individuals standing in flat-bottomed, motorized skiffs, anchored bow and stern, throwing what looked like a fairly heavy metal thing with teeth and a really long handle into the water. If they weren't throwing the thing into the water, they were using hand-over-hand movements to bring it up to the boat again. Or they were hunched over a flat board plopping what from a distance looked like rocks, into the water, or else dropping them in the bottom of the boat in what looked like a sorting action. There was a practiced rhythm to their actions, and it seemed a scene that had played out for a long, long time and might go on year after year after year.

But the shellfishermen and the grocery clerk-biologist had a surprise waiting for them.

Orleans was once part of the town of Eastham and when the towns split in 1797, part of the language inserted in the incorporation papers was a provision that the towns would enjoy a joint fishery. That meant that the inhabitants of both towns could enjoy the fishing privileges accorded the residents of either town. Later, it came to mean that a resident of either town could purchase a license in the other town for the resident fee, and that a person living in either town could obtain a commercial license from either town. Ordinarily in Massachusetts, commercial licenses were and are issued only to residents.

In 1937, Orleans voted by resolution to do everything in its power to prevent passage of a bill introduced by Eastham to the Legislature to separate the shellfisheries. That was not the only time the subject has come up. It seems that every time there has been an exceptional crop of one shellfish species or another, the town with the bounty wants to keep the other guys out. It's probably evened out over time — quahaugs are more abundant in Eastham waters of Cape Cod Bay and scallops have sometimes been more abundant in Orleans.

The idea of "managing" the shellfish resources evolved over many years, although the position of shellfish constable was focused mostly on licenses and limits.

Orleans hired a shellfish constable as far back as the early 1930s in accordance with state law, but the old town reports do not give much information about activities except for the amount appropriated for shellfish projects. Who the people were or what they did is sketchy at best — until Elmer Darling was appointed as Constable in the late 1930s.

Darling wrote detailed summaries for the annual town report that explained how many of each species were harvested from which bodies of water and also estimated the wholesale value of the harvest. He made observations of natural conditions and fully detailed any propagation efforts that he had undertaken. He identified what was probably a natural cycle of clams when he noted that for ten years clams had disappeared from the whole town.

There didn't seem to be any reasonable explanation available to Darling to account for the dearth of clams during those years. However, he did recognize propagation as a method to increase natural stocks and transplanted undersized juvenile shellfish (seed) from one part of town to another. He transplanted large "chowder" sized quahaugs from Cape Cod Bay to other parts of town as well. His reports, because of their detail, continue to serve the public well as historic documentation of an important resource. They follow in step with another Massachusetts author, Dr. David Belding, who wrote definitive manuscripts for the Commonwealth of Massachusetts in the early 1900s on clams, quahaugs, scallops and oysters. Belding's works, long since out of print, are scheduled to be reprinted, thanks to the Barnstable County Extension Service, sometime in 2002.

Elmer Darling was constable into the 1950s and was followed by Frank Burling, whose reports reverted to the sketchy model. By the time Skip Norgeot became constable in the 1960s, the town reports on shellfish activity were quite short. Very little information can be gleaned from them regarding management techniques, but Norgeot reported transplants of shellfish from one body of water to another. He had grown up on Pleasant Bay and was an astute observer of the natural world. He listened carefully to the stories the "old timers" told and learned much about the history of the bay. He remains a valuable resource for his breadth of knowledge. During his tenure in the town's employ, Pleasant Bay was the "hot spot" for quahaugs. Fishermen from Chatham, Harwich and Orleans — each town owned some of the bottom — all bullraked in the 10-20 foot waters of Big Bay.

Warren Goff was the next constable, taking up the post about 1967, and his deputy was Mun Richardson. They were quite a pair, with storehouses of stories and descriptions of old Cape Cod and old Cape Codders, some of which were doubtless true. The catch records they kept were very good though. They knew what species were harvested from what body of water. Warren and Mun knew everybody on the water, as a matter of fact, and knew pretty well how much each fisherman harvested each day. They knew every foot of the shore, and as Warren put it, Mun was a good choice for Deputy because he knew all the tricks of how to get away with something — he had invented a lot of them himself. There was little information about propagation in their reports except for notes about transplanting quahaugs from Cape Cod Bay to the other estuaries.

Warren retired in 1973 and Gardy Munsey was appointed Shellfish Constable while Mun stayed on as Deputy. Gardy had been a member of the Shellfish and Waterways Advisory Committee for many years and a recreational shellfisherman, but he had not fished commercially. He had been a property caretaker for a well-to-do family in South Orleans on Pleasant Bay for a good portion of his life but one of his greatest joys was scratching for quahaugs.

But the great quahaug set that had sustained scores of shellfishermen for two decades was not inexhaustible. And by the time Gardy took the job, new pressures were affecting the harvest.

By the early 1970s, a new crop of young people had flocked to the Cape. Many were avoiding a life their parents had dreamed for them, many were going as far east as they could in a reversal of the mid-1800s when the mantra had been "Go west, young man, go west." The newcomers to the Cape were independent, hard working and wanted to be left alone. Many were college-educated but did not want the traditional trappings that their education could provide if they chose to use their degrees as a ticket to a 9-5 business career. They wanted a simpler life, not in the mountains or backwoods someplace like others of their generation, but rather on the water. They quickly learned to be adept at many types of fishing — for shellfish, finfish and lobsters — because to survive, they needed to diversify.

With so many more harvesters out scratching, old-time observers of the natural surroundings began getting the uneasy feeling that for the first time, the inshore fishery had become something that couldn't be taken for granted anymore. Mother Nature couldn't seem to catch up to the effects of years of big harvests. Not only were the harvests of the old days no longer being provided by the early '70s, but there were more people trying to make a living from what nature did provide. Orleans folks realized that there was now a need to know a lot more about how shellfish worked. It was time, though nobody knew it for sure then, for something new to integrate the fundamental facts of shellfish and the ecology of the bays where shellfish live. That something new was biology.

And so, in a forward-looking town that looked to the sea for sustenance, Orleans would hire a green kid, a woman at that, to look at shellfish in a new way, taking into account the biology of the shellfish and the ebb and flow of life in the estuaries. But I'm still ahead of myself.

Chapter 5

Bountiful Harvest

The ecological situation when I started work for the town of Orleans was in flux all along shore. Ancient assumptions were giving way to new realities. Although my main concern was shellfish, the changing realities of all kinds of fisheries were having, and would continue to have, major implications for my work.

Imagine what Bartholomew Gosnold saw at the dawn of the seventeenth century when he wrote that the codfish were so plentiful on Cape Cod that you could walk on their backs. It must have seemed like an inexhaustible supply.

For 350 years, until the 1960s, it had seemed like an inexhaustible supply to local fishermen as well. Inexhaustible was not accurate, however, once factory trawlers from other countries began appearing not only on the horizon but almost at the Cape's back door. One of the most productive fishing grounds in the world, Georges Bank, within 200 miles of Cape Cod, was being systematically scoured of fish. For the first time, huge ships could catch hundreds of tons of fish, then process and freeze them on site before they returned home months later.

In the age of sail, fishing boats had stayed on the fishing grounds for many days, processing fish by salting them. Dorymen set out from the larger vessels to set the nets or hooks and haul in the catch, then returned to the larger boat. Later, as steam replaced sail, boats carried ice on board and the boats brought whole fish back to shore for the fresh fish markets. The fish were minimally processed at sea (head and guts removed), and land-based operations finished the job to get the fish ready for market.

Not all ports supported the large vessels. Some, such as Provincetown and Chatham, had boats that were not offshore for more than a couple of days and most were "day-trippers". These boats relied on fish that were closer to shore, still a plentiful supply with the factory trawlers focused on deeper waters, but numbers were nonetheless decreasing alongshore as well.

By 1976, the U.S. Congress would take action to reduce the impact of the foreign factory ships by declaring that the sovereign waters of the nation extended 200 miles offshore. But American factory ships continued to ply the waters, in fact their numbers increased. The declines in offshore fish stocks continued. Well before 1976, many small-boat fishermen on Cape Cod had decided their future lay in the inshore fisheries.

The inshore fisheries can be classified as those economically significant species that reside in the estuaries or relatively close to shore. The term includes finfish, shellfish, and crustaceans. Nationally, inshore fisheries are regulated by the states, but in Massachusetts, the towns manage the resources for some species.

From the New England perspective, fishing is sort of an inverse pyramid. The offshore component accounts for most of the fish harvested by the most number of people and yields the highest economic value. Fish found closest to shore, and lobsters that crawl along the shore, are in the middle, and the fish and shellfish found in the estuaries form the narrow apex of the upside-down triangle. As fishing decreases offshore, the fishermen move closer and closer to home and the pressure on the inshore fisheries increases. And so what happens on Georges Bank has a profound effect all the way down the ladder to the local level.

Some Cape people had never chosen to go offshore in the first place. That's still true. Such people like fishing in their own back yard. They like working with tides, working alone, choosing how hard they want to work, choosing what they want to fish for and when. They know weather patterns and can "read" the water. They follow the market prices, fishing for the highest cash crop when it is expedient to do so and eking out a living when prices are not as good. They have no one to answer to but themselves. The ones who are adept at this lifestyle are also keen observers who have intimate knowledge of the waters around them and the creatures that dwell within those waters. Generations of men from the Cape fit this grouping.

The inshore fishery is diverse but the main components are flounder, striped bass, bluefish, tuna, cod and haddock, lobsters, eels, clams, quahaugs, scallops, mussels and oysters. Other less prominent species also are harvested from time to time. All of those species are regulated by the Massachusetts Division of Marine Fisheries but as we've seen, the shellfish are managed by the individual coastal communities. The state is in charge of such items as size restrictions, night fishing prohibitions, and all issues of harvest when contamination enters the picture, but municipal shellfish propagation, harvesting methods, licensing and setting license fees, opening and closing areas (except for pollution decisions) and enforcement matters are managed by the towns. Towns are expected to hire a shellfish constable and other personnel as they deem appropriate and the duties of the constable are spelled out in the state law.

People from outside Massachusetts are often astounded by this management scheme because it means that the regulations can be very different from one town to another. Most other states manage shellfish either through county government or state government. The Massachusetts system means that the people who manage the shellfishery are generally very well acquainted with the shoreline on a miniscule scale — they know precisely where the shellfish are and where shellfish are less abundant. They attend to all the natural cycles of abundance and often profess the optimistic attitude that if one thing is down, another will take its place. When that happens, they are ready to switch gears and urge people to harvest the more prevalent stock.

Shellfish are harvested commercially by residents of the town who can sell their catch. Shellfish are also harvested recreationally by residents and non-residents alike who gather them for their own personal use. Although the price is reduced for residents, all across the Cape, thousands of non-residents also purchase a permit to get shellfish. The ability to buy a permit and dig shellfish has historically been a huge attraction on the Cape.

In Orleans, all the shellfish species are present in one place or another except for oysters. Natural populations of oysters have not occurred in decades but ancient shell middens left by the native peoples provide proof that oysters were once abundant in town waters.

At this point, a kind of primer of shellfish will be helpful.

Clams

Clams (*Mya arenaria*) — also known as soft-shell clams, steamers, "piss clams", and clams for fried clams — are found in sandy and sand/mud substrate combinations. They are difficult to harvest for several reasons. They are found 1-2 feet below the surface; their shells are brittle and break easily; and smaller ones are on top of the larger, legal ones — which means many sub-legal sized clam shells are broken in the harvest process.

To harvest clams, one uses an implement that looks like a garden spading fork that has been bent at least 90° but more often is bent inward toward the handle at closer to a 110° or so bend. So, not only are the small ones on top of the legal-sized clams, but the optimal angle of the spading-fork tines means digging into unseen clams, and the more brittle the shell, the more breakage that occurs. The faster clams grow, as in areas like Nauset Harbor, the more brittle their shells become. It takes a certain skill to harvest clams from this area without breaking them, which would render them unmarketable.

Digging clams is awkward, hard, backbreaking work. You're hunched over, legs spread apart in a half-split, digging holes or trenches in the sand for hours. Less agile or competent diggers get down on their hands and knees, but digging a hole from that position is difficult as well. When digging for clams, you are "up close and personal" with the sediment and all its inhabitants — holes that show in the sand indicate where the clams are, but not all such holes belong to clams. Worms make holes too, as do quahaugs and razor clams.

Anyone fourteen years of age or older can get a commercial license and dig (if they are able) two bushels of clams a day. In case you've never tried it yourself, that's a lot of clams to dig from a very uncomfortable position. Chatham has no harvest limit — the only limit is stamina.

Native clams generally are sold to restaurants for steamed clams and there isn't a salty Cape restaurant that does not serve steamers.

When demand is high, so is the price, and the summer pace is frenetic. Demand is sharply lower before Memorial Day and after Labor Day. Sometimes clams are simply opened and the shucked clams are canned and sold for the fryer market, but more often, fried clams you eat here are imported from off-Cape suppliers.

Quahaugs

Quahaugs (*Mercenaria mercenaria*), — or hard clams, also known as littlenecks, cherrystones, chowders (to repeat, all such terms relate to size, from small to large) — are also found in sandy or sand/shell/mud substrates. They live close to the surface and are harvested with a long-handled rake — which is called a "scratcher" because it has five or six sharply pointed curved tines used to scratch the bottom.

Some scratchers have a metal-framed "basket" attached, others don't and are called "open rakes". Some people feel more comfortable having a basket and feel it ensures they lose fewer quahaugs. Others prefer the relative lightness and ease of the open rake. In either case, the rake is dragged through the sediment with quick jerking movements until you "feel" the quahaug and you "hear" the sound of the metal tines on the shell. But more often than not, what you hear and dig up is the rock that your tine has hit. Eventually, you can tell the difference between the two but only through trial and error and lots of practice. The bull rakes I saw on my early excursions are used in deep water.

In Cape Cod Bay, a quahaug fishery has existed for over a hundred years. Before the combustible engine, people sailed from Rock Harbor out into the bay. There they fished with bull rakes attached to poles that were 40-60 feet long. It took a lot of knowledge and experience to make a 40-60 foot pole that was flexible enough to bend over the stern of a 24-28-foot boat, the end dragging in the water behind, yet also strong enough for the fisherman to work the metal-tined basket into the sediment below, searching for quahaugs.

Think about the dexterity it took to use a rake with a handle that long where the "T" end would be floating on the water while the basket was being emptied on the boat's deck. Think about the calluses the men built on their hands constantly working with the wet wooden handle. Think about doing all this from an anchored sailboat where walking along the gunwale was how you spent your day. Darling's 1984 booklet is a charming little book that preserves a bygone era.

Scallops

Scallops (*Argopecten irradians irradians*) are the darling of the shellfish world on Cape Cod. These beautiful-shelled animals are considerate enough not to dig into the sediment like clams or quahaugs or to attach to one another by some sort of glue or threads like oysters or mussels. Instead, they rest on the sediment surface, seemingly waiting to be scooped up by a dredge or basket rake. When the price is high, collecting scallops is like picking up quarters off the bottom.

One of the main differences between scalloping and other forms of shellfishing is that only the muscle that keeps the two shells closed is eaten. That means that scallops have to be "shucked." Shucking means someone has to insert a knife between the shells, direct the knife toward the part of the muscle that attaches to the top shell, cut it, scrape the remaining viscera away from the muscle, cut the other side away from the bottom shell and — if the shucker can resist eating it right on the spot — putting the tasty morsel into a bowl. It also means that after a fisherman has been on the water for hours getting his limit of scallops, he or she then must stand for hours shucking the scallops before retiring to bed to do it all over the next day. If he doesn't want to shuck them himself, he has to get his "significant other" (if he has one) to shuck scallops or he has to hire someone else to do it for him, reducing his "take" for the day significantly. The state allows ten bushels per day per person; the town can adjust that haul downward but they cannot exceed the limit.

Scallops can't close their shells tightly, which is good for shuckers, but it also means they are relatively easy prey for crabs. However, scallops have a unique escape mechanism. First, they swim. Maybe not swim exactly, but they can propel themselves through the water by squirting a jet of water in sort of a clacking movement — opening and closing their shell — and thus they can avoid predators. Second, they have a series of blue eyes along both shells imbedded in the mantle, a ribbon of tissue that lines the inner edge of the shell, which may be able to tell them that danger lurks. Third, they have sensory feelers that they extend into the water outside their shell, which tell them danger is really near and they should skedaddle or close their shells tightly. When they are small, they attach to blades of eelgrass, which gets them above their predators, but crabs are like squirrels — where there is a will, there is a way.

Mussels

Mussels (*Mytilus edulis*) occur in large colonies, attached to something — small rocks or each other. They are found on intertidal bars where they spend part of each tidal cycle out of water and part subtidally, attached to rocks or pilings or some similar structure.

From a marketing perspective, commercial shellfish species fall into something of a hierarchy of preference. Oysters (*Crassostrea virginica*) are king (or queen) perhaps because of their historical significance as an acclaimed aphrodisiac, but they no longer naturally appear in Orleans waters except a few that attach to the bulkhead at Rock Harbor on the Cape Cod Bay side of town. Value-wise, bay scallops (*Argopecten irradians irradians*) are second (and some would argue they should be ranked first, with an asterisk perhaps, because the demand is always high and the supply is generally low or non-existent). Quahaugs come next, valued primarily for their versatility as a food source since even the big heavy old chowders are used for chowder base or to make linguine with clam sauce. Next on the list are soft shell clams. There is usually a year-round supply and they can be sold for canned fried clams, but there is a cyclical rise and fall that can mean decent money one year and slim pickings the next.

Last, but not least, are the mussels. Quality can be erratic and it is essential in preparing them to make absolutely sure all the mussels are alive in the kitchen because one bad one can spoil an entire batch, but those concerns aside, mussels can be a significant resource.

Mussels are a "Johnny-come-lately" species. Although they are delicious and have been prevalent for years in some areas, most notably in Nauset Harbor and Town Cove, they were not harvested appreciably for food until the 1970s. Locally, blue mussels, as they are sometime known, have gotten a bum rap. In the town reports of the early 1940s, Elmer Darling pleaded with the townsfolk to eradicate the mussels. His message was to get rid of them any way they knew. He said mussels were smothering the clams below them, they were a nuisance, and for some reason, it was Darling's view that mussels were not fit for eating.

Then, in the mid-1940s, during the war, meat was scarce and the locals realized that Orleans had a bountiful source of protein in mussels. They were plentiful in Nauset Harbor, residents could get as many as they wanted and Darling changed his tune: Now he was urging them to get mussels. Right after the war, Darling switched again and put out more anti-mussel rhetoric to get rid of them and get clams back in the markets in abundance.

Growing in clumps, with larger specimens surrounded by smaller ones and all attached together by a mass of strong threads called byssal threads, mussels are easy to harvest. Break a clump off the bottom with a scratcher, tear off the smaller mussels and throw them back in the water, put the larger ones in your bucket and off you go. It doesn't take very long to gather a bucket of mussels when they are plentiful.

Mussel abundance is not only a function of man's harvesting efforts, however. Severe winter temperatures and ice or sanding in of the bars can reduce populations. Eider ducks visit the harbor every winter and they can completely wipe out the mussel resources in three or four months. Summer visitors in the early 1980s blamed the fishermen for the decline but photos taken in the fall, winter and spring belied that idea. On one particular bar where no one was harvesting the mussels because they were too small, the photos showed the bars completely clean by spring where they had been black with mussels in the fall. Thousands of eiders had their picture taken over the bar at high tide one day in late winter but they were there every day for several months before and after their photoshoot since mussels are their favorite food.

Mussels from Nauset Harbor are of a remarkably high quality. Those mussels that grow under water at all times have shells free of barnacles; they have no pea crabs inside their shell unlike those harvested near Woods Hole at the shoulder of Cape Cod; and they have a low incidence of jaw-breaking pearls in the meats, a major problem with mussels from Maine. Those on the intertidal bars in Nauset Harbor grow more slowly than those that live under water at all times, but they do not seem to grow so slowly that they develop multiple pearls. The largest mussel-harvest and mussel-shipping company in Maine, Great Eastern Mussel Company, uses the quality of Nauset Harbor mussels as the quality standard for their company to achieve.

Oysters

Oysters (*Crassostrea virginica*), a nationally important commercial species, does not appear as a natural population in Orleans. Sporadic individuals appear in Rock Harbor from time to time. They are cultured privately in Orleans through aquaculture. Wellfleet has the greatest concentration of oysters in the region.

Chapter 6

Opportunity Knocks

By the early 1970s, the Pleasant Bay fishermen's bullrakes, filled mostly with shack (pieces of shell, stones and other debris), were still being emptied on the culling board to be sorted, but most of the "catch" was thrown overboard. The tremendous number of quahaugs that had been there since the late '50s had finally played out, and nature had not provided any seed to replace what had been taken. A few fishermen continued to try to make a day's pay, but the majority had left quahaugging the bay to find alternative ways to making a living. What was wrong with the bay? That question was to occupy me for several years.

During the height of the fishing activity in the 1960s, David Gates had made a study of quahaugs at the request of the Orleans Board of Selectmen and the town's Shellfish and Waterways Advisory Committee. Gates was a local biology teacher, who had worked on oysters in Hawaii and had worked with marine invertebrates at the Marine Biological Laboratory in Woods Hole. Gates collaborated with Skip Norgeot, the town's Shellfish Constable, for the study. To obtain samples for Gates's 1964 study, Norgeot and his friend Tom Adams used SCUBA gear to obtain square-foot samples of the bottom. Gates estimated that they covered about 30 acres of bottom out of about 3500 acres of Pleasant Bay within Orleans waters. He broke the sampling down to seven discrete areas where most of the fishing activity was taking place. Extrapolating from 22 individual samples in Big Bay, Gates estimated the standing crop to be about 65,000 bushels worth an estimated $967,000 wholesale at that time ($5,630,000 in today's market). The report states that in some areas of the bay, quahaugs averaged 50 per square foot, a bountiful population, but

Norgeot and Adams had one sample as high as 180 per square foot and several near 125, phenomenal numbers.

By the time I came aboard, no such concentration could be found anywhere.

Gardy Munsey had been appointed as Shellfish Constable in 1973 and Mun Richardson, who had worked for the Shellfish Department for several prior years, stayed on as his deputy. Both men also comprised the Harbormaster office, responsible for maintaining channel-marker buoys, town docks, and Rock Harbor, the town's only marina on Cape Cod Bay.

The fishermen had gone to the selectmen, informing them that something was wrong in Pleasant Bay. As the responsible political body, it was up to the selectmen to do something. When the fishermen "suggested" that the selectmen DO something about a fishery, the selectmen usually listened and took some sort of action. In this case, they held a meeting in 1974 to gather information and hear specifically what the fishermen wanted them to do.

I attended the meeting as an interested resident, no more. But when the fishermen said they needed a biologist, someone who could study the bay and find out what was really going on, my pulse raced. Someone looked at the back of the room and said that there was already a biologist in town. The next thing I knew, Gardy was looking for me to see if I wanted to tackle the job, to see if I could find out why there weren't many quahaugs left in the bay. I couldn't believe it. Could this really be happening? It was just a six-month contract, part-time at that, but it was a start. Little did I know that it was the seed that would grow into a 25-year career.

I was still working at Ellis' Market and not quite ready to give up my "day job". I worked out a contract with Gardy and an arrangement at Ellis' where I worked at the market in the mornings and went out in the bay in the afternoon. My experience at the store came in handy later since I had met a lot of waterfront property owners and got to know them.

The two-person department was strapped for equipment and Gardy and Mun couldn't spare me much time. If I was going to take the job, Gardy said, I needed to know that the Shellfish Department couldn't help me out with manpower or equipment. I would be on my own.

Chapter 7

Where Did All the Quahaugs Go?

I had just begun to learn a bit about running outboard engines. The only other boating experience I had was back at the boat shop when I was about 7 or 8 and then I was rowing, not using a motorboat. I had almost never been out on the water alone.

Bruce loaned me an extremely heavy but stable 14-foot fiberglass skiff with a 6hp motor to use for the detective work on quahaugs. He moored the boat in Paw Wah Pond, about a mile or more journey from the prime quahaug area. He knew I was inexperienced but felt that I couldn't get into too much trouble with such a weakly powered engine trying to push the hefty boat through the water.

Getting there was one hurdle but the quahaugs were on the bottom in 10-20 feet of water and I needed to find out about what was happening where the quahaugs were. I didn't want to dive solo (thereby breaking the cardinal rule of diving: Never dive alone) to observe life in the depths through a mask. The next best thing was to sample the bay bottom. But how?

Bruce suggested a post-hole digger but one rigged with longer handles than would be needed for a fencing project. It would be an implement that was similar to the oyster tongs used in Chesapeake Bay.

The tongs look like two long-handled basket scratchers. The handles are attached to each other with the baskets facing each other with a pivot bolt, forming an X. The mechanical theory is that the teeth get under the shell of oysters on the surface of the bay bottom. By manipulating the handles, the baskets can open or close. When the handles are close together, the baskets open up and when the handles are splayed out the farthest, the baskets close.

My posthole digger would do the same thing but it would be a smaller version. The blades wouldn't open up too much but if I could keep the handles somewhat apart when bringing my haul up to the boat, it should contain some sediment. It wasn't exactly a core sample, like those provided by more sophisticated samplers, but I figured I could get some idea of the bottom.

There I was, a woman with naturally well-developed pectoral muscles, trying to increase them even more by using this gizmo. It worked, but only marginally. It was OK in mud but totally unacceptable in the hard bottom. Sampling the latter type would require another gizmo.

The best way I could figure to do that was to use a rake similar to the bullrakes the guys were using. My brother-in-law made a long-handled but small version of a bull rake for me. The basket was lined with quarter-inch-mesh galvanized hardware cloth so that I could see the type of sediment I was digging into. I had dug a few clams and scratched a few quahaugs before but I certainly had never done anything like this before and definitely not with a bullrake. This was going to be quite an adventure and I had no idea how it was all going to work out.

But I was happy — a golden opportunity had just been handed to me: I would be working in the natural resources field and on the water no less! I wanted to make the most of the chance.

One of the advantages of a background in conservation of natural resources and ecology is that the principles are pretty much the same regardless of the habitat you're working in. So all you have to do is think about the big processes and then just plug in the particulars about the resources you're working with. Piece of cake, I thought innocently.

I worked at the market until noon most days and then headed out of Paw Wah Pond in the afternoon and inched my way to Big Bay against the prevailing and usually intensifying southwest wind. "Intensifying" meant whitecaps most of the way there. My tools were the post-hole digger with ridiculously long handles and a modified bullrake attached to a 20-foot pole that stuck out beyond the 16-foot boat. I was ready to take on the challenge and find out things about the bottom and its inhabitants that I couldn't see simply peering down from the bobbing boat.

For the most part, the guys out in the Bay ignored me. Many times I was sampling areas where there were no quahaugs and I must've looked ridiculous. For starters, I was having a devil of a time getting samples. What did I know about bullraking? Trial and error was my teacher and my assignment gave new meaning to the phrase "on the job training." Even if Darling's book had been printed earlier and I had read it in '74, I probably wouldn't have known what he was talking about. What is a "rode", for example, as in Darling's phrase, "Running the Rode"?

I knew enough to anchor the boat bow and stern, a challenge in itself, and I tried to rake along the side of the boat, but it was extremely hard work and a battle just to get the teeth in the bottom. Then, because of the finer mesh of the hardware cloth basket liner, I was pulling up all the mud, sand and shells that the basket could hold, doubling or tripling the difficulty. I found out why they called them bullrakers.

Then one day, one of the guys came over to my boat. I had been watching him and he had seemed like a loner, always off by himself and never talking with the other watermen. He said he had been watching me and couldn't stand it any longer because I was so awkward. He said I was fighting the rake and using it all wrong, that I had to slide the rake down the rode, which I finally learned was the bow anchor line. He showed me and I began to understand. Then he asked me what I was doing out there and I told him I was trying to get samples of the bottom to see what was there and try to figure out why there were not a lot of quahaugs left. He asked me why I was scratching where there weren't any quahaugs and I told him that I needed to see what a lot of the bay bottom looked like. Instead of giving me a hard time, he gave me valuable hints on how to work the rake into the bottom. I was extremely grateful.

I sampled the bay, zigzagging across most of the western portion of Big Bay, putting special emphasis on the bottoms where fishing activity had taken place, using Gates's report for a reference point. Fishermen start their day early, so by mid-afternoon, when I got out there, I often found that most of them had already gone home. When the afternoon wind came up, I had few competitors in the most productive areas. Which was a good thing because I could work without being laughed at, but it also struck me that if I ran into trouble, there was no one out there to help.

I drew a crude map of the bottom sediments and the density of quahaugs. Mostly, I found piles of "shack" in the part of the bay that had been heavily fished. There was so much of this debris that it was difficult to get the rake into the bottom. I thought that if there was so much shack, how could a new set of quahaugs get established in the bottom? But parts of the bay that did not have the shack didn't seem to have much of anything either. In those areas, I found few shells, fewer live quahaugs, and only some small, thin, red worms in the sediment. Once in a while, I found a mollusk species that I'd have to take back to identify — like a Gould's pandora (*Pandora gouldiana*) or a Baltic macoma (*Macoma baltica*). Some areas had a sulphurous sponge on the bottom and some areas were thick mud but the most productive areas had been a sand/shell/silt mixture. When I identified the various species I was finding, I often also found some useful information about the particular habitat each favored. I learned that in the areas with the Macomas and the sulphurous sponges, for example, the bottom was naturally inhospitable to quahaugs. That little tidbit was filed away for future reference.

The contract with the town lasted six months and was extended for another six months. During that time, I also helped the Shellfish Department with their propagation efforts. I had found my place.

Gardy made the case to the selectmen that my contract position should be deleted and instead a new-full time position with the Shellfish Department should be created. After debate at Town Meeting, the new position was approved and I began working for the Shellfish Department as a full time shellfish biologist, the first such position established in Massachusetts.

I was elated and couldn't believe my good fortune. I would be working with shellfish, a marine natural resource. I would be on the shore and in boats. I would be spending hours on the water in a job where I hoped I could be useful. And although I had my own insecurities and felt overwhelmed with the breadth of things I didn't know, I knew I had an incredible opportunity. I would learn and find out about quahaugs and other species of shellfish and I would actually be getting paid for this luxury.

I gave my notice at Ellis' Market.

Chapter 8

Foot by Foot

I had this great job. Now what was I going to do with it?

Aside from the shellfish that were my primary responsibility, I also had to know all about the other aspects of the estuaries — who used them and for what purpose? Which activities would ultimately affect shellfish and how?

Each estuary was so completely different from the others. There was Cape Cod Bay, the large expanse of water that rims the entire shoreline of the flexed arm that is the Cape. Nauset/Town Cove, an exquisite mixture of coastal environments that remains incredibly productive despite being adjacent to a major highway and a busy downtown commercial area. Pleasant Bay, the largest estuary of its kind on the Cape and a true gem any way you look at it.

These three diverse systems were my own laboratory. What made them distinct from one another? Why were some plants or animals found in one and not another? How could they be so different and yet be so close as the gull flies? Why did certain species of shellfish do well in one place and not another? Would I ever be able to answer those questions?

Numerous researchers have described Cape Cod as a geographical and biological dividing line. It is the northern limit of southern species most commonly found near the Gulf Stream, one of the world's longest and most influential currents, and the southern limit of northern species found inhabiting the colder boreal waters along the Labrador Current. Orleans epitomizes that dividing-line with its three separate estuaries exhibiting different natural regimes. Northern species could be found in Cape Cod Bay and sometimes

Nauset, for example, while southern species were found in Pleasant Bay but rarely Nauset and never Cape Cod Bay.

The first thing I needed to do was to get acquainted in a more up front and personal manner with the shoreline and estuaries. I devised a check list of plants and animals common to the region, added sediment types to the list, got a pair of hip boots, bought a basket scratcher and lined it with quarter-inch galvanized hardware cloth, and set out walking, looking, and recording my observations. I'd park at a town landing and walk all around and then back again.

Town landings weren't always convenient to where I wanted to go and the customers I had met at Ellis' Market came in handy since many of them owned waterfront property. I'd go to a house and ask if I could park in their yard. Not only was I never refused, most of the time I was invited to stop for a visit or a beverage or was the recipient of some other neighborly gesture. The people were terrific.

As I walked along, I was struck by the diversity of the shoreline. Sand, gravel, cobble, silt, shell, mud and all combinations. Coarse sand and fine sand, gravel with rocks — every conceivable combination of sediment types, often changing abruptly from one to another in a matter of a few feet. Animals were present in some areas and absent in others, those patterns also changing abruptly.

Then there were the creeks that led to salt marshes. These were shoreline indentations, once coves, that had gradually filled in with sediment. They had developed over thousands of years into some of the most productive ecosystems in the world. Some of the marshes were no bigger than an acre or two and others were vast systems covering tens of acres. The bigger the marsh, the bigger the creeks feeding it. The sediment at the bottom of a creek was usually soft, a function of the slow water velocity constantly depositing fine materials, except at the mouth where the fine materials were washed out of the creek. Often there was a sand delta at the mouth, beyond which was often a bottom of soft sediments.

There were always birds foraging as the tide went out, searching for that morsel that would tide them over until they found the next morsel. There were large boulders, dropped in place by the glaciers, with barnacles or mussels or various types of seaweed attached, depending on what body of water I was at.

As I walked along the shores of both Nauset and Pleasant Bay, I was struck by the rivulets of fresh water coming from the land. In the summer old sneakers replaced the clunky hip boots and I could feel a marked difference between cold fresh water and the warmer salt water. Often I noticed red sand where the water coursed from land, and in that red sand there were rarely clams and almost never quahaugs. But slightly offshore, where fresh and salt water intermingled, was a different story. Quahaugs were often found there. Wherever there were fresh water rivulets, there were usually large colonies of mud snails seemingly gliding along the bottom.

Scratching around large boulders usually revealed a little group of quahaugs on one side or another. Clams lined the shores in places and in other places there were hardly any. Sometimes there were no shellfish for a long distance alongshore and I'd try to figure out what was so different around the corner. Sometimes there would be shell fragments but no live specimens and sometimes I'd find other species of shellfish that were not commercially important. Once in a while I'd find a real oddity, something that the guide books said was rare for the region.

There were clams on sand bars as close to the ocean as the inner harbor and as far away from the ocean as the upper reaches of the estuaries. There were mussels in Nauset but none in the Orleans portion of Pleasant Bay. Quahaugs were almost everywhere in Nauset and the only difference was how many were where. But they were few and far between in Pleasant Bay. There were worms that looked like beige ribbons and worms that looked like red thread. I saw gelatinous masses attached to the sediment that, when closely examined, held tiny eggs.

Even better than walking the shores, however, was use of the town workboat whenever I wanted. Gardy had shown me how to operate the 25hp engine on the flat-bottomed work skiff and was willing to launch it for me at almost a moment's notice. I told him I needed a "look box" or bucket or something with a clear Plexiglas bottom that I could use to peer into the water from the boat and he immediately had a fiberglassed box with handles specially made for me.

My favorite use of the boat was to observe the watery world by travelling slowly in shallow water, either with the engine idling or by letting the boat drift in the tide. Using the boat that way didn't do much for the engine but it was incredibly revealing to me. I compared areas when the tide was low and the critters were hiding and when it was high and they were all moving about. In the summer, I also snorkeled in Pleasant Bay. I was fascinated to see tiny seed scallops attached to eelgrass before they were large enough to fend for themselves on the bottom.

As the boat drifted over the immense eelgrass meadows that existed in the bay then, I'd often see pipefish, which resemble seahorses, or various species of other small fish darting through what must have been a forest to them. I'd see tiny snails attached to the blades of grass and tinier, circular, white hard-shelled worms seemingly glued on to the grass for decoration. There'd be patches of sand with no grass and then thick grass again. Why?

I'd drift over the shores that I had walked at low tide, watching the multitude of animals move around in their element. I'd watch the struggle for survival among species. I'd dig something up and watch and time how long it took the animal to dig back into the sediment. I'd dig up small conchs, predatory animals that can drill a perfectly round hole in the shell of a clam or quahaug, and wonder how it found its prey. I'd watch a moon snail wrap its "foot" around a clam and then cover it with a gelatinous substance so that the clam couldn't siphon water. Seeing all this wasn't much like work to me.

There were starfish in Nauset, none in Pleasant Bay, and blue crabs in Pleasant Bay and none in Nauset. Tiny gem clams that looked like baby quahaugs were extremely common in Pleasant Bay and almost non-existent in Nauset. The amount of life I saw was endless — I always saw something new. I bought an array of guide books to help me identify what I was seeing.

In lousy weather, I often traveled to Woods Hole to the Marine Biological Laboratory library, one of the foremost libraries of its type in the country. There, because I was working for the town, I was able to obtain journal articles on all aspects of marine science. I was beginning to plug in those variables that make marine ecology different from forest ecology.

I could learn to identify the marine life, which was only what might be expected of a shellfish biologist but that, to me, was only a small part of the picture. I needed to know the whole picture. What interacted with what? Where did the users, man, fit into the scheme? What areas were heavily used and what ones were less popular and why? Actually, "why" became my favorite word. I needed to look critically at each separate body of water throughout the year to get a sense about how each fit into the bigger picture.

Cape Cod Bay

Cape Cod Bay was probably a large fresh water lake many millennia ago. It came into existence during glacial melt and filled with seawater through the sea-level rise that followed. Indentations along its margin are classified as separate estuaries. Among them are: Barnstable Harbor in Barnstable, Sesuit Harbor in Dennis, the Stony Brook-Paine's Creek drainage in Brewster, the marsh creeks in Orleans and Eastham (Namskaket, Little Namskaket, Rock Harbor, Boat Meadow Creek, and Herring River), Wellfleet Harbor, Pamet River in Truro and Provincetown Harbor. Marsh creek systems are transition areas between land and sea and inherently different from drowned kettle holes and connecting rivers. Each type of system has its own set of environmental attributes, including the plants and animals that inhabit them.

The most intriguing aspect of Cape Cod Bay is the tidal range, normally about ten feet. When the tide is high, the marsh creeks along the margin fill with water and the deeper ones like Rock Harbor are even navigable and support a large fishing fleet. But when the tide is low, sandy tidal flats extend from the shore out to about one-and-a-half miles and the passageway to the creeks may be no more than knee-deep. This fluctuation means that boats can navigate the channel only during the two hours before and after high tide. Fishing from Rock Harbor means constant attention to time and tide.

The extensive flats of Cape Cod Bay are not productive for shellfish, at least in Orleans. Because the Orleans flats extend from the inner crook of the elbow, the shoreline bears the brunt of harsh northwest winds in the winter, the predominant winds in that season. They are especially fierce when the wind hauls to the northwest after a northeast storm has passed.

When the temperature drops to the teens for several days, the shallow water over the flats freezes and as the tide comes in, it pushes the ice into the crook, which is the gut of the bay. If the cold snap is long enough, no blue water can be seen from Rock Harbor, since ice can build up for three to five miles offshore. People who visit the area only in the summer would not believe this awesome sight. When the ice moves, it scrapes the sand from the surface of the flats and deposits it somewhere else. Even large adult quahaugs can't dig down as far as larger clams can, and when the ice scrapes the sand, it lifts the quahaugs out of the sand too. Even if the clams can dig down deeply, clams don't like to be in shifting sands and often perish in such conditions. Meanwhile oysters and mussels need something to attach to and there isn't anything on the flats. The only place where shellfish might survive is close to the marsh on the extreme landward portion of the flats but even there, with some protection from the marsh, shellfish are hard to find. In sum, none of the commercially important shellfish can tolerate such conditions and need some sort of protection that they simply can't get on the bay flats.

One exception to this scenario is the razor clam (*Ensis directus*), a species that has just recently become important commercially. This long, thin bivalve's shell resembles an old-fashioned straight razor — and is almost as sharp. It has a powerful foot that allows it to burrow very quickly plus it has a mechanism that enables it to propel itself through the water, as if swimming. This behavior is especially useful for small razor clams.

Offshore of the flats, in waters that are up to forty feet deep, it's a different story. Quahaugs are plentiful out there. Quahaug harvesting was mechanized after the development of the combustible engine. Gone are the sailing vessels and Darling's bullrakers, replaced by 30-40-foot "draggers" that pull heavy steel dredges behind them as they motor along.

The dredges are rectangular box frames. The forward edge of the rectangle, nearest the boat, is a knife-edge that digs into the sandy sediment to dislodge the quahaugs, which are about six inches below the surface. The box frames are narrow on the far end, with bars spaced about two inches apart to allow smaller quahaugs to fall through as the dredge is raised in the water. As the boat moves forward, the dredge "rocks" forward a little, stops and rocks forward again, creating what is known, not surprisingly, as a "rocking chair" effect. The dredges are called, also aptly, rocking chair dredges. The boats need to be sturdy because the constant tug and pull of the dredge is hard on the boat.

Sea clams (*Spissula solidissima*) — also known as surf clams — are harvested with hydraulic dredges on the north side of an area known as Billingsgate Shoals, about five miles or so offshore. The hydraulic dredges are similar to the rocking chair dredges except that instead of the knife blade at the forward edge, there are small hollow pipes called "jets." The jets are connected to a larger diameter pipe or "manifold". The larger pipe is connected to a hose that is attached to a pump on board the boat. Seawater is pumped via an intake hose to the manifold hose and out the jets. The jets of water loosen the substrate ahead of the steel basket that is dragged along the bottom, and with the sediment loosened, the sea clams are easily scooped up as the dredge moves along the bottom.

These clams are made into chowder base, and the mantle edge (the strip of tissue attached to the shell around the entire edge of the animal) is edible as well. These are the "strip clams" often seen on restaurant menus as fried clams. Refrigerated trucks wait on the dock for the boats to return. They'll carry the clams to a processing facility, usually off-Cape.

Bay scallops make infrequent appearances in Cape Cod Bay and when they do appear, it seems they almost always straddle town lines. They provide another reminder that town lines are politically and socially important with respect to shellfish harvesting since each town manages its own shellfish resources.

Most often, scallops are found south of the Billingsgate Shoals in Eastham and Wellfleet waters — north of the Orleans-Brewster flats. Not since 1976 have scallops been found in shallow waters off the Orleans-Brewster flats.

Back then, a large set occurred straddling the town line in a depression or guzzle offshore of the flats. Harvesting them took place for only about six weeks because bad weather set in after that. But they were very intense weeks with a lot of people involved in the fishery in all manner of small craft, some of which should not have been there since Cape Cod Bay can dish up some pretty nasty weather very quickly. A lot of the scalloping took place on either side of high tides so that if you ran into trouble with nasty weather that came on suddenly, you could run for the harbor. But once in a while, boats braved the eight-hour shift over the low tide, when the harbor couldn't be reached for lack of water. They were taking quite a chance.

One day, after a couple of weeks of "loose" enforcement of the legal harvest limit of this 1976 bounty, Gardy had received some complaints that some of the fishermen weren't playing fair. The language of the law said "bushels" but used "bags" as well, clearly intending the two to be taken as synonymous. Some smart alecks were using huge grain bags as their measure, taking way more than the legal limit. Gardy had let the harvest go relatively unchecked because he knew that the bay could ice over at any time and the scallops would be dead by spring. But things were getting out of hand and so he had to clamp down.

It was blustery, the day we put up signs that said that beginning the next day, scallops would be measured by bushel limits. It was cold, gray and damp and the wind was increasing over the high tide while the boats were out. Some of the boats were just skiffs, better suited to the more protected Town Cove or Pleasant Bay, than Cape Cod Bay.

Bruce told me later that he and his partner had nearly reached their limit of 20 bags that last day of "loose" enforcement but the weather was coming on snotty and dangerous. Bruce said he wanted to go in. His partner said he wanted to stay and get their limit because no one else was leaving. Bruce, who was uncanny about danger, said he didn't care about anyone else — it was getting too dangerous to be out in the boat that they were in. They pulled in their drags and headed home.

And when they looked back, the fleet was lined up behind them. Someone had to be the first to cry "uncle". Why there were no serious accidents that year, I will never know.

Orleans's boundary in Cape Cod Bay is somewhat odd and is also contentious.

Most town jurisdictions extend 3 miles from shore but because Orleans is in the "elbow" of the Cape, its jurisdiction is oddly shaped and extends about 6 miles from shore, including, as we've seen, approximately one-and-a-half miles of intertidal sand flats. The actual boundary line has been in question for years. Orleans was once part of Eastham and when the two towns split in 1797, the official Town Record of Eastham showed the compass direction of the line from a point on shore. It headed off in a somewhat northerly direction to a point in the bay where Eastham and Wellfleet boundary lines also meet. The result gave Eastham a pie-shaped piece of the bay and Orleans a trapezoid whose offshore line was larger than the landward edge.

At some point the state Division of Marine Fisheries produced a map that showed the same line heading in a northwesterly direction, giving Orleans a smaller piece of the bay with the same geometry except that the landward edge was larger. The confusion has never been resolved although Orleans officials have repeatedly tried to iron out the matter. But since Orleans and Eastham have a joint fisheries agreement when it comes to shellfish, the line has not been enough of a problem to warrant the expenditure of effort it would likely take to clear it up.

The Cape Cod Bay waters are fished heavily for striped bass, bluefish and flounders from the charter boats that may hail from Rock Harbor, or Wellfleet or Sesuit or Barnstable Harbors. Even though it is a tidal harbor, navigable only two hours before and after high tide, the Rock Harbor fleet is the largest charter boat fishing fleet in New England. Fishing trips are either four hours — over the high tide, or eight hours — over the low tide, but the four-hour trips are most popular. The charter boats often conduct two trips a day, an exhausting schedule for the captains and mates, fishing for 12 hours and repeating the sequence the next day.

Rock Harbor provides an impressive and entertaining scene when the boats, following a crooked line of trees set in the bottom to mark the "channel," race for the harbor. A flotilla of large charter boats and smaller private craft steam at full throttle from all over the bay, heading into the harbor at essentially the same time in a continuous line of boats. The charter captains tie up for just long enough to say goodbye to their first clients, welcome the next group and then head out again. Somehow, it all works. The timing is critical at the end of a four-hour trip because if the boats try to push the envelope of time and stay out too long, they may end up high and dry on the flats for a long eight hours.

The harbor is uncommonly picturesque at sunset when the sun sinks into the bay and the hues of gold and red and purple fill the sky. Rock Harbor is an amazingly busy place on a warm summer evening, between the folks at the harbor just to watch the sunset, those there to watch the boats come in, and the charter clients.

Judging by the number of fish caught on a daily basis from Rock Harbor, fish are abundant, because there are a whole lot of fish out there in the bay during the summer, and a whole lot of them end up on the dock.

Such was not always the case. In the 1950s, '60s and early '70s, tremendous numbers of fish had been landed at Rock Harbor. There was no catch restriction on the number of fish, nor on the size. The name of the game when the boats returned to the dock was to have the most and biggest fish laid out so that everyone on land could see which boat was the "high liner." That boat would inevitably get a new customer as a result.

Then, calamity. Either because of overfishing or a natural cycle, or both, stocks of striped bass plummeted all along the eastern seaboard.

Fisheries management officials from all the bass states agreed on an unprecedented action. They halted harvesting of bass everywhere for a number of years, hoping that the stocks would rebound. The first year of the moratorium, many people were furious. With bass illegal, bluefish became the target species for recreational fishing. After several years, bass fishing was again allowed on a very limited basis. But again there was an unprecedented move — in allowing fishing, all the states agreed to uniform regulations on size and number of fish allowed. Stock abundance progressively improved. After a few more years, states again went their separate ways regarding size and catch limits. But fisheries managers from the states talk together during the winter to discuss strategy.

In Massachusetts, the size limit went from 36 inches down to 28 inches, where it is as of this writing. There is a catch limit of one fish per day.

Most of the early naysayers to the program now laud the efforts to bring this magnificent gamefish back to the Atlantic's waters. Others still claim the lack of bass was just a low part of the natural abundance cycle. Bluefish are still harvested and they provide exciting "action," but they are less desirable to many as an eating fish, so many are caught and immediately released.

Some boats are rigged for tuna fishing. Tuna appear in Cape Cod Bay toward the end of summer but are found on the "backside" (the Atlantic-facing side of the Cape) throughout the summer season. An eight-hour or twelve-hour trip from Rock Harbor around Provincetown and down the backside can sometimes net a big bluefin tuna. Buyers from Japan are often on hand when they know a tuna is coming in on a boat so that they can take a sample of the meat. If the fat content is high, a fish can bring $40 per pound or more, so a fairly typical 400-600 lb. fish makes a trip very worthwhile. The guys hope for a tuna of any size but they also hope for a big tuna like the 1100-pound giant landed in Provincetown in August 2001. It is why tuna fishing is locally referred to as "tuna wishing" and creates something known as "tuna fever" in the fleet.

The bay is seasonal home for other large species, especially in the spring, summer and early fall. Whales, especially the endangered North Atlantic Right Whale, use the bay as a feeding ground, and slightly offshore on Stellwagen Bank, several species of whales are abundant, including humpbacks and fins.

Al Avellar, a Provincetown captain, made an interesting observation one day in the late '70s. He operated a fishing boat for tourists called a "head boat" where he supplied all the gear and bait for several dozen eager anglers. He noticed that whenever a whale was spotted, all the people on board left their fishing positions and crowded to the rail on the side of the boat where the whale had been seen, "oohing" and "ahhing" at the sight. Being resourceful, Capt. Al began advertising trips just to see whales and they filled up immediately. He abandoned fishing excursions, bought another boat and began running trips throughout the day to the "whaling grounds" instead of to the "fishing grounds." He filled his boats several times a day and is widely credited as having single-handedly launched the regional whale watching industry in the North Atlantic. Regional whale watching fleets now operate worldwide.

Avellar soon saw that if he provided commentary to the passengers about what they saw, his natural history business would grow even more. A coincidence helped make that happen.

At about the same time he had begun whale watching trips, the Center for Coastal Studies in Provincetown began scientific studies to observe whales in their natural habitat. The two purposes clicked together. What better way to combine their two objectives than for the center to provide interpretive naturalists aboard the Avellar boats? The naturalists could educate the patrons, while Capt. Al provided boats and skipper and fuel to the center so the naturalists could make many more trips than they might otherwise be able to, greatly expanding their observations and records on whale activities.

The naturalists photographed the whales they saw, and when the images were analyzed, they discovered that the same whales returned year after year. Whales have distinctive markings on their tail flukes that don't change, and with careful observation the naturalists could detect other characteristic differences among whales. And so the Coastal Center staff began naming the whales. The names were popular with the tourists too. The symbiotic relationship between the Dolphin fleet (Capt. Al's family business) and the Center for Coastal Studies continues, although there is extensive competition now for the whale watching tourist dollar in Provincetown (and elsewhere) because this eco-business is booming.

Nauset Estuary

The Nauset system is small, about 3,000 acres, but it is packed with natural resources that make it an extraordinary body of water. Its main physiographic features include two salt ponds (Salt Pond and Mill Pond), a drowned lake (Town Cove), as well as an extensive salt marsh (Nauset Marsh) (Map 5).

Within the area known as Nauset Harbor, intertidal flats are numerous and constantly changing as a result of the tremendous amount of sand movement within the harbor. The speed with which the benthic creatures (those that live in the sand) change habitat is amazing to us humans, who can't even detect the slight change in the currents or other environmental trigger that gets the creatures moving. One bar I watched for years changed from worms to clams to worms to mussels-and-clams to worms in a matter of ten years. Another changed from clams to worms just before the clams were large enough to be harvested and when we dug for clams, all we found were clam shells and worms.

A bar can have clams one summer and have inches of sand covering it the next. That condition is known as "sanded in" for obvious reasons. Clams have a foot but it is not nearly as powerful as that of a razor clam, for example, and so the clams can't effectively use their foot to dig up through the new sand so that their siphons reach the surface. Instead, they are suffocated by the new sand piled on top of them. It seems a shame that clams do not have some mechanism that would allow them to move up in the world.

There is no harvest from Northeast waters with higher total value than the American lobster, quite an interesting attitudinal change since in earlier times, lobsters were fed to prisoners — it was the last thing anyone else would eat.

The lobster is enigmatic; its habits and migration patterns are not well understood. It sheds its shell regularly, leaving few options for traditional population dynamics studies. Tagging studies are also out of the question as a means to study the lobster's early life history because of the molting process, but as they reach sexual maturity, they molt only about once a year. As they get older, they may molt only every few years, giving scientists an opportunity to study their migratory behavior with tags, and the results have been useful for several discrete populations. Lobsters can be found in estuaries, especially near their mouths, and Nauset and Pleasant Bay have been no exception.

The Massachusetts Division of Marine Fisheries sponsored a state lobster hatchery in Martha's Vineyard that has been in existence since the 1950s. During the first 35 years of operation, John Hughes was the director of the facility. John hatched and raised millions of juvenile lobsters that he transported to other Massachusetts bays and coves, and over the years hundreds of thousands were released in Nauset and Pleasant Bay. Neither John nor the DMF could track the numbers of juveniles that reached maturity through his hatchery program because of the molting problem, so John set about to raise distinctive strains of lobsters.

When a fisherman would bring him a blue lobster or a bi-color one or a red one (prior to cooking, that is), he would use that genetically unusual lobster as breeding stock to see what the progeny would be like. He was able to raise a small number of blue lobsters but other color combinations were more problematic. The relatively few lighter-colored ones he raised turned out to be easy prey and he couldn't raise enough blue ones to really assess their survivability in the wild. But he continued to raise and transplant the tiny lobsters because he felt that even if only a small percentage made it to be harvested, his efforts would help the Commonwealth's lobster fishery, given the high value of every animal. By the late 1980s, his hatching program was curtailed and the hatchery turned more to research.

In Nauset, most of the adult lobsters have been harvested from the marsh creeks, in the area known as Nauset Marsh, or up the Town Cove as far as Hopkins Island. Juvenile lobsters had always been found in the traps too, mostly no more than several inches long. No one knew where these naturally occurring lobsters, both juvenile and adult, came from originally, or where they went in the winter. From reports of fishermen, we knew adults and sub-adults were in Nauset for at least six months. No one knew about the juveniles.

The National Park Service contracted Rutgers University to conduct an ecological assessment of the Nauset system. Their report, published in 1989, states that the American lobster was abundant in Nauset Marsh and was collected consistently in samples except in December. Not only were the researchers finding juvenile lobsters at all times of the year, they were finding tiny lobsters as well, ones that would not be noticed in traps or ones that would have fallen out of the one-inch wire mesh of the pots. They found small juvenile lobsters mostly in peat reef habitats, chunks of marsh peat broken off along the edge of the marsh, and from their sampling, they concluded that those smaller than 10 mm (three-eighths of an inch) had settled in the peat shortly before the sampling.

For the first time, scientists had found an actual natural lobster nursery where lobsters of a very small size found refuge. Whether the eggs had hatched inside Nauset was still unknown, but Nauset Marsh had been the first location shown to be a true nursery area for the American lobster. It was a very important discovery. Fishermen have been braving the dangerous Nauset Inlet for decades to catch lobsters on the backside of the Cape. But at least some of the lobsters they seek were probably not born in the off-shore canyons beyond the continental shelf. Some of them may have been born less than a mile from where the lobstermen moor their boats, on the inside, in the protected waters of the Nauset estuary.

The habitat and species diversity of Nauset estuary is high, according to the Rutgers ecological analysis mentioned above. It is an important embayment for commercial species of shellfish (clams, quahaugs, mussels and occasionally bay scallops), fish (especially winter flounder) and crustaceans (especially lobsters but also crabs that are shellfish predators). It is also important as a nursery area for many other species such as cod, Atlantic tomcod, pollock and hake, not to mention feeding ground for the important gamefish of bass and bluefish.

Species of commercial importance do not tell the whole story of the estuary however. The analysis revealed a total of 49 species of fish and 11 species of decapod crustaceans (10-legged lobsters and crabs). During their sampling in 1985-6, the researchers found 31 species of mollusks (shellfish), 20 species of crustaceans (other than the decapods) and 32 species of polychaete worms. In addition to those species in the water, they found 47 species of birds utilizing the estuary (probably low, as the researchers' observations were limited to daylight hours). These numbers are an impressive indicator of species diversity and diversity is a prime reason the Nauset system is so productive.

The rare times that scallops appear in the Nauset system is a time for jubilation. When they occur, they often appear in the Town Cove in water so shallow that people can gather them simply by walking along the shore. Boats are not even needed. A large set occurred in 1985 and the majority of scallops were found south of Hopkins Island near the main channel. On opening day, Asa's Landing, the only town landing on the east side of the Town Cove, became the focal point in town as hundreds of area residents were out on the exposed flats in the crisp October weather to scoop up these succulent morsels.

Since the scallop season runs from October through April, this opening-day gift from the gods was a real treat for year-rounders. This bounty seemed to be meant for those who work on town committees, for those who pay the taxes to live near the sea, and for those who buy a shellfish license just so that they can take

advantage of such a windfall. On that opening day, everywhere you looked at the shore, people were grinning. It was a magical day.

Pleasant Bay

Pleasant Bay is the larger of the two ocean-fed estuaries. It is over 9,000 acres, three times the size of Nauset. Although Pleasant Bay has only oceanic water, it was not always that way. For years, water from Nantucket Sound also flooded in. The mixing of water from the Atlantic Ocean and Nantucket Sound produced an estuary of uncommon diversity because of the number of predominantly southern species that found a home in the bay, coming in from the sound at the northern extreme of their range.

The two features of the bay that are unique to the area and give the Pleasant Bay its sense of tranquility are the islands and barrier beach that protect the bay from the open ocean (Map 4). Seven islands are strung along the eastern portion of the bay. Strong Island is in Chatham, while Sipson's, Little Sipson's, Sampson, Hog, Pochet and Little Pochet are all in Orleans. All have limited or non-existent development. Sampson, Hog, Pochet and Little Pochet lie within the National Seashore Boundary while the remainder are in private

Photo courtesy of Kelsey-Kennard

ownership or are protected through conservation trusts or other restrictions.

Historically, boating has always been important on the bay, but boating years ago was not always strictly for pleasure. Fishing was the most important aspect of the bay. Fishing and transport, that is. In the age of sail, hundreds of boats plied the waters of the bay and along the coast on the "outside," using the bay for refuge or to unload a catch. River Road Landing in Orleans used to be known as Packet Landing for New York-bound packet ships that docked there. At that time, the bay was much deeper than it is now.

Bay scallops are elusive animals — here one year and absent the next. Historically they have exhibited a type of yo-yo population dynamic, and when they are abundant, happiness bordering on glee overtakes the town, for as we have seen, the fishery occurs in the fall and winter when other fisheries have slowed. In very good years, even more people benefit because shellfishermen hire additional hands to shuck.

Pleasant Bay scallops have often been larger than others in the region and since scallops are sold by the pound, it takes fewer Pleasant Bay scallops to make a pound of meats. Town Cove scallops are noticeably smaller and scallops found off the flats in Cape Cod Bay are often about the same size as those in the Town Cove, so scallops in Pleasant Bay are coveted animals.

Every time I go out in the bay, especially in Little Pleasant Bay and especially when I am rowing, I am constantly amazed at the shallowness of the water in the middle of Little Bay. Although most of the bottom is covered with water at all tides, my oars constantly hit sand.

It is heartening that 1600 acres of eelgrass continue to thrive in the Bay, though the extent of the eelgrass meadows may be dwindling, which is cause for concern. Although eelgrass is the bane of motorboats, it is vital for a host of marine animals, including bay scallops, that thrive among the blades of underwater grass. But eelgrass is a sensitive plant. It requires sunlight and if conditions are not right, and it does not get enough sun for the photosynthetic process — because other seaweeds are mixed in that compete with it, or there are other organisms present that foul the blades of grass — the eelgrass will die. If it dies, the productivity of the Bay decreases as well.

Eelgrass is an indicator of threats to water quality, analogous to the terrestrial warning signal, the canary in the coal mine. As we shall see later, scallops, eelgrass and water quality all play a big part in the story of coastal issues and changes that have taken place on the Bay.

When I'm out in my Cape Dory, I sometimes stop rowing in the middle of Little Bay and just turn my boat in a circle and look around. Out there, thinking about the tremendous number of plants and animals that gain sustenance from this bay, I feel small in comparison to the grandeur around me. I recognize that although humans are the largest user, in all senses of the word, we are only one of many, not the only one involved in the "budget" of the Bay.

The biodiversity of Pleasant Bay is immense. The Massachusetts Division of Marine Fisheries found over 60 species of fish and shellfish alone in one survey conducted in1967 and they did not sample for crustaceans or other invertebrates besides shellfish. In 2002, the state's Natural Heritage and Endangered Species Program listed 7 species that were Endangered, Threatened or of Special Concern. Not only does the Bay have much of the same species diversity found in the Nauset system, but because it also has undeveloped islands, the bay has the added biomes of upland and transitional areas between land and sea.

Pleasant Bay helped me gain a true understanding of the complexity of estuaries and the surrounding upland. I don't mean I understand everything about them. Quite the contrary. I mean that I view them as interrelated systems and I hope I will always be learning more about them. I see the whole but I also see the parts, each part a discrete habitat with transitions from one part to another.

Traveling from the inland areas surrounding Pleasant Bay to the ocean, the habitats include upland, coastal banks, marshes, beaches, tidal flats, cobble beaches, submerged lands and overlying waters. Then there are the islands with more beaches, marshes, thickets and upland. Lastly one finds more tidal flats and then the dunes of the outer beach with the Atlantic Ocean beyond. In the upper parts of the bay there are the semi-enclosed quiescent ponds, some of which lead even further inland to fresh water ponds. The flowing water between the fresh water lakes and ponds and the salt ponds is the pathway for the herring (an extremely important food source for larger fish) to swim annually from the sea to the lakes in the ancient ritual of procreation.

These separate habitats and the transition zones between them contain a complexity of interdependent life that is truly amazing, from large mammals — we have coyotes, red fox and deer — to tiny beach fleas and all manner of life in between.

From oaks and pines, to beach plums and Scotch broom, to beach grass, the land slopes down to the water. Grasses that can tolerate salt water fringe the land, protecting the upland by dissipating wave energy as waves hit the shore, and providing the proper ingredients for ribbed mussels (*Geukensis demissus*) that are found in the peat created over hundreds of years. Indentations of the shoreline often mark extensive salt marshes where red-wing blackbirds flit and marsh hawks hover overhead and a fox searches for small animals for her pups. The marsh creeks may be filled with mummichogs and stickle-backs, small fish darting through the water as the tide comes and goes. And yes, the marsh is also home to the interminably pesky greenhead fly whose worldly "value" we may not know but whose bite we surely do know.

The intertidal and nearshore area is home not just to clams and quahaugs, but also home to crabs and worms and other forms of life that provide food for the thousands of shorebirds that stop to rest and feed on their yearly migrations north and south. The water is teeming with plankton, the young-of-the-year that will become the fish and shellfish and predators of the following year. The islands provide refuge to some animals because they are islands, where predators may not be as numerous as on the mainland. Ospreys have made a comeback out by the islands, thanks in part to the platforms erected by humans for their nests. The fish that find themselves gripped in the osprey's talons may not be grateful to us, but ospreys were part of the landscape before humans nearly killed them off with DDT. Now they are back.

The horseshoe crab, related to spiders and a member of earth's community for hundreds of millions of years, plows its way across Pleasant bay's shallow waters in search of its favorite food, the gem clam. The gem clam is a mollusk that looks like a miniature quahaug, except that the purple is on the outside of the shell and not the inside as with the quahaug, and the gem shell doesn't get any bigger than one-eighth of an inch. There are probably billions of them in the bay.

This is merely a sampling. Just imagine the number of terrestrial, intertidal, aquatic, and avian species that utilize the bay's complexity during a normal year!

When you look at Orleans as a whole, the town's coastal resources are extraordinary because of the three separate and highly productive estuaries within its borders. They provide habitat for four of the major species of commercially important shellfish: softshell clams, hard clams or quahaugs, bay scallops and blue mussels. They also provide habitat for spawning, nursery or feeding of dozens of fish and other invertebrate species in addition to habitat for the huge populations of migratory and non-migratory birds, whose interactions with one another were not quite clear to me in my early years on the job. I learned very early that species diversity and complexity of habitats is what makes the area so special, but I also learned early on that its exquisite complexity is what makes it so fragile.

I got to know the waters quite well. Lots of people knew them a lot longer than I did and maybe better than I did, but I knew them intimately, foot by foot. Some stretches of shoreline I felt compelled to walk again and again, often not really knowing why they struck me so; others I walked once and lost interest and didn't go back to for a long time. I realized quickly that scouting, even scouring the shoreline just once in a while was not enough. The shoreline may look the same but it is constantly changing and the animals that make their home there might be there one year but not the next, possibly pushed out by something else that was more efficient for living in just that space at that particular time. The shore subtly evolved as much as I did.

It didn't take me long to realize that plugging in the variables for this ecology exercise was not going to be a piece of cake. I was at the bottom of a steep learning curve.

Chapter 9

Half Moon

There was more to the learning curve than just walking around the bay, enjoyable as that was. My bullraking experience would convince anyone — even the novice that I was — that there weren't many quahaugs left in Big Bay. Big Bay bottom was littered with shack so thick that it seemed it would be difficult for another set to dig in where there had been $1,000,000 worth a decade earlier. My walking tours scratching along miles of shoreline convinced me that the situation wasn't much better for Little Bay either. I was hired to find out why such was the case but there was much more behind the word why in my assignment. Why really didn't matter to many in town. The reality was that everyone just wanted more quahaugs.

How to get more quahaugs in the water became my problem. Desperation can be inspiring and I desperately wanted to find a way to help Mother Nature produce more quahaugs.

I began to learn about quahaugs by talking to people and finding scientific papers at the Marine Biological Laboratory library in Woods Hole. I found papers written about the habits of quahaugs, predators and their habits, sediment conditions necessary for their growth and survival, current conditions, and a host of other technical information. Some reports conflicted with one another but I kept reading, trying to understand as much as I could.

I found journal articles about other species of shellfish too, and one particular paper intrigued me. Written by Dr. Herb Hidu, the paper described a process for increasing sets of oysters in Chesapeake Bay. The theory was that oysters exude a chemical pheromone or scent into the water that attracts juvenile oysters to set nearby, a process called gregarious setting. The pheromone also cues predators where to find prey so it acts as sort of a natural population stabilizer. Dr. Hidu had moved since publishing that paper and was working at the University of Maine Darling Marine Center in Walpole, Maine, experimenting with clams in an effort to further demonstrate the theory of gregarious setting with clams. He used netting to protect the juvenile clams from being eaten by the predators.

What amazed me was that clams and other shellfish are plank-tonic during their larval stage and float where the currents take them for about two weeks. How, then, when they got their hard shell and sank to the bottom, could they find other clams? As they were developing their hard shell could they somehow move closer to the adult clams? Did they crawl around the bottom until they found other clams? I couldn't find the answers to those questions but Hidu was conducting experiments to test the gregarious setting theory.

I knew there probably was something to this theory since clams are often found in groups and in layers with small ones on top of big ones. In fact, the layers of clams were among the biggest reasons clams were a pain to dig because so many little ones got broken in the process.

Hidu's experiments used field plantings and sample plots to illuminate his theory. He'd plant some plots with adult clams and cover them with netting and have some plots that were covered with netting but had no clams. (Earlier experiments had shown that juvenile clam survival was far better when netting was used than without netting because the netting protected juveniles from preda-tors.) These test plots both had netting, but only the plots with adult clams produced baby clams. The plots with just netting and no clams did not produce any juveniles. Theory proved. Gregarious setting did work for clams.

If it worked for clams, would it work for quahaugs? I knew that sometimes a few quahaugs might live close to one another as they seemed to do around rocks, but that didn't often happen in big num-bers. Though I looked for papers where experiments like Hidu's had been done for quahaugs, I couldn't find any. But I had an idea. And I had a boss who let me try it out.

Gardy, the genial Shellfish Constable and Harbormaster, loved scratching for quahaugs and had fished recreationally most of his life. Mun, his deputy, was a crusty fellow, physically imposing with a shock of black hair, and fingers that were three times the usual circumference. The size of his fingers was the result of nature's responding to a life on the water, working in constant cold weather and icy waters, mostly fishing but finding other ways to earn a dollar in lean times (including rum running, or so he said). He came from a family of fishermen — his brother was notorious both for the speed with which he could dig clams and for the tests he imposed on every new shellfish enforcement officer, seeming to say to them, "Catch me if you can". Mun was also around the age of 60 in the mid-1970s and was of the school that believed that a woman's place was in the home or anywhere except for a boat and certainly not working for a shellfish department. I was suitably intimidated. But Gardy, our boss, listened to me when I explained my idea and gave the go-ahead.

I told Gardy that quahaugs didn't seem to behave like clams naturally and maybe what was needed was a way to enclose them so they would set in a group. Maybe we should build an enclosure with sand on the bottom. We could plant adult quahaugs in the bottom like the adult clams in Dr. Hidu's experiment but we would capture the larvae the adults produced so they wouldn't float around to who-knows-where for two weeks. Then, the larvae would stay in the enclosure and set in the sand. It sounded feasible. Maybe we could create the right environment for gregarious setting to occur. The enclosure would have to be high enough so that the larvae couldn't float out at high tide but there would have to be some exchange of water.

We would need a few sheets of plywood, some strong netting, 2x4s and nails. We needed to find a way to let the food-sized plankton in while also keeping the quahaug larvae from getting out of the enclosure and thought about the problem as construction began.

Supplies on hand, the two men — the guy who would agree to anything if it meant more quahaugs and the cagey Cape Codder skeptic — made two rectangular boxes that were eight feet wide on the sides, four feet wide on the ends and eight feet high. On one end was a "door" for us to access the inside to take samples of water and sand, and we finally decided to cut "windows" on all the other sides, covered with netting for the filtered water exchange.

We loaded the first one onto a flat-bed trailer and brought it to the Mill Pond. The Mill Pond is a picturesque and quiet place, a saltwater pond used as anchorage for larger lobster fishing boats when there's a storm, but it does not generally have a lot of boating activity. An old rock mill dam blocks the pond entrance, making navigation in and out rather difficult. On the opposite side of the pond from where our experimental box was going, however, was one of the most exclusive residential developments of the whole town with large, expensive homes on a hillside overlooking a postcard-perfect Cape Cod view.

We carried the box from the trailer to the water where I supervised the placement, with a "that looks about right" precision. Stakes, previously cut, were sledgehammered into the ground abutting the box and then nailed to the box. Sand, brought from an inland site — so it would not have any natural predators or other marine unknowns in it — was shoveled into buckets, carried to the box, and spread on the bottom in a layer about six inches thick. We got some chowder and cherrystone quahaugs to use as parent stock and planted them in the sand.

When I looked at the box in the water, with openings on all sides to have some exchange of water, I thought that maybe the netting was too large a mesh and the larvae would easily flow out of the box. I left the pond and came back with an old bedsheet, cut pieces to fit the openings, stapled them in place and then closed the door and took photos.

Mun never said a word while building the boxes but he knew what they were for and his expression spoke volumes. He kept pretty quiet until we got the things to the water. Then he really couldn't hold back any longer and said that this was the goddamnedest fool thing he'd ever seen and it'd never work.

We plodded on and loaded up the second box to put in the Town Cove. The sediment around the box there didn't cooperate as well as at the Mill Pond since there were small rocks wherever we tried to pound in the stakes. The end result was that the box in the Cove also was not anchored nearly as well. The Cove was not as calm as the Mill Pond and we thought we might have problems at that site.

The quahaug boxes stayed for the summer. It seemed like the execution of my idea was just a bit askew. We needed a covering on the "door" and "windows" that would allow for an exchange of water, but keeping planktonic larvae inside without starving either them or their parents just didn't work. Quahaug food and the potential juvenile quahaugs were the same size — microscopic. The bedsheets we used for the covering had a tight weave that severely restricted water flow. Not only that, but we didn't count on fouling of the sheets probably preventing *any* water exchange, nor did we count on a summer storm with wave action that succeeded in lifting the Town Cove box so that the sand-filled netting bulged visibly below the wood. With no exchange of water, if the adult quahaugs spawned, the larvae would then become food for the parents. This was not part of the plan.

Gardy and I discussed the newest wrinkle at one point and decided we needed to do something — namely bail water into the box at the Cove. There he was, the Shellfish Constable and Harbormaster, on a step ladder, in the briny, pouring buckets of seawater into a plywood box anchored into the Cove sediment, as

his young biologist kibbitzed. Both of us laughed and laughed at the ridiculousness of our endeavor but neither of us was willing to give up.

The boxes were sort of out of the way, not anchored near town landings. Even so, a few folks saw the odd-looking and out-of-place wooden structures and asked what on earth these things were. We wondered what the folks in the big houses on the hill above the Mill Pond thought but never heard from any of them. When we explained to the folks who did ask what we were trying to accomplish, they nodded in a bewildered acceptance that said it all must have seemed like a good idea at the time and if the boxes could produce quahaugs, finest kind.

They didn't. Well, it's not exactly that they didn't work, but a total of five new seed didn't seem like much of a success. We were hoping for thousands.

Oddly, even though the boxes didn't work, Mun decided I had some spunk to even dream up the scheme. He still thought I was crazy but now somehow OK. He became much less intimidating and actually started sharing stories and his vast knowledge with me, a great gift.

In my study of technical journals, I never read about a project that had been tried but didn't work. I knew this experiment wasn't going to be published in a journal either but I wondered how many other people had tried crazy ideas to get quahaugs to set near their parents and wished there was a forum for an exchange of ideas, no matter how loony.

Gardy, always willing and ready to share any new information about shellfish, encouraged me to tell other shellfish officers about our experiment, and since I had taken slide photographs, I had visual proof of our adventures. I gave a presentation at the next Massachusetts Shellfish Officers Association meeting. Nothing like advertising your folly.

After the laughter subsided, someone remarked that all that was missing was the half-moon over the doors. Terrific. Quahaug outhouses. Great beginning on this learning curve.

Chapter 10

Replenishing

Luckily, we didn't have to depend on our outhouses for quahaug seed because a hatchery in North Carolina was selling seed. Buying seed from a commercial hatchery to use in a municipal propagation program was a radical departure from tradition.

Most towns were buying adult stock from places like Cape Cod Bay or they were participating in a state-sanctioned relay program whereby stock was harvested from a bacterially contaminated area, then transplanted to a clean area that was closed to harvesting for at least one spawning season. The state believed that the program was a win-win — available stock was harvested and used as parent stock in other locations, while the public was protected because once quahaugs are left in the water long enough, they completely purge contaminants. Harvesting for human consumption would not occur until all harmful bacteria were purged.

Gardy didn't like the idea of bringing shellfish into town that were even remotely tainted, especially since Cape Cod Bay quahaugs were clean and could also be transplanted. The major difference between the approaches was that towns were promised sub-legal quahaugs from the state-sanctioned relay program, a more desirable size than the large cherrys and chowders from Cape Cod Bay. In reality, towns that participated in the state program sometimes received mostly cherrys too so Gardy was glad he didn't choose to transplant the contaminated stock.

Bringing seed quahaugs into town from a hatchery in North Carolina raised a lot of other questions in town, starting with the basics. Would they survive the transport and if they did, would

they survive in the Massachusetts climate? We started small and ordered ten thousand seed which we picked up at the local airport. They arrived in great shape. We planted in ten locations through-out town, not wanting to put all our eggs into one basket. The method was simple: Rake an intertidal area of ground to remove any obvious predators such as crabs, sprinkle 1,000 seed on the surface, cover them with a frame made of wood strapping with netting stapled on top, and then stake the frame into place. We monitored them through the summer and fall and saw that many of them survived, so we expanded the program the next year and bought 250,000.

Most of them went into larger bottom boxes but 50,000 were put in floating rafts. The rafts were based on a design by George Souza, the Falmouth shellfish constable, who had successfully experimented with floating sand boxes. We altered his design to suit our needs, ending up with 6X9-foot rafts. The bottom was a wood frame with one-inch vinyl-coated wire mesh stapled to it. Thick orange Styrofoam flotation blocks were bolted to the frame and painted green so the

rafts would be a bit more acceptable aesthet-ically. A window-screen-sized mesh was placed over the wire mesh to hold the sand we trucked to the site. We shoveled the sand onto the rafts to a depth of about 5 inches. After about a week or so — to allow for the sand to leach silt — we planted

25,000 seed on each raft, one in Mill Pond and one in Lonnie's (Kescayogansett) Pond. We floated them across the pond and moored them on one end so that they would swing in the tide.

We were amazed at how well the rafts worked. We started with seed that was about one-quarter inch long and ended up with seed that was mostly three-quarters to a full inch by the fall with virtually no mortality. I checked their progress throughout the season, sometimes by boat and sometimes swimming across the pond, especially at Lonnie's. I often had friends with me swimming across to the rafts and we would dig through the sand and come up with handfuls of seed quahaugs. If a person came with me more than once, he or she too was astonished at the growth of the "kids". We emptied the rafts in October and planted the seed to various shorelines around town, most of the sites in Pleasant Bay. After a few years, we dropped the Mill Pond site because the seed didn't grow as fast there and the pond was not as protected from damaging winds, especially in the spring when the seed were small.

This rather promising beginning led to an innovative quahaug propagation program that lasted for 15 years. Orleans was not alone. Other towns, including our neighbors in Eastham and Chatham, also used hatchery seed for their propagation programs and the successes in the towns led to successes in private quahaug aquaculture on the Cape, currently a fledgling industry.

Bottom culture had not been easy. It had seemed like a good idea to plant quahaugs in their natural environment, protected from predators, but we ran into many problems. None of the bottom areas even came close to matching the rafts for either growth or survival. We tried boxes at many different areas of town, different substrate types, different box designs to improve predator exclusion, varying densities of plantings, and a host of other variables. But we consistently lost seed with the boxes.

We checked the boxes frequently and learned a lot about the nature of quahaugs in their natural environment, about growth with respect to sediment and currents, and about survival.

We learned a lot about the vexing issue of predation and the difficulty involved in excluding predators. We could usually exclude larger predators but they began life as small animals too, cued by a powerful chemical pheromone that signaled to them that here quahaugs were clustered closely together, as in trapped in a box. They merely had to penetrate the netting on top, which was there to allow for an exchange of water. The slightest separation between the box and the cover enabled the small predators to enter a box full of quahaugs. Some found a way through the netting. If we tried to plant seed subtidally (under water at all times) so they would have better growth, we could not get the boxes tight enough to prevent predators, and so we devised new box designs every year. However they got in, the upshot was that many predators grew up in the box munching on the seed that had been planted there by us.

We learned that winter can be beautiful, but learned that it can be deadly to seed quahaugs for a few reasons. Massachusetts is near the northern extent of their range. Quahaugs can dig very deep in the winter when they more or less hibernate, but if they do not have sufficient energy reserves when spring comes to enable them to crawl back up to the surface to feed, they can die when they are down deep. Ice can tear apart boxes and netting, leaving seed exposed to the cold elements or to predators. If the seed is exposed and the water temperature is below 38°Fahrenheit, the quahaugs can't dig back into the bottom because they are hibernating. They too die. The decay process produces hydrogen sulfide (the same compound that makes the "rotten egg" smell). Too much hydrogen sulfide can kill other quahaugs, and a dead patch can occur in a box of planted seed.

When surviving seed do begin to feed again, the right food may not yet be in the water in early spring, and lots of seed can die then, abetted by the decay process.

Bottom culture was challenging, and each year we were losing a lot of seed using bottom culture methods.

Since the rafts were so successful, we dropped bottom culture after three years. We never found areas or box designs that allowed us to grow quahaug seed in a relatively short time. Our experience with the winter conditions of 1976-1977, the coldest in many years, taught us to hope for the best and prepare for the worst winter conditions. If we hadn't had the rafts, perhaps we would have continued to experiment with the bottom boxes to come up with an appropriate method. But after losing so many seed, I hated bottom culture.

We didn't know how lucky we were to buy quarter-inch seed for $8 per 1000 when we started. By the end of the '70s, inflation had taken a big bite out of the dollar and we had to buy smaller and smaller seed for the same price, ending with one-sixteenth inch seed, only 25 percent the size of the original stock. These later seed were so tiny they hindered our program. The rafts no longer worked with the really small seed. We tried to start earlier in the season so the quahaugs would have more time to grow, but this was Cape Cod... and the weather hadn't calmed down. Any boat wake or storm waves would wash out the sand and seed. We joked and called it "premature planting" but it really was no joke to us. We were losing seed.

Our choices were to decrease the amount of seed purchased so we could buy larger seed at substantially higher per-unit cost, or to continue with the small seed — delivered a bit later in the season — but hold them over in the winter to give them a second year of growth before being transplanted. Overwintering was problematic at best since everyone who was trying overwintering methods had failed to come up with a winner yet. If we held them all over for the winter, we knew a lot of them would be dead by the spring. We ended up planting some at less than optimal size and holding some to do our own experiments with overwintering methods.

We also searched for another option. Some people, most notably researchers at the National Marine Fisheries Service Shellfish Laboratory in Milford, Connecticut, had had success with holding seed in long narrow tanks called raceways through which seawater was pumped to flow continuously over the seed. If we went that route, we would be changing the entire program dramatically since we would need equipment, pumps, electricity and land to implement the method. We reasoned, however, that it could well be worth the effort: If it were successful, the seed would survive the winter so we could grow them to a point where we could use the rafts successfully. We ended up with a land-based facility.

We had been buying, growing and planting seed since 1975. We used bottom culture in 1975-1977 and raft culture for many years after our initial success in 1976.

Meanwhile, Town Hall had outgrown its space. New personnel hired to address emerging development issues in Orleans had no space to work. Our office, a 16X24-foot building with attached shed, was behind Town Hall. It was to be demolished for a parking area and we were to have a new, smaller office in Town Hall and storage space elsewhere in town.

While this new arrangement was being discussed, we considered the fact that seed prices had been steadily rising — faster than our budget — and we were being forced to buy smaller and smaller seed. We realized that 250,000 seed per year was not much for a town with 45 miles of shoreline and wondered if we might not be better off to try our hand at creating a small hatchery of our own, using models from Martha's Vineyard and Eastham. We had the building — why not move the 16X24-foot building to the water and design our own hatchery? The selectmen agreed.

We moved the building to the shore of Town Cove, in a business-zoned area, and set it up as a hatchery (Map 5). I never called it a hatchery but always referred to it as the shellfish lab or just the lab. We set up the lab with a flowing seawater system and a small room set aside for algae culture that would provide food for the minuscule seed. We continued to use the rafts to hedge our bets (and would continue to use rafts for six more years).

A hatchery has certain requirements in order to operate efficiently. Large tanks are needed for the millions of larvae that are produced to go through their two weeks of free-swimming larval development. The tanks need to be drained every other day, and the water being drained must be directed through a series of varied mesh-size sieves to size and hold the larvae. The water in the tanks and the algae culture must be aerated and so the hatchery must have an air pump. Microscopic food must be grown in a temperature-controlled environment to feed the larvae, or else purchased from a commercial supplier (at a substantial cost). Finally, the hatchery must have separate tanks for development of post-set animals, those that have metamorphosed and developed their hard shell and are no longer free-swimming.

We designed our facility on a nickel-and-dime budget with few back-up systems. We really needed a dual intake for the seawater system so that we could shut one down and clean it while using the other, but it was too costly. But making do with one intake was costly in another way — it meant a loss of efficiency.

We used plastic trash cans for larvae tanks instead of the expensive fiberglass conicals used in most hatcheries. Conicals are large cylinders with a cone-shaped bottom to which a valve is attached so that a tank can be drained easily.

We needed variable meshed-size sieves to capture larvae when the trash cans were drained. We made them from free 5-gallon buckets obtained from restaurants rather than the typical large-diameter PVC pipe.

We designed the building and installed all the equipment and plumbing ourselves. We used free glass jugs, also supplied by local restaurants, for algae culture. We made do with an air conditioner in the window for temperature control. Everything we did was as frugal as possible.

We had taken a giant leap into the unknown.

The building was situated at the top of a naturally inclined shore at the town landing and our intake pipe simply ran over the ground to the water. On

either side of the landing, the shorefront property owners (a small marina and an old inn) had built, years earlier, vertical walls made of wood and steel defining the edge of the land. These were called bulkheads. About a year after we moved to the site, the town approved construction of a bulkhead in front of our building at the landing to tie in with adjacent bulkheads. The town added a dock with a ramp and float to be used to access boats moored just off-shore. As soon as the Town built the bulkhead, the town landing became much more popular, leading to problems for us. But I'll get to those later.

Quahaugs were not the only species that concerned us. Clams were also part of the shellfish program. For several years, an intertidal bar in Lonnie's Pond, also known as a clam flat, had produced seed clams that were way too crowded, so most could not make it to maturity. There were over 500 per square foot and it was physically impossible for 500 two-inch clams (the legal size) to fit in a square foot. We decided to utilize this bounty by thinning out the crop, sort of like thinning out a vegetable garden.

We used a pump rig that acted as a vacuum and removed some of the one-half to one-inch clams and transplanted them to other

areas. We used a machine called a "twister" that was essentially a harrow and we literally plowed the receiving area on the low tide. Then we transplanted the clams in the loosened sand during an incoming tide. The clams dug in quickly and we lost very few either to breakage or to preda-tion. We transplanted so many seed that when they matured, they had turned into hundreds of bushels of marketable clams. We transplanted clams from this one flat to all three estuaries over the course of three years. Even clams we transplanted to the generally inhospitable flats of Cape Cod Bay survived.

Granted, the receiving area there was close to the clam-friendly marsh, but it was survival on Cape Cod Bay.

Because the transplant method was successful, we experimented a bit and tried to get clams to set on a barren flat on the west shore of Nauset Beach. It was generally accepted wisdom, going back to Belding's reports of the early 1900s, that clams set better on ground that had been previously "worked" — the bottom had been turned over, to use the gardening analogy again. Our program was a joint one with Chatham, and we pooled our resources.

In the Chatham part of the Nauset Beach flat, we (Gardy, Chatham's shellfish warden Kass Abreu, and I) plowed up a huge area, several acres, and then placed frames with netting on the plowed ground. We also put some frames with netting in untouched areas adjacent to the plowed area to see if the netting would catch a set, and if it did, to see which area would be more productive. In other words, we wanted to know if plowing was really necessary to gain a set or if the netting itself would provide refuge to seed clams so that they would set under netting on unprepared areas. There were some wild clams in the general vicinity, so if the theory of gregarious setting worked — I hadn't given up on the idea — there would be clams under the netting by the end of the summer.

In Orleans, we plowed up another huge area and anchored some frames within it. The major difference between this site and the not-too-distant Chatham site was that there were no living clams anywhere near the Orleans area. About two feet underground, we did find a set of clams that had died, presumably buried by shifting sands that had moved quickly, probably from a storm. The shells were large (about 4-5 inches long) and all were still oriented in the way that they would have been if alive. They looked like praying hands buried in the sand.

An individual clam (or any other shellfish species) will spew out millions of eggs at any one spawning, and once those eggs meet up with sperm somewhere in the water, the resulting microscopic larvae swim and drift with the currents as part of the zooplankton community. And adult clams are filter feeders, which means that they ingest water and filter out the plankton for their food. Clams — and every other creature in the water that ingests the water — ingests the larvae. With the odds against survival so high — some estimates are that only one-tenth to one-one hundredth of one percent of the larvae actually make it — it takes millions of eggs to get a relatively tiny number of survivors.

We checked the frames and netting of our experimental sites at least once a month. It was always a lengthy excursion because of the distance down the beach to Chatham and because of the tides. We worked the low tide first in Chatham because the turn to flood stage came first there. Then we moved to the Orleans site as the tide was just coming in. Spending most of a day on the beach didn't hurt anyone's feelings and we enjoyed what we considered an adventure. It was never the same twice — there was always something new to observe and document.

The results of our experiment were interesting and unexpected. We sampled everywhere — under the netting, outside the netting but still in the plowed area, and outside the plowed area. In Chatham, we found clams had set under the netting, but very few set in the plowed area outside the netting, and none had set in the area nearby that hadn't been plowed. In Orleans, there wasn't a clam to be seen anywhere. Even though the area we chose for the experiment was not far from the main channel, neither the larvae from Chatham's clams nor from any other clams in Pleasant Bay reached our area.

Under one of the Orleans frames however, a couple of horseshoe crabs had gotten caught. They had burrowed beneath the frame but somehow were not able to burrow out all the way to safety — or perhaps they had found safety beneath the frame. By the frame-checking excursion of mid-August, there wasn't one clam to be found but thousands of tiny horseshoe crabs had been born there. The eggs had been protected from voracious birds by the netting just as seed clams are protected from their predators.

In all, it was a successful project. We presented our joint experiments at a clam conference in Maine and later learned that managers Down East later used some of the techniques we had discussed for their clam flats.

Mussels are of higher quality from a cook's perspective when they live below water at all times. But they prefer to set in intertidal areas. So we also developed a program to move mussels. We chose a bar in Nauset Harbor that had long strings of thousands, perhaps millions, of mussel seed. It was relatively easy to use a pitchfork to get the strings off the sand bar and into the adjacent deeper water. It was a low-priority project and we couldn't come close to moving all of them but we moved several hundred bushels. It would have been more efficient if we had used heavy machinery but we didn't want to overly disturb the established intertidal community that the mussels had helped create in the intertidal mud/sand of the bar.

For scallops, in those early days, hatchery methods had not yet been developed, so the best propagation plan was simply to transplant some from heavily seeded areas to other less-populated ones. It was rare that we found scallop production high enough for transplants however. But scallops were an important species, as we shall see later.

Municipal shellfish propagation is a difficult concept to explain to people, and especially hard to rationalize on a financial basis. Shellfish propagation had not in the early days, nor has it yet, arrived at a stage of predictability. It was and continues to be experimental. Some methods seem to work better than others but the same methods may have completely different rates of success depending on the natural conditions of the site.

Municipal propagation projects follow the timing of natural shellfish production, which means that towns buy seed in the spring from the hatcheries. The hatcheries generally produce enough seed to fill orders and to satisfy the needs of their own grow-out procedures. They have nothing more to sell by mid-summer.

Propagation and natural production both take place in the summer months when water temperatures are high, dissolved oxygen is low, predators are active, the waters are filled with competing human users, and a lot of things can go wrong. But if something goes wrong and you lose the seed — regardless of the cause, human error or the vagaries of nature — you can't get more seed, you're done for the entire year. Winter is also hard on seed and winter is when you have to go before the finance committee and other town officials to plead your case for funding the following summer.

The town officials ask about survival to harvest size, but you're talking about survival of seed. It takes another five years or so for quahaugs to reach maturity when they can be harvested. When budget time rolls around, it's difficult to obtain funding on faith that there will be something to harvest in the future. It's very difficult when you have to admit that things did not go as planned the year before. Finance committee members aren't always particularly well versed in the vagaries of natural systems and they don't take kindly to programs that can't prove their worth well in dollars and cents.

Given its 45-mile coastline and thousands of acres in three separate estuaries, it's also difficult to make a substantial difference in the amount of shellfish the town can propagate given inadequate financial resources either to provide parent stock for natural spawning or harvestable shellfish. No matter what we could accomplish to replenish stocks, it was a mere drop-in-the-bucket because Orleans was a big town estuary-wise. In essence, what we could afford to do with propagation methods was extremely limited in the broader scheme of things. We were successful but it often didn't seem like it.

Chapter 11

Hypothetical Problem?

Since I keep my boat in The River now, near Meetinghouse Pond in the uppermost part of Pleasant Bay, I have to row the entire length of The River, about one-and-one half miles, until I get to the buoys at Namequoit Point (known also as Viking Point, named for Camp Viking), the entrance to Little Bay. When I go by Jack Knife Cove, I often find myself smiling as I remember days spent in that cove. When I'm trying to avoid larger boats in the channel, I often come very close to running aground on a spit of sand, covered at high tide, that parallels the channel and forms the western side of the small horseshoe-shaped cove.

The cove itself is a mooring area for families living in the vicinity, not for the general public, as there are no town landings on that side of The River for at least a couple of miles. Many of those families have ties to this part of town that go back for generations, and much of the land is still in relatively large tracts, not chopped up into small house lots. But the land is becoming so valuable that it is becoming difficult for the families to keep it in the large acreages.

Former customers from Ellis' Market allowed me to park at the Jack Knife Point Association landing. I got to know the neighbors better the more time I spent there. The shoreline had been one of our heavily used sites for both quahaug and clam seed transplants since both species did very well there. Tucked away on the eastern side of the cove is a smallish salt marsh of perhaps five acres, and prior to the spring of 1980, no houses were visible around its shoreline. Just to the south of the marsh creek and delta was a great spot for quahaug bottom-culture boxes and just offshore of that was one of our favorite transplant sites. The cove was out of the way since the general public rarely walked the shore there, and so we were relatively unencumbered in doing our experiments. The neighbors loved seeing the activity there.

Jack Knife Cove thus was ideal, a model. I was to use it as a model of a different sort as well.

I was three years into my job when, in 1978, the newly elected president of the New England Estuarine Research Society (NEERS), asked me to be a member of his Executive Committee. NEERS is a group of about 400 people, most of whom are researchers at marine labs and academic institutions throughout New England. The majority of the work being conducted at that time was basic research on specific well-defined aspects of the marine environment. Tying the research to real-world management decisions was foreign territory to most of the members, few of whom were involved in management. I was an oddity, a municipal employee, but I had been a society member since shortly after I started my job with Orleans. I was always trying to learn from other NEERS members so I could use the science they were involved with in the management decisions that had to be made throughout the town.

When the president asked me to join the Executive Committee, I asked him if the format of the meetings ever varied. It had always been composed of a day-and-a-half of 20-minute presentations interspersed with breaks. He said no, and asked if I had an alternative in mind. I suggested a change that would feature a panel discussion for an afternoon session. He gave me a green light and I organized a session a year or so later, based on the hypothetical situation of development around a marsh. I used Jack Knife Cove as the theoretical model.

The first really big building boom was just beginning across the Lower Cape at this time, and although the negative connection between development and shellfish had not completely penetrated my consciousness, I was beginning to feel uneasy about what loomed as inevitable development of the Orleans shoreline. Jack Knife Cove was a "pristine" area where there were no houses for probably 500 feet or more around the marsh. I drew up a hypothetical scenario where a developer wanted approval for several components of development. The developer was proposing to build 10 condominium units close to the marsh, dig out the marsh to create a boat basin and marina, and also build a golf course in the field beyond the marsh.

I asked five people to serve on the panel. Four represented separate disciplines of estuarine science: benthic ecology (concerned with animals that live in sediments), water chemistry, salt marsh ecology, and fisheries. The fifth expert was versed in permitting. I also named a moderator. All participants were given the scenario ahead of time and each had the same task, to discuss the potential ramifications of the proposed development from their distinct perspective. It was a gamble that the people would actually "play" at this exercise, and if they didn't, the whole episode would be a colossal failure.

The night before the session, the then-president and the newsletter editor of the Estuarine Research Federation (ERF-the national umbrella organization) had arrived from the South to observe a NEERS meeting. I told them about the session I'd set up for the next day and expressed some anxiety that it could be pulled off. Bob Reimold, the ERF president, asked if he could be a devil's advocate and catalyst if things didn't work and I said, "Please. Be my guest".

The next day, I introduced the session and the members of the panel, and then sat back. It was awful. To a person, the panelists said they could not possibly answer the questions of what would happen if this development went in because they did not have enough information. I understood their professional reticence but my experts wouldn't let their guards down even for a hypothetical situation among their peers. I felt wretched. Here I was, a relative newcomer and not a research scientist and I had tried something new that was failing miserably.

Then Bob Reimold stood up and because he came from Georgia, few NEERS members knew him by sight. He said that he was fed up with these scientists. This land had been in his family for generations and he had a right to do what he wanted. He knew that digging out the marsh would have no effect because he could create a marsh somewhere else and have it function just like the original marsh that had taken thousands of years to develop. He said the sewage from the condos would not get into the water because he could put in a package treatment plant that was more efficient than the traditional septic systems. We were worried about fertilizer on the golf course? He knew of fertilizers that were taken up by the plants so fast that there'd never be a problem. As for the fish, well everyone knew that pilings attracted marine life and there would be more fish there with a marina than with a marsh.

Reimold's intervention started the ball rolling, the rest of the audience began participating, and I began to grin. It got raucous, but a lot of good ideas were thrown out. I ended the session by thanking the participants for their willingness to take some heat. I also pointed out, however, that all the people in that room had expertise in some aspect of marine affairs. Someday, someone in their own community might come to them because they had that expertise. I suggested they pay attention not only to their own research but to what was going on in the community so that they could contribute accurate and timely assessments when issues arose.

I was so grateful that our two southern friends had paid NEERS a visit because they not only saved me from a programming disaster but also planted the seeds for a new way of thinking in the minds of a room full of people who could have critical roles to play in difficult situations all over New England.

Since that meeting in 1980, NEERS has added special symposia to their meeting schedule, five of which have related to human effects on estuaries while three were devoted specifically to estuarine management. The title of the latest symposium on the subject, in 1998, was, "Is Science Helping in Community Decision-Making?" I guess I have to admit that I'm no longer the oddity in NEERS.

Chapter 12

Beautiful Blue Mussels

Elmer Darling may have urged the people in town to eat mussels during the war, but mussels remained the low bivalve on the popularity hierarchy for over 30 years afterward. A few fools continued to gather them to eat, but not many.

Then, in the winter of 1976-77, Orleans and the rest of the Cape experienced the coldest winter in years and mussels came into their own. With the exception of a few swift-running channels, the entire town was frozen for 14 consecutive weeks. Saltwater and fresh, wide rivers, bays and coves, everything was frozen. One of the very few exceptions was a place called Roberts Cove channel. A man-made rock dam, built in the 1800s to provide power for a mill, served to increase the velocity of the tide going in and out of the Mill Pond, keeping Roberts Cove channel open for a short distance around the dam. That meant a cornucopia of mussels.

Mussel harvesting was unregulated — perhaps the last free enterprise left in the local fishing world. Over ten weeks, I watched about 12 guys harvest over 12,000 bushels of mussels, all from an area that was only about one acre. At the time, it was the only shellfish they could get and it kept them solvent for the winter. The fishermen used pitchforks to gather the clumps of mussels and then they threw the large clumps into small skiffs. They brought the skiffs to shore, did some very minor cleaning, and bagged them, getting about $3 per bushel for their effort.

Large mussels attach to other mussels or stones by their strong byssal threads, and because of gregarious setting behavior — indisputable in the case of mussels — smaller ones surround the big ones.

If the clumps are not broken apart, the small seed gets marketed (though later thrown away) along with the larger mussels.

After the ice left, a few men continued using the pitchfork method but a father-and-son team decided that pitching and cleaning was too laborious and so they used a scallop drag in the remainder of the channel. Another 12,000 bushels were harvested but the dragging method was too efficient and the number of mussels in the channel quickly dwindled from the dragging effort.

The pair of guys dragging for them were not cleaning them at all. Instead, they were shoving large mussels, seed mussels, mud, snails, stones and anything else that came up in the drag into the bag, dragging as many bags as they could in a day, and getting only about $1.25 per bushel from a wholesaler. They felt it was not worth the effort to clean them when they could just pile everything into the bag and still make a "day's pay." Of course they got such a low price because their quick-and-dirty method meant that someone had to clean them before they could be sold to restaurants or retailers. Meanwhile the town lost all the mussel seed from an extraordinarily productive area.

To me, watching the mussel activity that winter, it seemed the fishermen were fishing themselves out of a resource where it seemed as if Orleans had the potential for a goldmine. This was my second winter as the town's shellfish biologist and I thought that if we could manage mussels so that the channel was left alone until we had another bad winter, then, when that harsh season came, the men could keep fishing. When I watched the dragging, I found it disconcerting because absolutely everything was being taken out of the system, most importantly the seed mussels but also the stones and cobbles that mussels need to attach to in order to build a clump.

I suggested to Gardy that we might want to consider putting some regulations on mussels. Gardy and I worked together on draft regulations that included a minimum size limit of two inches to give them a chance to reproduce. We also wanted a requirement that seed be put back into the water, and proposed a bag limit of 25 bushels per day.

The Shellfish Advisory Committee held a hearing in the winter of 1978. Wow, what fireworks!

The minutes for the hearing don't come close to suggesting the animosity exhibited in the room that night. Many of the men there had been fishing all their lives, as had their fathers before them. Others were the newcomers of the early 1970s who resisted authority as a matter of principle and didn't want anyone telling them anything about what they could or could not do. Both groups knew I had never fished commercially and was not responsible for feeding a family on what I gathered from the sea. Gardy wasn't much better in their eyes. He had worked for years as an estate caretaker in South Orleans and had been Shellfish Constable for a mere four years. What did he know? Some in the hearing room were Mun's friends and family, guys he had worked with or competed against all his life. Mun didn't say a word.

The fishermen said what they thought about our proposal in such a manner that their meaning was impossible to misconstrue. They had no use for Gardy or me or for mussel regulations. How dare we suggest regulations for something that was just beginning to bring in some real income, something that was truly a free enterprise, and something that the town had stupidly tried to get rid of before? Who did we think we were preventing them from making a living from these mussels? The state didn't even have any regulations on mussels — not even a size limit, as there was for every other commercial species. If the Division of Marine Fisheries of the Commonwealth of Massachusetts didn't care about mussels, why should we?

Gardy tried to explain that we thought the regulations were appropriate to maintain a fishery for them for the future. They didn't buy it. The Advisory Committee held more hearings. The opposition didn't diminish one iota. We gave in and dropped the idea of regulations.

The mussel harvest for 1976 was 12,500 bushels and for 1977 was 12,600 bushels, with almost all them harvested from December 1976 to May 1977, the nasty winter. For 1978, the harvest dropped to 3,090 bushels. There are a lot of possible explanations for the decrease, including the fact that other shellfish was more plentiful and therefore worth more fishing effort, but to my mind, there was no denying the fact that Roberts Cove channel had been just about fished out. But the time for regulations still had not arrived.

Over the next several years, mussels gained in popularity among ethnic markets, especially around New York City, and prices increased. Restaurants on the Cape also began serving mussels and they began gaining popularity among mainstream diners. Guys who got into musseling learned that if they took the time to thoroughly clean the mussels on the shore, they benefited from better prices. They also found that if they sold directly to restaurants, the price increased — from the original $3 per bushel for mussels that had been somewhat cleaned to $5 to $9 to $15 to $18 per bushel. The cleaner the mussels were, the higher the price.

The fishermen did what I called the "Orleans Stomp" to clean mussels. They put about half a bushel of clumps at a time in a wire bushel basket and put the basket in the water so that all of the mussels were covered with water. With the heel of their boot, they stomped the mussels to break up the clumps. The water acted as a cushion between the boot and the mussels and remarkably few were broken with this method. As they swished the basket of separated mussels around in the water a bit before bagging them, the remaining sand, gravel and seed mussels fell though the wire mesh. They wound up with clean, marketable-sized mussels in the basket, and seed mussels were left to grow.

Stomping clumps didn't take that long, perhaps 5-10 minutes for each half-bushel, but multiply that by 30 bushels or more per day and it became an arduous chore. Some men tried using a mechanical tumbler, using water again as a cushion, but few of them found that method totally satisfactory and most went back to the stomping method. One innovation did take hold: The men found that if they held the mussels in the water overnight after cleaning them, the byssal threads would regenerate and the mussels would have a greater shelf-life when they reached the market than if they were sold directly after harvest.

Four years after the original harvest of Roberts Cove, as more and more shellfishermen went into the fishery, taking mussels from Nauset Harbor and to a lesser extent, the Town Cove, a couple of fishermen came to me and said they needed some mussel regulations. There were too many harvesters and not enough stock to go around. I asked what they suggested and they said they wanted a size limit of two inches, all mussels to be culled on site and seed returned to the water, and a 10-15 bushel daily limit. I smiled and said I'd see what we could do.

The recommendations became regulations. At the height of the mussel industry, about 15 guys were working at it almost full time.

The price steadily increased over the years to the point where mussels were definitely competitive with other species. Mussels may be the lowest bivalves on the economic ladder but there is no longer talk in Orleans of eradicating them. But the huge mussel resource that was once in Nauset Harbor has dwindled dramatically, even with regulations in place. Perhaps the lack of mussels is a cyclical event. Whatever the reason, far fewer fishermen have been harvesting them for a decade or more. Nauset Harbor quality still counts — they fetch up to $80 per bushel now.

Over twenty-four years later, there are still no mussels in the Roberts Cove channel.

Chapter 13

Hunter-Gatherers

The commercial fishermen taught me a lot over the years. They taught me about independence and diversity of skills, about resiliency and self-reliance, love of the water at all times of the year, and even how to argue a case. They showed me what hard work really is and why dawn is a special time of day.

They also call it like they see it and leave no doubt as to what they mean. They are principled and for the most part, follow the rules, but they will debate the wisdom of fishery regulations for as long as it takes to make their point and often well after their point has been made. If a regulation is passed that they don't agree with, they will grumble loudly but will still follow the rules — although some of them just can't help themselves in testing the resolve of the enforcers of those rules.

The fishermen — women make up only a small percentage in the commercial ranks — professed a way of life that is fast disappearing on Cape Cod in general and in Orleans in particular, as the town evolves rapidly to a community of affluent retirees and second-home owners and the well-to-do business people who provide them with goods and services. The fishermen were proud individuals who did what it took to survive and make a living along the shore. For many, that meant shellfishing when shellfish was plentiful, then codfishing or lobstering when shellfish waned, or harvesting other stocks to make ends meet.

Economic survival also meant some needed bigger boats so they could go codfishing or lobstering. It meant they would have to endure daily trips through one or the other of the inlets from the Atlantic — two of the most dangerous inlets on the East Coast.

Every fisherman who has gone through Nauset Inlet or the Chatham Break has a story to tell of a near miss when they tempted fate.

When they just couldn't find a way to make a living from the sea, they went to work on land "banging nails" in the building trade, but most still kept a boat in the water or on a trailer and trained their eyes on the bays and ocean to get back into a fishery when conditions warranted.

Some fishermen shared their astute observations of the marine world with me and when they did, I felt privileged to be given insights culled through years of days on the water. To me, that meant I had gained some respect in their eyes.

They loved the water and so did I, but we didn't always see eye to eye. In fact, if truth were told, there was rarely agreement. Their love of the water was different from mine. The sea was in their blood and they wouldn't be any other place if they could help it. We were on the same page there. But every fish, every lobster, every scallop represented to them a percentage of a bill that had to be paid, food to be bought. Many had kids to be housed and clothed. A sword was always over their heads. Life was tough enough without some woman telling them that they couldn't fish harder because of long-term ecological issues.

I represented change and a different way of doing things. Change in propagation methods and shellfish management. Change in attitude, from harvesting today and worrying about tomorrow later, to trying to plan for tomorrow. Fishermen said planning never worked because you could never tell what Mother Nature was going to dish out; a fish in the bucket was better. I said if you took it today, it not only wouldn't be there tomorrow, but if it was too small or too many were taken, there may not be any left for tomorrow. We were probably both right. They may not always have known it but I respected them and respected the way they chose to live their lives. It's a hard way to make a dollar.

Countless changes occurred over the years I worked for the town — biological, physical, social, political and economic. I was a catalyst who orchestrated many of the changes in shellfish management. I was hired because quahaugs were sparse in Pleasant Bay after years of super harvests and the selectmen asked me to do what was necessary to bring quahaugs back. They wouldn't have hired me to do that if the fishermen hadn't complained to them about the lack of quahaugs. However, by hiring someone with some science background and a college degree, it meant they recognized the problem was complex and understood there might have to be some changes in how things were being done. But the nature of change is funny.

Most of us don't like change even though it is life's most enduring constant. Fishermen are no different. A fisherman's lab is at the end of his line or on a culling board. You can imagine how enthusiastic they were about establishing a lab that was part research and part propagation. What they knew was what they saw and they saw plenty and that was enough for them. Raising quahaugs from tiny seed with questionable "parents," seed bought from a hatchery somewhere off-Cape, well, that simply was not the traditional way of doing things.

It was a big change and there was to be little reward for the fishermen for many years because of the learning curve of the new methods, the long timeframe from seed to harvestable adult, and the cost of large-scale culture. They didn't see direct benefits. They felt a lot of years had been invested with little to show that a real difference had been made. It was no wonder they scorned new methods and thwarted the efforts in order to get back to tradition.

The irony was that tradition hadn't worked either. Too many people fishing or wanting to harvest had resulted in too few shellfish. Relying strictly on what Nature provides without putting much back to replenish stocks no longer worked. It added up to a depressed fishery and emotionally and economically depressed individuals.

Before we planted seed, the only significant propagation program was to buy chowder-sized quahaugs (three inches and larger) from Cape Cod Bay and transplant them to the Cove or Pleasant Bay. But watching large quahaugs during the spawning season in the lab convinced me that those old quahaugs needed *perfect* conditions in order to spawn. How often do the perfect conditions occur in nature? What seemed like a good approach for years may have been marginally good at best. There was NO proof of its success because it is the nature of shellfish to float with the currents for two weeks, making it impossible to link transplants and their progeny. Another peculiarity of quahaugs added to the ambiguity — they do not necessarily set in large groups like mussels or clams.

If there are enough quahaugs in a bay, of course there will be good sets that follow if conditions are favorable. But we didn't have enough quahaugs to start with in Pleasant Bay. Other towns had shown that if a semi-enclosed area like a salt pond has a lot of quahaugs, it might produce a bounty of quahaugs annually. Our natural stock in Pleasant Bay was slim everywhere. At least with the seed program, my reasoning went, we could buy seed that had been bred for fast growth and distinctive shell markings so we could track success rates with those non-native animals.

I never liked using those well-defined animals because I thought that the selective breeding done for fast growth and markings — a way to visually distinguish a cultured clam from a wild one — may not have produced the appropriate traits to select for in a wild population. In the wild population, survival rather than fast growth was the key trait. I used the stock for the same reasons that everyone else did. They were available, they let me track the survival of the seed, and hence they gave me a way to determine whether the program was working.

It seemed that two issues escaped the consciousness of the commercial fishermen and, by extension, the selectmen. One was that commercial harvesters were not the only people involved in shellfishing. Orleans and every other Cape town had huge numbers of recreational harvesters as well, maybe as many as ten times or more the number of commercial fishermen. These were ordinary folks who were willing to buy a permit just so that they could go to the shore and dig a mess of clams or scratch a bucket of quahaugs. A large percentage of non-commercial harvesters were residents who also paid the freight for the Shellfish Department activities through property taxes. But the commercial fishermen were often more vocal.

The second issue was that we were responsible for the whole town's resources and to the whole town for our programs, not just to commercial interests. After all, commercial fishermen made a living harvesting a public resource. Why should his or her opinion carry more weight than that of anyone else? The answer was that commercial shellfishing was a traditional way of life that we all wanted to preserve. But the conflict led to innumerable disagreements about shellfish management.

In the early days of my tenure, there were 90-100 commercial licenses issued on average. In contrast, there were 700 recreational shellfish permits issued. Licenses were inexpensive: $25 for commercial permits and $4 for resident non-commercial permits. Some residents bought commercial permits only because of the possibility that there might be a good scallop year in the fall. After a scallop bonanza year of 1983, when 336 commercial licenses were issued, the license system changed. No longer could the carpenter decide at the last minute to buy a license just before the scallop season opened, or just after it opened, which many would do in bountiful years to take advantage of the windfall.

The regular commercial fishermen though it unfair to those who made the majority of their living from the water to have the "fly-by-nights" take "their" scallops. A licensing window seemed a way to level the playing field a bit. Under the new system, if a person wanted a commercial license just for scallops, he or she would have to take a chance on what nature would provide because licenses were sold only during a window of opportunity that ran from January 1 through April 30 annually.

Once in a while, a species other than scallops also lead to increased permits. In 1996, the town issued the highest number of commercial permits ever — 428 — because of a super-abundance of clams in Nauset Harbor. But by 2001, the number of commercial licenses was 173 — a sign of the times as far as shellfish abundance was concerned. And yet, 1035 recreational shellfishing permits were issued the same year, an indicator from the public of the continued importance of shellfish and the privilege to harvest shellfish. Out of the commercial licenses, only a handful belonged to guys who made the majority of their living from shellfishing. Other licenses went to guys who were lobstering or codfishing for their principal income, to people who wanted to get more than the recreational limit, or to those who had always held a commercial permit just in case something good happened with shellfish.

Scallops have not made a comeback since the mid-1980s; more guys are fishing in Cape Cod Bay for quahaugs than in recent years; clams have been abundant in Nauset Harbor off and on; mussels are hard to come by; and a new fishery has opened up for razor clams.

The old adage is still heard on the waterfront — Mother Nature will provide — but these days, she seems to provide what constitutes a living for fewer and fewer people.

But now, there are more trying to farm the sea through aquaculture.

Chapter 14

Farming the Sea

After the first municipal seed experiments proved successful, private aquaculture for quahaugs mushroomed in Wellfleet, a town with a history of private oyster aquaculture. Culturists out there found that they could get the seed to market in three years. I never found an area in Orleans where the seed would grow to legal size in less than five years and in some cases, it was closer to seven.

In Chatham, a town with a huge commercial fishery and an almost non-existent private aquaculture industry, the town used volunteers for their propagation program and raised over four million seed while we were struggling to raise a million. But in Chatham, the fishermen agreed in 1983 to a substantial increase in their license fee ($50 to $200) if a considerable portion of the fee (75%) went directly to a dedicated fund for propagation. In 2001, a typical year for the number of permits, with 533 commercial permits issued (including junior permits), Chatham fishermen put nearly $75,000 into their dedicated fund. The wholesale value of their industry is $5.5 million. Back in 1983, when Chatham established its fund, Orleans would not allow volunteers to work on propagation and would not agree to a dedicated fund.

Frustration spilled over in meeting after meeting. Fishermen wanted to see tangible results from our propagation. They repeatedly said they never found any of the stock we planted. Fishermen looked at Chatham and Wellfleet, both towns where bottom culture was used, and said we had not found the right places to grow shellfish in the ground the way Nature intended. They said the lab was merely my pet project. Shellfish in the other towns took only 3 years to get to harvest. We must be doing something wrong and crazy.

Meanwhile, we were running our operation on a shoestring and never had enough money to expand the number of shellfish we were growing. So we were frustrated as well.

The state required that the towns prepare a shellfish management plan in order to receive state funds. It was my responsibility to write a draft plan.

Native populations of shellfish had dwindled to a low level for almost all species. In 1983, thanks to scallops, the total harvest in Orleans was valued at over $2 million wholesale, but three years later, the total value was just $197,000. Clams were abundant some years but we couldn't count on them either. Since Pleasant Bay stocks had declined so precipitously and the only good news on quahaugs was the stock in Cape Cod Bay that continued to muddle along, our propagation efforts were even more important. However, the quahaug program had not made a dent at that point since we were only able to buy 250,000 seed annually, and using the lab as a hatchery had not been as successful as we had hoped.

Could private farming take some of the pressure off the wild fishery?

One of the questions the state asked was whether or not the town allowed private aquaculture in town-owned waters. The history of Orleans was a "yes." Historically, the town allowed people to harvest quahaugs from Cape Cod Bay and "bed them" in privately leased areas in other town waters until markets improved, a practice going back to the early 1900s. Additionally, there were other areas held by lease-holders and used for private culture.

The history of the town gave some credence to the notion of allowing private aquaculture in town-owned waters. In order to expand private aquaculture and issue new leases, however, the state required the town to prove there would be no adverse impact to the town's natural shellfisheries where the activity was going to take place.

I looked at the existing grants (the state law's term for private leases of town waters), and at the reasons leases had been approved in the past, and then reviewed the applications coming to the selectmen. There were not many existing grants, and all but one were small, an acre or less. Some grants dated back many years. One large tract, ten acres, had been abandoned because the grant-holder had not satisfactorily proven that his use of the area complied with the purpose of the lease. New applications were coming in for a variety of areas.

The most problematic applications from a policy standpoint were those from individual waterfront property owners. Some of the applicants apparently wanted a grant in front of their house as something to play with, but it seemed very likely that some property owners merely saw a grant as a way to keep others from fishing in front of their house.

With the paucity of shellfish along the shores of Pleasant Bay, the mandatory "shellfish survey," required to be performed by state staff prior to the issuance of a grant, would often come up with few shellfish and hence, a finding by the state biologist of "no adverse impact." Unless the town could show that the application would cause an adverse impact to the town's shellfish resources, it was difficult not to allow the lease to go forward.

Waterfront owners were beginning to take advantage of this situation and many applied for grants. As grant-holders they wouldn't have to do all that much to satisfy the law and could keep others out of their area. This was clearly a "not in my back yard" (NIMBY) way of looking at shellfish. Shellfishing was an activity allowed by state law that went back to the Colonial Ordinances of 1640-1647 and the NIMBY attitude was potentially very damaging to the entire shellfish industry, wild harvest as well as aquaculture. Allowing people to have a grant for such reasons would set a dangerous precedent for the future.

Was there another way to address the issue in the management plan I was to write?

I wondered if perhaps we could find a relatively large area that would be acceptable to set aside for private aquaculture, without serious impact to the town's existing shellfish resources, that would prevent the lot-by-lot grant designations that seemed to be on the horizon.

Two areas looked promising — both in Pleasant Bay — and there was one possible site in Cape Cod Bay. In each case, there had not been significant native populations of clams, quahaugs, scallops, mussels or oysters in at least 40 years, so there would be no adverse impact. Both areas in Pleasant Bay were "out of the way" of major boating interests and were either inaccessible by land or accessible only to Off Road Vehicles (ORVs) via the beach but even so, they were not near established ORV beach trails. The flats of Cape Cod Bay were significantly less hospitable for shellfish to set and the waters were subject to ice and high wave action, especially in winter's frequent northwest gales. Plus, the flats were easily accessible for people on foot and the waters were used heavily for boating and fishing, so there might be problems for a lease-holder as a result of public use and trespass. Nonetheless, the draft management plan included all three areas as proposed for private aquaculture.

The proposal called for 25 acres to be set aside in one section of Pleasant Bay, provided for the possibility of several acres to be desig-nated in the second area of Pleasant Bay, and allocated some territory in Cape Cod Bay to be left in abeyance for possible future expansion. The first area would be divided into five 5-acre sites.

Talk about resistance to change! The fishermen recognized immediately that if the proposal were approved, they would be "giving up" those 25 acres for the foreseeable future and they knew that it would probably be extremely difficult to get the acreage reverted to public wild fishery. The "what ifs" started from the very beginning. What if conditions changed in the future such that today's infertile area, infertile for 40 years, somehow became pro-ductive later? What if the barrier beach broke through (that was a when, not an if)? What if scallops set in the area? What if fishermen tore up gear on the bottom while dragging for scallops in a leased area — would they be liable? What if something else of value settled there? Giving up public land for private business stuck in their craws on general principles and the vocal fishermen made it very clear they didn't like it. The subject was debated for two years.

Finally, the Shellfish Advisory Committee agreed to a plan calling for 30 acres and 15 potential farmers, giving more people a chance to develop and utilize culture techniques for private business while making aquaculture less attractive for large corporations to get into the act. The fishermen felt that if the town were to open this area to aquaculture, it would be more equitable if more people could become involved, just in case it worked well. Each applicant could ask for a half acre to start and could eventually increase to a max-imum of two acres.

During the time the proposal was debated, the grants in Wellfleet increased both in number and success. Word spread quickly that aquaculture was not necessarily a bad way to live off the water, but regardless of the successes in Wellfleet, some guys up my way just didn't like it. They pointed to Chatham, which had a history of denying grant applications, but Chatham had a much greater wild shellfish resource than Orleans. Chatham may not have been able to find potential grant sites that met the state criteria of being barren or not adversely affecting the town's natural resources, or their stance may just have been philosophically anti-grant. I don't know.

The Orleans selectmen accepted the management plan and adopted it in its revised form in 1986. A few applications came in almost immediately, but most people took a "wait and see" attitude, not wanting to invest heavily in something that might not pan out. If the area was naturally unproductive, the condition mandated by state law for aquaculture to proceed, was there perhaps a reason we didn't know about as to why it was unproductive? Might there also be no success with aquaculture on such a site?

The early aquaculturists — many were not traditional commercial fishermen — made some headway slowly, but they were shocked to discover that the animals did not attain legal size in three years as they had in Wellfleet. Some didn't become legal in four years either. Some of the plots took more than four years to get quahaugs to harvest size despite the state's decreasing its size requirement by almost one-quarter of an inch from the time I had begun growing seed. (The size was two inches across the shell when I started growing seed and was changed to one inch thick to be consistent with other states' requirements and to provide uniformity in the marketplace. That meant an average decrease in shell width of about a quarter of an inch).

For the farmers, slow growth had several consequences. It meant keeping the quahaugs in the water longer and hoping — hoping for a longer string of ice-free winters, hoping for good growth in following years, or simply hoping to see positive effects from any other combination of factors thrown in the mix. It also meant that they couldn't add new seed until the old seed had been harvested, and so they lobbied to speed up the process of lease-site expansion. Slow growth meant that growers could not see a return on their investment, and cash-flow going only one way meant they were increasingly strapped.

Expansion became a contentious issue because at one point, the selectmen allowed additional people to obtain grants in unused portions of the original area that had been set aside. That meant that if all the growers expanded to their maximum of two acres each, the amount of land necessary would be more than the allocated 30 acres. That issue has not been totally resolved. A rift developed between the aquaculturists and the wild harvesters because of additional territory being taken out of the public domain, which led the selectmen to question the wisdom of allocating more territory for grants. Several aquaculturists left the industry, which freed up some acreage, but not all that was requested. An uneasy alliance among the principals exists to the present.

A chicken-and-egg scenario took place several years ago when clams set naturally under netting placed on the bottom to protect planted quahaugs. Lease plans changed to include clams. Fishermen argued that clams were a proof of natural productivity but it wasn't clear-cut. Was it the netting that afforded the clams protection as we had seen earlier in our experiments with Chatham a decade earlier? Or had the new flow of water that resulted from the break in the barrier beach at the mouth of Pleasant Bay in Chatham aided in natural productivity? There had to have been some clam larvae in the water in order for them to settle under the nets. We will never know the dynamics for sure but the clams gave the growers some breathing room while they waited for the quahaugs to grow.

The shellfish grants and the idea of private aquaculture in town-owned waters will probably never be totally accepted by Cape fishermen as a good management alternative to wild fisheries, regardless of how depressed the wild fishery is. That conviction is one of the principal impediments to expansion of the shellfish aquaculture industry in Massachusetts, and it stems from the inherent conflicts in competing uses for the same area.

The inshore fisheries continue to dwindle and those who make a living from them continue to fight for a way of life that is integral to the town's history and tradition. But their numbers and political clout are steadily decreasing. Even with all the odds against them — from poor harvests to water quality degradation and habitat loss, plus some waterfront property owners who don't like the "look" of someone shellfishing in front of the big house on the bank — it's understandable that the fishermen have not embraced leasing public land to private individuals as an alternative even when that land is unproductive for shellfish.

But there are growing numbers of people who have embraced aquaculture for its positive environmental effects. For the Cape, one of the benefits of lots of shellfish in the water is their ability as filter feeders to help "clean up" the waters that have become overburdened by nutrients that caused unusual plankton blooms. With that benefit in mind, some wonder if aquaculture can actually help rather than harm an area.

To some commercial shellfishermen though, aquaculture is too much of a departure from tradition. And aquaculture is new. Changing from hunter-gatherer, where nature provides the bounty and all you have to do is harvest it, to farmer, where you have to pay for the bounty up-front and nurture it yourself in order to realize greater bounty several years later — that's a major change. Most people don't like major change.

Chapter 15

Hand-me-downs

What does a small town department do when its rescue fleet no longer meets the rigorous demands of the state? Obviously, the department replaces the inadequate emergency transport. But what happens if trade-in value is a pittance? In the case of thrifty Orleans, the unwritten policy was that if some other department could use the old relic, then give it to them. The Fire Department was in such a predicament several times when state regulations forced medical-transport replacements. The firefighters had old but serviceable vehicles that could use a new home. I was the recipient of three such vehicles that they could no longer use.

The first was a gray utility truck. It was ancient but it allowed me mobility to carry out my responsibilities without relying on Gardy or Mun to drop what they were doing to get me somewhere. With my basket scratcher in the back along with a few other necessary tools of the trade, the "Gray Ghost" took me wherever I wanted to go.

Several years later, by the end of the 1970s, the state-mandated ambulance design shifted from hearse-type to multi-purpose vehicles that were more boxy-looking. The Fire Department had to ditch their 1967 International Travel-All, and by that time the gray truck was getting mighty tired so we took the new gift. The Highway Department painted it Army green, the only color they had on hand, and delivered it to us.

It was a "stretch" model, about 2 feet longer than the traditional Travel-All and it also stood about a foot higher. It still had the now non-functional ambulance lights across the top of the sides and rear, plus the spotlights next to the side mirrors, and was altogether a strange-looking sight. I took one look at this monstrosity and had two immediate thoughts: "Beggars can't be choosers" was one and "This is ridiculous" was the other. I was going to be driving around town in that thing?

That night, I tried to think of names for my new conveyance and came up with a few: clam mobile or quahaug or scallop or shellfish or mussel mobile didn't quite capture its essence. Then I shifted gears and sounded out quahaug ambulance, scallop ambulance, clam ambulance. Hmm. Clam ambulance. "Clambulance". That was it.

The next day, I told Gardy my new chariot's name and said we should paint it on the door. After he had gotten himself under control, he said he loved it, but this time, we'd better ask the selectmen about officially painting something so outrageous. After the selectmen stopped laughing, they said it was fine just as long as "Town of Orleans" was in big letters and "Clambulance" was printed in small letters. We said fine.

There must have been a slight mis-communication with the sign painter however, because when we got it back, the lettering format was just the opposite. "Town of Orleans" appeared in smallish white letters painted in a half circle, and "Clambulance" was in big

letters below in a straight line. In between, not the official town seal as on every other municipal vehicle, but a lovely rendition of a clam. Perfect.

The one thing I had neglected to take into consideration was the reaction of people when they saw this ugly duckling and its sign. Locals smiled or laughed but tourists were mystified. A zillion times people stopped to ask, "What's a Clambulance?" If the questioner asked, "Is it to take sick clams to the clam hospital?" the answer was, "No, it's to take baby clams and other healthy shellfish from one place to another as quickly as possible." They'd usually look quizzical but often shrugged and left smiling. We even went so far as to drive the laughing stock of the town in the 4th of July parade, grinning the entire time.

The Clambulance never did have very good steering and was actually bordering on dangerous when the Fire Department came through again. This time it was the town's first boxy ambulance, ready to be replaced, and re-painted bright blue and white. It was impossible to sneak up on someone for enforcement because this enormous van was unmistakable amidst the fishermen's pickup trucks. With all the vehicular oddities used for the job over the years, it was always pretty easy to find me.

We thought the Clambulance was ready for the junk yard but the Town of Wellfleet disagreed and bought it from Orleans for a song to use at Wellfleet Harbor. It could go fom the harbor to the town dump but not much further. The Harbormaster kept it going for another 3-4 years and although they removed the white paint on the doors, if you looked closely, you could still see Clambulance on the side.

Small town antics, impossible to get away with now.

Chapter 16

Raising the Stakes

The decade of the '70s, spilling over to the early '80s, was a transition period nationally, with big consequences for Cape Cod. Parents of the war babies and baby boomers had gone through the Great Depression and Second World War. Many had moved out of cities and into suburbs, and were starting to get ahead financially and looking forward to retirement. If they were lucky, they bought a piece of real estate on the Cape where they built a small house for their vacations and eventual retirement. They had found their niche.

Their children, fresh out of school or the service, defined the crazy and tumultuous '60s. This was an era that, to my mind, didn't really start until 1963 with the Kennedy assassination — an event that shook the nation to its core. It lasted into the early 1970s, to about the end of the Vietnam War, when many hoped the divisiveness that convulsed the country would be healed and the nation could be glued back together. Children of this era, like me, looked for a meaningful place to live and many gravitated to the Cape. We too found our niche.

The Shellfish Department in Orleans had begun the decade of the '70s with a change in personnel — Gardy first and then me. No longer was the Shellfish Department simply going to transplant available stock to other areas as the principal propagation method. We immediately departed from tradition when we bought our first shipment of seed quahaugs, creating a new niche for ourselves.

Those first years were an adventure, filled with experiments. We never knew ahead of time what we would find out. Our decision to plant quahaugs in 20 different locations in three estuaries proved to be a wise move because we were able to learn so much, not only about the preferred habitat for quahaugs, but also about areas that were less than ideal for them.

Our focus was to try anything, even a few wacky ideas, that might increase stocks of shellfish in the waters. We also tried different management techniques, including the launch of a regulatory strategy for mussels, just to keep them in high supply. We transplanted clams using a harrow. We plowed huge acreage in Chatham and Orleans just to see if it would catch a set of clams. We built floating sand-boxes and put them in two separate ponds. And, as we shall see, we even got risqué checking out the sex lives of scallops.

We were in our own little world in the late '70's. Other shellfish officers in neighboring towns were doing similar things, but it got more and more difficult for the towns to pay for shellfish propagation. We were lucky. We had the opportunity to do something even more daring — move a building, scheduled to be demolished, to the water, and then install a running seawater system and create a shellfish hatchery. If it worked well, we would be able to plant millions of seed. Our hopes were high.

By the end of that period, the late 1970s, economic shifts had taken place on the Cape. Local property taxes had increased — the new people meant expanded services, especially for schools and public safety. At the same time, the oil crisis, with its accompanying long lines at the gas pumps, fueled distrust in Washington that filtered down through all levels of government.

Massachusetts taxpayers, fed up with high property taxes, passed landmark legislation in 1980, called Proposition 2½, whereby municipalities could not raise taxes more than 2½ percent over the previous year's levy whether or not the residents thought a new program was a good idea or that an existing program needed an infusion of extra money. Towns were allowed to ask voters for an override to raise additional money but that action required not only success on the floor of Town Meeting but also success at the ballot box in a special election. And operating expenses could not be included in an override request.

Orleans town departments began to hear terms such as "level funding" or "zero-based budgeting" and were told to "do more with less" when the budget process began. Orleans taxpayers had been generous, approving expenditures if they thought a program was a good idea, and would benefit. But in the beginning stages of Proposition 2½, towns like Orleans found it difficult to cut back programs that had begun as a result of increased population, just to get budgets under the maximum percentage increase mandated by law.

It was a period of double-digit inflation and money wasn't going very far. There now wasn't enough money for us even to maintain the level of seed that we had bought in the second year of our program, let alone expand. And yet, we were still trying to expand because we believed doing so was essential. So other facets of the department budget suffered instead.

Inflation meant that since our propagation dollars were not worth as much, we were forced to buy smaller and smaller seed. For commercial hatcheries to keep feeding the seed until they got bigger, they had to grow a tremendous amount of food, which was costly, and the hatcheries passed on that cost to us. Our choices were to buy more small ones and hope they survived in more areas, or buy fewer large ones and plant in fewer areas. We opted for smaller seed. The problem with that choice was that smaller seed were more likely to wash out of the rafts and would not grow big enough to avoid being eaten by predators when we planted them around town in the fall.

When we created the shellfish lab, remember it was done on a nickel-and-dime budget. If we spent money on seed, we had less for the lab, already operating on a shoestring, but we kept the propagation program going the best we could, despite the constraints.

Meanwhile, the whole character of the town was changing. Swirling around us, beginning at the end of the '70s, was the first of several big building booms that changed the Cape dramatically in a quarter-century. Cottages like the one I grew up in were becoming a nostalgic memory, replaced by substantial retirement or second homes, although sometimes on small lots more suitable for a summer cottage than a year-round house. The population was steadily increasing — the year-round population of Orleans more than doubled, from 2,500 to nearly 6,000, in the years 1970-1980 while the summer population doubled, from 7,500 to over 16,000. Subdivisions were plotted and new roads were cut into the woods.

Some of the homes were not used by vacationers but rather by retirees who moved to the Cape to relax, dig a few clams, play a little golf almost year-round and join the community at large. Some of the new building was along the waterfront but a greater portion was inland and in our innocence at the time, those houses didn't seem to affect the water at all.

To service the new people, Orleans became the business center of the lower Cape. It began early in the '70s, before stringent wetland regulations were adopted. We noticed a cranberry bog was sanded over, a common practice for bog maintenance. Nowhere was there a definition of how much sand meant bog maintenance and how much meant filling the bog. As the truckloads continued to dump sand, it became obvious that this bog was being filled. Not long after, a supermarket and large discount department store filled what was the old bog. By the end of the next decade, another large developer cut down acres of woods to build a strip mall, anchored by another supermarket. The supermarkets were like bookends sandwiching the town.

At town meeting, people still voted for shellfish propagation. But they also established a golf study committee to see if there was enough land someplace to build a golf course. Shellfish was losing its competitive edge as new residents, with new priorities that didn't revolve around the traditional waterfront uses, began deciding how to spend tax dollars..

By the mid-to-late '80s, houses were popping up at the water's edge, not just inland, in another big building frenzy. These houses were bigger than in the earlier building boom. There were so many new people in town, both during the summer and year-round, that everything connected with shellfish had to be explained over and over. We felt it was time well spent to explain why shellfish were important to the town, what the maritime history was all about, and something about the ecology of the estuaries where shellfish lived.

An important piece of the education was to explain the Colonial Ordinances of the 1640s that said waterfront property owners may own title to land down to the low tide mark, but they didn't own the shellfish there. Anyone properly licensed could dig anywhere along the shore. Many of the new waterfront owners didn't like that. They didn't like the "look" of someone digging in front of their house.

However, many more people liked the idea,that they could dig shell-fish for a small fee. Recreational permits hovered between 1,000 to 1,500 from 1970-1982. Tourists, at the Cape for a couple of weeks, couldn't believe that they, too, could go out and dig shellfish. It was a family outing for many people.

Fishermen faced ever greater odds during this period. Those who chose to fish offshore were faced with the beginning of restrictions that would completely alter the nature of fishing in the North Atlantic. Some of them moved from offshore to inshore, to fish on the back-side of the Cape or in the inshore bays and estuaries, putting additional stress on those resources. Our propagation program couldn't make a real dent in the demand when there was less pressure; our efforts seemed downright puny with the added fishing pressure.

The stakes were changing. The cost of development, known to be higher than vacant land, was about to become incredibly high for the estuaries. By the end of the '80s we had to deal with drastic changes. The second major building boom of larger homes meant open land was disappearing at an alarming rate, but worse even than that was pollution, once a word reserved for metropolitan areas. Now it was about to hit our shores, and with a vengeance.

The effects of the building booms became apparent as shoreline vistas were transformed from natural landscapes to views of man-made structures; as houses that were built too close to fragile coastal banks became endangered; and as effluents from the houses began to wend their way to the estuaries. It would not be long before the long-term consequences of the building booms became painfully obvious.

Suddenly, I was dealing with more than just growing quahaugs. The job I was hired to do, to find out about quahaugs and get more shellfish in the town, starting with learning to bullrake, was getting much more complicated and complex. Fortunately I was active in professional societies where I could learn some of what I needed to know to deal with the changes that were happening at a frenetic pace. But there were also a lot of issues emerging that had no ready-made solutions.

Great natural fluxes were at work too. Pressure was building not only politically but also in the natural world, and the barrier beaches protecting both Pleasant Bay and Nauset were under siege by the sea. A period of incredible turmoil on all fronts was being ushered in.

Chapter 17

Blood Red and Tropical Green

I had been in the workboat one day in 1980 going slowly down The River. I looked at the water and was startled. The water was blood red. It was so noticeable that I took a sample to look at later under the scope. The slide I made indicated a single species of algae in the water — The River was having a bloom of one particular algae species at the expense of almost any other type of plankton, and the organism was a cousin of the Red Tide organism. I was glad to see that the organism was not one of the toxic species of plankton, but I was disturbed that it was so prevalent that it turned the water red. It was unusual and not a good sign.

We had experienced a few outbreaks of Red Tide (Paralytic Shellfish Poisoning or PSP) but that was from a specific species of algae that had blown into Nauset in 1972 from a storm in the Gulf of Maine. The organism (*Alexandrium tamarense*) has two phases to its life history. It is seen first as a cell that multiplies and is part of the plankton community; then the cells transform into hard-shelled cysts that falls to the bottom and stay in the sediment as part of the benthic community; and then, when conditions allow, the cysts germinate and "bloom" as plankton again.

Each cell in the water changes to a cyst when the conditions are no longer appropriate for it to be in the water column. A big bloom results in a large number of cysts left behind in the sediment — seeds for a subsequent bloom. A large bloom was cause for great concern.

Although PSP isn't harmful to shellfish, ingesting shellfish affected by PSP is potentially very dangerous. The state monitors the water regularly and if there is PSP, the area is automatically closed until the bloom subsides.

The Alexandrium organism attacks the central nervous system in humans and causes a tingling sensation around the mouth. But if the toxicity is great enough, the person's breathing may be paralyzed, hence the name paralytic shellfish poisoning. If the person does not receive medical treatment (often a respirator), death is quite possible. With proper treatment, there are no long-lasting ill effects.

Scientists researching blooms of toxic algae don't know exactly what the triggering conditions are that cause blooms in the first place. It might be nutrients entering the water after rain storms in the spring and fall when the temperature is just right, but it might be something else too. What would cause the water in Pleasant Bay to have a monospecific bloom of another species of plankton? While the shellfish area closures due to PSP in Nauset were distressing, it was certainly not the same thing as a shellfish closure because of pollution. Or was it?

By the late '70s, we had begun hearing laments from some of the shellfish officers from the larger towns of the Upper and Mid-Cape (Bourne, Falmouth, Barnstable, Yarmouth and Dennis), as well as other officers from around the state, about areas that had been closed to shellfishing because of pollution. We listened, but we were smug, sympathetic but smug. Our water was clean. We said, privately, thank God we live in the Lower Cape where we don't have to worry about pollution, and we kept doing our thing with shellfish propagation. But one of the shellfish officers from one of the Upper Cape towns that was much more developed than Orleans, said that it was inevitable that all of the Cape would experience pollution. He said that all the pollution around the big cities of New York to the Cape's south and Boston to the north, was heading our way, converging on the point of land forty miles off the coast of Massachusetts as if the Cape were the tip of an arrow. We still weren't worried.

We had seen some changes though. In addition to the water color I noticed that summer day in 1980, other subtle changes were visible. Green and brown seaweeds had increased along the shores and there were patches of seaweed floating in the ponds. The rafts we had made for our Lonnie's Pond propagation effort were lower in the water from the weight of the seaweeds trapped within the flotation logs and under the chicken wire we had added to prevent predation by birds. The rafts needed to be cleaned more often to prevent the quahaugs from being smothered but we weren't greatly concerned — we just made sure that raft maintenance was done regularly and well. The eelgrass in Little Bay seemed less lush too. Fuzzy growth appeared on the grass blades while branched brown seaweed congregated on the sand among the grass.

Still listening to other folks talk of their woes and the amount of area closed to shellfishing elsewhere compared to us, we still thought we were in relatively good shape. Although we were noticing changes, the whole town was still open to shellfishing, so we were still smug.

In 1981, clams were prolific in Meetinghouse Pond. The fishermen requested that a new type of harvesting be used, called pumping or hydraulic harvesting. We weren't sure about the new method but allowed it on a limited basis just in the pond — not in The River — and I did an analysis of its effects on the clam populations. I was focused on the effects on the seed.

Pumping for clams is similar to the hydraulic harvesting method used to harvest sea clams in Cape Cod Bay but on a smaller scale. The guys in the pond generally used a 5hp motor to run a pump in the boat. On the intake side of the pump, they attached a flexible hose, generally three inches in diameter, to which they added a sieve-type attachment at the end to prevent seaweed or debris from getting in and damaging the pump. This hose they put over the side into the water. On the output side, they attached a long hose, about two inches in diameter. At the end of this hose, the guys attached a reducing coupling in order to attach a one-inch diameter metal tube, a kind of wand, which was crimped on the end to produce a jet of water.

The fisherman walked along the shore, dressed in waders and blasted the sediment as he walked. Once the clams had been dislodged and lay on the sediment surface, it was easy to scoop them up with a net and dump the contents on the culling board. The men would cull the catch and throw the small undersized clams back into the pond. The others would go to market. All together, the fishermen using this method harvested about $100,000 worth of clams that summer.

Pumping became a controversial harvest method. It allowed the shellfishermen to scour an area, getting even subtidal clams that were buried in areas that were difficult to harvest under water by conventional methods. Resuspension of the sediment made the water "dirty" at a season, summer, when a lot of people were boating in the pond, adding to the controversy. But clam prices were much higher in the summer and the fishermen wanted to use the pumping method when the price was highest.

Unfortunately, my analysis suggested that summer was not the optimum time to use the pumping method, further fueling the controversy. I had a couple of reasons.

First, pumping ravaged the population of clams that weren't taken to market. Small baitfish such as mummichogs and sticklebacks, which are around in huge numbers in the summer, would descend on a pumped area after the shellfishermen had finished culling. The fish would bite a piece of the foot of the larger, but still sub-legal clams as they tried to dig back into the sediment. Once the foot was bitten, the clam could not re-burrow and was left on the surface for other predators to gorge on — a free lunch.

Second, summer is the time of procreation, and pumping blasted the sediment where baby clams had settled. Although it was impossible to tell if tiny clams, dispersed by the pumping, had been killed or just displaced, it was clear that there were fewer seed clams in the pumped area vs. an unpumped area.

The method might be preferable from a resource standpoint in almost any other season but summer, but of course the price was lower in the other three seasons. I never had an opportunity to compare the method at different times of year, however; so non-summer pumping might have been problematic as well.

But hydraulic harvesting was a moot point the next year. There would be no harvesting by any method.

When the notice came in 1982, we were shocked. Meetinghouse Pond had been closed to the harvest of shellfish because of bacterial contamination. Not for a week or a couple of weeks, but indefinitely. The town had received a loud and jarring wake-up call from the Massachusetts Division of Marine Fisheries that we were no longer immune to closures of shellfish areas because of bacterial pollution. The pond would be closed to shellfishing until further notice. Until further notice. Those words sent a shock wave throughout the Orleans Shellfish Department and the shock rolled through the community at large. This wasn't just a plankton bloom.

Just the summer before, over $100,000 worth of clams had been harvested from the pond. But in the time it takes to open an envelope, it had been closed due to bacterial contamination. Pollution. In Orleans. Our reaction was the usual one from people in shock. We wrung our hands. We questioned the state officials who had done the testing and issued the edict. We talked and attended meetings. We listened and we learned. And the pond remained closed.

"Have you seen the water in the Town Cove today?" the concerned caller asked in the summer of 1986. "It's a strange color." Sure enough, down by the Orleans Yacht Club at the head of the Cove, the cul-de-sac of the estuary, there was a patch of blood-red water adjacent to a patch of tropical-green water. Neither was normal. I took some samples and found that each color represented a single type of microscopic plankton. Great. This was another incidence of a bloom of one particular type of algae. A few hours later, the colors disappeared. A few weeks later, the whole estuary was closed to shellfishing by the state because of contamination. Nauset had followed the same sequence — plankton blooms and then high bacteria counts. There had to be a relationship between the colors of the water and the closures.

This was the entire Nauset estuary that was closed. We were dumbfounded. This was not the infamous Boston Harbor, one of the dirtiest bodies of water in the country back then. This was the Lower Cape, home to the pristine Cape Cod National Seashore. Our regional cocoon had been broken wide open. Pollution affected us now. What was going on?

Our meetings with the state began to shed some light on the problem. We learned that the contamination in Meetinghouse Pond, followed by the contamination in Nauset, was the same as had been found in the Upper Cape towns we had been so smug about. We were being hit with bacterial contamination. We learned that the bacteria could come from several different sources and failing septic systems were the first possible culprit to consider. No surprise there. But we also learned that road drainage could actually be one of the primary contributors of the contamination. Our first reaction was, how could that be? We were moving slowly and cautiously and there was a steep learning curve.

The first thing we had to learn was how to tell if a body of water is polluted. Exactly what were the tests the state had conducted and what did the results mean? We needed to know how testing the water related to the safety of shellfish. We needed to learn about the standards — how they were developed, why they tested for an "indicator" organism, and what all the terms meant. And most important, we needed to know what, if anything, we could do to solve the problem in order for shellfish to be harvested again.

People asked us how it was possible that storm drains could cause such a problem. We told them what we had learned about a complex process.

We explained that when water is tested for shellfish-harvest quality, the test that is used measures the amount of fecal coliform, an "indicator" organism that is in the water. Bacteria grow in "colonies" and the test supplies the proper conditions for any bacteria present to flourish, and if the amount of fecal coliform exceeds 14 colonies in 100 milliliters of water, an area can be shut down to shellfishing. Because shellfish can be consumed raw in the United States, the law requires very high water quality standards in order to harvest shellfish. The count must reach 200 colonies for an area to be closed for swimming, for example. The coliform bacteria being tested were not a threat to human health per se but they indicated the potential of more serious bacteria that can be a threat, hence the term "indicator organism".

We explained that fecal coliform bacteria originates in warm-blooded animals including birds, dogs, cats, skunks, deer, mice and any other creature that falls into the category, including us humans. We said that if you walk along a road and look down, instead of scanning your surroundings, you'd see droppings left behind by animals patrolling the road or by birds flying overhead. All of that substance accumulates until a rainstorm comes to wash it off the roads and when that happens, it gets flushed down the drain, literally, and into the estuary.

We told them that as far as the legal mandate was concerned, it didn't matter if the bacteria came from a dog or a human, there was no differentiation in the testing — fecal coliform bacteria were fecal coliform bacteria and that meant there was a risk.

We had been told that there was no hope of any new testing regime that would differentiate between bacteria that were harmful to humans and bacteria that posed no such risk. Shellfish sanitation fell to the state and the towns were prohibited from allowing shellfishing in an area closed because of bacteria. So, even if the towns sampled for human pathogens and found none, they could not fine tune the state program on their own; all they could do was test the waters under state protocols to determine what was happening in the estuaries. If the counts in the samples taken by the state exceeded the legal limit, the area was closed. Case closed until the problem was solved.

While we were still learning about bacterial contamination in general and how it affected Orleans resources specifically, June Fletcher, a resident of Meetinghouse Pond, became convinced we were moving too slowly. We told her what we knew and she asked if a group of concerned citizens might be more effective dealing with the town leaders and committees than her single voice. We said definitely yes. And so, after discussions with her neighbors, the Friends of Meetinghouse Pond was born. From the beginning, the group worked with the town to solve the problems at the pond and repeatedly asked what they could do. For several years, we really didn't know what they or anyone else could do.

Finally, we learned enough to work to try to solve the problem. We conducted a "sanitary survey" of the shoreline to identify any potential source of contamination, using the system approved by the National Shellfish Sanitation Program. Working closely with the Board of Health, we quickly ruled out faulty septic systems since we didn't find any as a result of a major septic inspection and maintenance program that they had been implementing. We began taking water samples that we brought to the Barnstable County lab. The Friends of Meetinghouse Pond learned how to take water samples and they brought the samples to both the county lab and to a private lab, all at their own expense. We went further and further upstream. We tested stormwater drains and discovered to our horror that the drains were indeed a major contributor.

Roads were traditionally designed to get water off roads as quickly as possible for safety reasons, and the conventional method had always been to shunt the water to a lowland or lake or pond or estuary. No one knew when the roads were built that road drainage carried bacteria, toxic chemicals such as hydrocarbons from the cars, and other potential pollutants, including excess nutrients, into the receiving body of water. It was just common sense to dump it in the most logical place, the nearby lowland or a body of water.

Dick Gould, the Highway Manager, had worked for the Highway Department for over 30 years and all of a sudden, he was hearing that his department's standard operating procedure might be a cause of serious problems. With the new information, the Highway Department had to re-think all of its maintenance procedures. Rather than balk at the new information, Dick embraced it and immediately began to change the way he approached road drainage.

The Friends of Meetinghouse Pond were vigilant in their search for answers. We informed them of what we knew and what we were doing to search for the sources of the pollution. They continued to offer to help in any way they could.

It began to dawn on all of us that our bays were no longer the pristine places they had been and that we were in for a long battle.

Chapter 18

Simulated Systems

Operating a hatchery is innately frustrating, and often depressing. Operating one in a 16x24-foot poorly equipped building is even worse. Anything that can go wrong in any aspect of the hatchery process will go wrong. Tiny shellfish can succumb to the subtlest change in their environment in the blink of an eye and in staggering numbers. People either like hatchery work or hate it — there is no in-between.

With an animal as low on the totem pole of life as quahaugs, it's surprising to learn they have certain requirements for procreation that are mystifying to us humans. They often just won't cooperate when you want them to spawn.

Most commercial hatcheries spawn shellfish out of season so they can sell them in the spring. Hatchery staff "conditions" the animals in the winter by raising the water temperature and feeding them, essentially "tricking" them into thinking that it is June and not January. In nature, environmental cues trigger the spawning process and although scientists are not sure what all of them are, water temperature is one of the cues.

Hatcheries keep the quahaugs in tanks with the water temperature warmer than winter water temperature but not so warm that the animals will spawn without being coaxed. That way, all it takes is a spike in water temperature and they will spawn. Once they have been "conditioned" — their gonads having been ripened so they are ready to spawn — heating the water to spike at about 10° Fahrenheit higher will usually get the process rolling. Heating the water in the winter was too expensive for our budget, so we opted to use the animal's natural rhythm. We hoped we would be getting the quahaugs to spawn in June.

Some people use a "mass spawning" technique where a lot of animals are placed in a tank and are coaxed into spawning by the raising and lowering of the water temperature. Others use a method where individuals are placed in Pyrex loaf pans and the water temperature around them is raised and lowered. We did not have a good means to do a mass spawning but we did have shallow tanks where we could manipulate water flow, and so we used the loaf pan method.

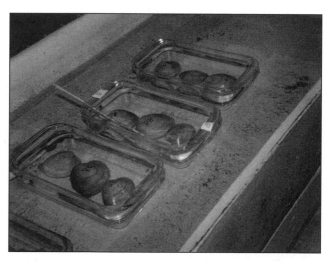

We could be at it all day. Raise the temperature. Lower the temperature. Raise it. Lower it. Cycle after cycle for hours. We were beginning to wonder what aphrodisiacs we needed to get quahaugs to do their thing and created many biologists' jokes to release the frustration. Just before we were about to call it quits for the day, a male might finally spew out a cloudy white stream and a female might follow, discharging a stream of white substance seemingly dotted with pinpricks. Finally, reluctantly, maybe a few others would let go. Then we'd be there for several more hours getting everything ready for the next phase.

The eggs were placed in plastic 30-gallon trashcans. After 48 hours, the trash containers were drained through a fine-mesh sieve that we made from five-gallon buckets with tight fitting lids. We made the sieves by cutting the bucket about five inches from the top, using the bottom of the bucket for other purposes. We removed most of the lid, keeping only the tight-fitting rim. We placed netting over the top of the bucket, snapped on the lid and caulked the interior seam with aquarium sealant. Every other day from then until the larvae went through a metamorphosis stage, the larval containers (trash-cans) were drained through a sieve, washed thoroughly with soap and water and then with a bleach solution, and carefully rinsed.

If they spawn, quahaugs may eject millions of eggs in one spawning. (The number of eggs is duly counted by extrapolating from a small sample). But two days later, when the eggs have become swimming larvae, the number has dropped precipitously. The number keeps dropping for the next two weeks until the larvae have gone through a metamorphosis, gained their hard shell and foot, lost their swimming organ, and dropped to the bottom. All of this means that in order to plan for a final number of seed to plant outside, you have to start with an incredibly higher number. A colleague told me of a commercial scallop hatchery he operated in Chile where he needed 2.5 *billion* larvae to end up with 6 million seed — meaning roughly 399 out of every 400 larvae died. How depressing to see all those animals die at various stages of development.

There are certain requirements to operate a hatchery for which there just aren't any alternatives. First and foremost is access to high-quality water that can be pumped around the clock or on demand, or else stored in a gigantic storage tank set high enough so that you can have water available for gravity-feed to the tanks, an expensive proposition. The second item is a high degree of attention to detail. Third is the ability to produce enough high-quality food for the microscopic and then larger but still tiny seed.

There was a steep learning curve to operating a hatchery on an inadequate budget in a setting that was less than optimal for the task. In one of our early years, a boater tied up to our intake buoy, the buoy that marked the position of the end of the long pipe that drew water from the Cove and transported it to the building above. With the boat constantly tugging all night on the buoy attached to the pipe, one of the connections tore apart and the water stopped flowing. On another occasion, we were growing algae, food for our animals, outside the building in large opaque cylinders into which air had to be constantly bubbled. We made a cover to keep out foreign materials and had the air tube threaded through a small piece of thick-walled plastic tubing, placed at the top of the cylinder to prevent the cover from crimping the air hose and shutting off the air supply. We found the air had stopped bubbling one morning because of a crimped air hose. A peanut butter sandwich was in the cylinder. A security fence was needed but it exceeded our budget. Clearly, we were always concerned about stupid acts or accidents happening as a result of the very visible nature of the site.

On the plus side, the location afforded us an excellent opportunity to educate people — to talk about the project specifically but also to answer general questions about marine issues. We had 200-400 people visiting our facility each year during the summer months. The people who stopped in were fascinated that shellfish were actually being grown in this little building.

Town decision-makers, most of whom were relatively new residents, understood the hierarchy of municipal service — police, fire, highway, water — but they never really seemed to understand that public education about natural resources was also a public service, or if they understood it, it didn't count for much in their eyes. This type of education was not an essential service to the community like the schools were, to be sure. The educational value was an intrinsic bonus, not a value easily measured in actual dollars spent for benefit accrued, the classic cost/benefit ratio used in business or municipal government.

Luckily, after a few years in the hatchery game, a new nursery technique came across the Atlantic from Europe. It was based on what are called upwellers. With an upweller setup, tiny seed were placed on netting inside a cylindrical container called a "silo," water was pumped up to flow through the mesh and silo, and then was discharged through a pipe at the top of the container. With this method, we could buy really tiny seed from a hatchery, the size of the head of a pin, and not go through the hatchery hassle ourselves. Plus it allowed us to grow a million seed in our small facility, four times the amount we had been growing on the rafts. We re-designed the water system in the interior of the building, bought a more powerful water pump, made silos from our free buckets, bought a million tiny seed and were off and running.

In order to have enough water flow up through the seed in the silo, we needed to create a tank-within-a-tank and we used inexpensive commercial plastic containers, called fish totes, which held two silos apiece. Fish totes are about three feet long, two feet wide and almost two feet high. The silos were made in essentially the same manner as our sieves, from five-gallon plastic buckets with tight fitting lids, except that the silos were higher. We cut off two inches

from the bottom of the bucket and attached the lids, again caulking the inside seam. We then turned the bucket upside down with netting on the bottom and drilled a one-and-one-half inch hole near what became the top and another hole, the same size and at the same height, in the tote. We cut pieces of one-and-one-half inch black plastic pipe to go through the bucket and tote overhanging the tank. Thus the water entered the fish tote, flowed up through the silo containing the seed and out into the tank in a flow-through system. As the seed grew, we replaced the netting with gradually larger-sized mesh to allow for the maximum flow through the netting without losing seed.

I walked into the lab one day in July 1985, and my assistant said, "They're all dead." When I looked at sample after sample from each separate tote, all I saw were floating bodies with just a few quahaugs still intact. I turned to Lauren and said, "If anybody wants me, I'll be at home" and walked out the door. How could this have happened? What went wrong this time?

The next day, I searched for answers and by chance, one of the guys that worked at the Goose Hummock boat rental shop next door said he had seen oil coming out of a discharge pipe that was about 100 feet from our intake pipe. I investigated further, following the discharge pipe back across the street to its source. There, I found a track of oil from a large gray metal machine behind a large supermarket.

When questioned, the manager of the supermarket acknowledged that a maintenance company based in New Hampshire had emptied hydraulic fluid from a trash compactor behind the building. The supermarket complex sat on a filled cranberry bog that was part of a larger wetland system — it had been built before environmental laws prohibited such development. It was adjacent to the lagoon that still drained directly into Town Cove via a 36-inch pipe. The compactor was separated from the small lagoon by a bermed asphalt roadway, built for delivery trucks that serviced the supermarket and adjacent discount department store. A cut in the berm to drain the road happened to be directly across the road from the compactor. The trail of hydraulic fluid flowed over the pavement, down the cut in the berm and into the lagoon. Ten days after the careless discharge, 95 percent of the million seed we had been raising in the shellfish facility were dead. I saved all the shells for future reference.

I did a lot of research at Woods Hole on the effects of oil on marine organisms, and after I convinced the selectmen that the supermarket corporation was liable, the town sued the company. The case inched forward for two years during which time the Town Counsel imposed a "gag order" to silence everyone involved.

I got a call in early April 1987 from our Town Counsel asking me if the building was operating as it had been at the time of the incident and if not, could it be operational by the following Tuesday? The request came before the intake pipe had been put out for the season and so the pump wasn't running. I asked a few women to help me over the weekend to lay the pipe and get the pumps started. For me, that had always been a pain-in-the-neck job, but to them it was different and exciting and they had a blast doing it. By Tuesday, the building was operational.

I met the town lawyer, one of his associates, and a corporate insurance adjuster at the site of the initial spill. We looked at the trash compactor (a new one), toured the site of the spill, and examined the pipe that discharged into the Town Cove.

The lagoon where the fluid had first been discharged was one of the last vestiges of Jeremiah's Gutter — a man-made canal built in the 1800s connecting Cape Cod Bay to Town Cove that served as an important route for ships avoiding the blockade of Boston Harbor during the war of 1812. At the time of the spill and when we looked at it later, it was a dirty, muddy pool that appeared to be good for nothing except to drain a road.

At the Cove discharge pipe, the insurance adjuster looked at me and said, "Do you mean to suggest that 7-10 gallons of fluid flowed out this pipe and affected a million quahogs out there?" gesturing to the expansive Town Cove. I said, "No. I'm suggesting that 7-10 gallons flowed out this pipe and into another pipe located approximately 100 feet away and into that building (pointing to our little red lab) where it killed a million seed quahaugs." He looked at me like I was crazy and his expression said the town didn't have a chance.

We walked up to the building. As we entered the cramped space, my visitors were greeted by the sound of the rushing water splashing simultaneously into three tiers of tanks on the right and two tiers on the left. The water splashed loudly into eighteen fish totes, up through the silos and out of the silos through 18 black pipes to the tanks. To the uninitiated, it was an unusual sound and spoke volumes about the work conducted in the tiny building.

Each person in this small investigative group was accustomed to remaining expressionless. But as I watched my guests' eyes, I detected almost indiscernible changes in their attitudes and instantly felt that I had gained the home-court advantage. The insurance adjuster's mask said "Uh-oh" and our lawyer's said, "We've got them".

I tried to remain nonchalant and matter-of-fact as I explained the process of growing seed quahaugs. I explained that the system they were looking at was called an upweller system. The netting held the seed and the water was pumped into the fish tote, flowed up through the netting holding the seed quahaugs and out the pipe into the tank. From the tank it then flowed into a drain and back into the Cove. It was a flow-through system as opposed to a system that did not require flowing seawater. I showed them the algae room, 6x6-foot and painted white, that had banks of fluorescent lights on the walls and an air conditioner in the window to provide a well-lit, temperature-controlled environment. I explained that the seed fed primarily on the natural plankton in the water flowing through the tanks, but noted that we supplemented that with food deemed to be nutritious for seed quahaugs, food that we grew ourselves.

Town Counsel had prepped me not to say much else on the tour but to explain carefully how the system worked. Prior to the visit, I had explained to him that certain fractions of oil products were water soluble, odorless, and did not produce the typical "sheen". The higher the refining process, the more water-soluble fractions there were. I explained that research had shown that the water-soluble fractions were lethal to marine organisms, especially small animals, and that hydraulic fluid was highly refined oil. Research had demonstrated the lethal connection in flow-through systems as well as static ones. What I said on the tour was that hydraulic fluid was highly refined and contained odorless, invisible, water-soluble fractions that I wouldn't have been able to detect in a flow-through system.

My final contribution was to show them the five-inch-high sieve containing the inch or so of tiny shells that I had saved for two years. As they looked, I said that what was in the sieve represented a million seed quahaugs. They thanked me for my time and the tour ended.

Within about six weeks, the town received a check in the total amount of the damages I had outlined, which included the cost of the seed, pumps, pipes, and assorted contaminated gear. But I had also listed as a loss the wholesale value of a million littlenecks that could not be harvested five years down the road as a result of the spill. I assumed sixty percent survival in my calculations. It was a lot of money — nearly $100,000. If the case had gone to trial, by statute the corporation could have been liable for "treble damages".

The following year, we were back in business, growing a million poppy-seed-sized juveniles. One of the more technical problems we always faced was what to do with the seed at the end of the season. Even though we could get the seed up to a half-inch or better in the summer through the upweller technique, that was still pretty small and we knew that overwintering still hadn't been solved. So we experimented with planting times.

We found that planting in September and October was unacceptable because we could count on severe losses due to predation, but if we waited until November, when the bay's water temperature dropped to 45-50 degrees Fahrenheit, the survival rate was high because predators had begun to hunker down for the winter and weren't as interested in quahaugs for food. We grew a million seed a year for five years at a 95 percent annual survival rate in the lab and an estimated 50-75 percent survival in the field. The field survival rate held for seed transplanted to both Nauset and Pleasant Bay.

We had three separate estuaries and over 40 miles of shoreline to think about with our quahaug program. Early on, we eliminated Cape Cod Bay as a transplant site for the seed we grew because of the harsh conditions on the flats, especially in winter. It was difficult to concede that a mile-and-a-half of sand flats were entirely inappropriate for quahaug transplants, but after losing the ones we planted because of ice or volatile sand movement, we gave up. Town Cove was naturally productive and we wanted to keep it that way, so we planted some in the Cove each year. But by far the major portion of transplanted stock went to Pleasant Bay in an attempt to recover the former productivity of the Bay.

Big Bay had been such an economic boon to the town in the past that we dearly wanted to replenish the stock there, but between the amount of shack and the water depth in Big Bay, we were not able to fully assess our efforts. Our resources were limited so we decided to concentrate our efforts on shorelines that would be accessible for monitoring. Over the years, we transplanted millions of seed to Pleasant Bay waters.

In our initial efforts, where we used the bottom and raft culture, we were searching to find areas where transplanted seed would survive to become adults. We didn't care how long it took them to grow but we wanted them to survive so that they would contribute progeny and eventually re-seed the bay themselves. At the same time we planted the seed, we were buying cherrystones and chowders from Cape Cod Bay and transplanting them to Pleasant Bay as well, figuring that the more adult parent stock in the water, the better the chances of a "set" taking hold. We knew that some of the larger stock we were planting would be harvested but we did not want the program to be simply a "put and take", where we put them in and someone promptly came along and took them out. We later learned through our hatchery experience that it didn't matter much:

Chowder-sized quahaugs rarely spawn. We joked about those tired old quahaugs, endowing them with human qualities.

Many areas proved suitable for transplants and they survived well. We ended up planting buckets of juvenile quahaugs along long stretches of shoreline. Grown in upwellers, they were broadcast from a slow-moving boat at high tide so that when they had become adults they would be accessible to harvest at low tide. We hoped to bring quahaugs back to the bay, but even a million seed per year didn't go very far, and the 5-7 years they took to get to legal size was a long time to wait to see something tangible from the program.

In retrospect, maybe we should have been more concerned about the length of time it took to grow quahaugs as well as whether they survived. To us, survival was the key ingredient. We were trying to repopulate the fishery so that the seed could grow to spawn and reproduce naturally, eventually to be harvested. To others, harvest statistics were the key ingredient, the best way to show visually and incontrovertibly that the program was working. If quahaugs weren't being harvested, how could our assertions be trusted when we said that the quahaugs eventually reached maturity? "We've never found any" was a common refrain, but when I sampled an area I had planted, I always found them. We weren't publishing specifics about planting sites but we did annually produce generalized maps of the areas that had been planted.

Regardless, between the hydraulic fluid incident that made us lose an entire year and the amount of time our plantings took to grow to be legal size, some very vocal fishermen were more and more restless in discussing the quahaug program and less and less in favor of continuing it. But even though a few commercial fishermen had philosophical problems with the propagation effort, the recreational harvesters thought the project was terrific and that Orleans was lucky to have such a program. I heard those comments all the time and the appreciation those folks voiced about what we were doing and about me personally sustained my own conviction that the propagation work was a worthwhile endeavor for the town.

But Orleans wasn't alone in its propagation efforts. There were other small hatcheries in the region too. One of them was next door, in Eastham. Operated by Henry Lind, it was an old boathouse on the shore of Salt Pond, where every conceivable space was utilized for raising shellfish. Henry, the Director of Natural Resources for Eastham, was the lightning rod for the project. A trained biologist, with a wonderful dry wit, Henry has worked for the Town of Eastham full time since 1976, first as Deputy Shellfish Constable and later as department manager. He is an innovator and brilliant at fixing things and making something work from inexpensive, borrowed or scavenged components and he is masterful at operating a complex department on short funds. We have shared stories, methods, insight, problems and solutions and often joked about our shoe-string operations. I was glad to have him nearby.

A second hatchery was on Martha's Vineyard. Operated by Rick Karney, the operation took a different approach. The hatchery was funded by five member towns, all of whom were represented on a board of directors of the Martha's Vineyard Shellfish Group. Rick raised oyster, quahaug and scallop seed in the hatchery and the member towns did the nursery work and planting within their towns. Rick's ability to raise bay scallops in the hatchery has resulted in higher and more even annual harvests on Martha's Vineyard's than other Massachusetts communities. Rick used more standard equipment in his hatchery than either Henry or I. But we all had similar problems, many of which are just part of the hatchery business.

Towns without a town-operated hatchery, raised seed in more conventional ways, most often utilizing bottom culture methods. Chatham was probably most successful, raising four million seed annually for many years.

But although the towns were busy raising seed to be transplanted throughout the towns, there were always people who complained about the programs. Orleans was not alone on that score either.

Chapter 19

"Send Sandy to China"

Some of the fishermen may not have been enthusiastic about the quahaug program but the general population was. I heard their support wherever I went around town. I heard the enthusiasm in townspeople's voices when they stopped at the lab to visit and said they were very glad Orleans was involved in this type of shellfish propagation. Then they showed their support, not only of the program, but also of me personally, in a most rewarding and humbling manner.

I received a letter in November of 1986 from People to People Citizen Ambassador Program, an organization initiated by President Dwight Eisenhower and headquartered in Spokane, Washington. When I opened the letter, I was astounded. I was being invited to participate in a shellfish production and research delegation to China and Taiwan, sponsored in the US by People to People and overseas by the Ministry of Agriculture, Animal Husbandry and Fisheries of the People's Republic of China and its counterpart in the Republic of China. The host agencies in both countries were requesting a delegation of shellfish researchers to share their knowledge and expertise with Chinese colleagues who were working on problems similar to those challenging the US. The delegation would be visiting production facilities and research arenas in both countries.

The letter also stated that Chinese officials requested participating delegates to prepare written documentation of one aspect of their work to be presented at formal meetings. The agenda for the trip was jam-packed, with meetings at research institutes in Beijing, Dalian, Quingdao, Guangzhou, and Shenzhen in mainland China and in Teipei and Lukang in Taiwan, leaving little time for non-technical activities.

I didn't know how I had been selected for the invitation but there were several possibilities. I had participated in developing a quahaug (hard clam) culture section for the 1978 National Aquaculture Plan in Washington, DC; I was the past president of the New England Estuarine Research Society; I was a member of several other professional societies including the National Shellfisheries Association and the Estuarine Research Federation; and I had been chairman of the county shellfish advisory committee for many years. Whatever the reason for being selected, I felt honored. I knew that this was an opportunity of a lifetime and if there was any way possible, I should take advantage of it. But it was expensive.

Just after I read the letter, Mary Smith, one of the selectmen, walked by the Shellfish Department office in the basement of Town Hall and I showed it to her. She was exuberant and said I ought to go, and that it was a great opportunity for both the town and me. She also said that the town should not send me, as it was not a budgeted item and it would be inappropriate. I heartily agreed. But then she really stunned me by saying she thought the selectmen could help me go by being innovative, perhaps by endorsing the trip and accepting donations. She said she'd talk to her colleagues about it. The next day the board agreed and essentially established a "Send Sandy to China" fund. I was dumbfounded.

I needed to reach full-funding by mid-winter — in just a couple of months — for a trip that would take place in May, 1987. Winter was not the best time to try to raise funds in a northern retirement community since many people leave town for warmer climes during that time, but checks started coming to Town Hall. By the deadline, over 200 people had donated to the fund. I had also received a grant from the Edward Bangs Kelley and Elza Kelley Foundation, a Cape philanthropic group. The trip was entirely covered, including incidentals. The people of Orleans were sending me to China and Taiwan for three weeks. Stories surrounding the generous nature of the townspeople move me to this day and I will forever be grateful to them.

When I arrived in Seattle, I joined 13 colleagues from vastly different backgrounds and expertise. Our leader, Dr. Anthony Provenzano, was a Professor in the Department of Oceanography of

Old Dominion University in Virginia. His specialty was aquaculture and he had worked both with fish and with such crustaceans as blue crabs and giant freshwater shrimp. Dr. Clyde Roper, Curator of Mollusks at the Smithsonian Institution, specialized in cephalopods (squids, octopuses and cuttlefish). Several television documentaries have been made regarding Dr. Roper's search for the elusive giant squid. Six delegates were all interested in or working with bivalve shellfish. I was in that group along with a professor from University of Rhode Island, a researcher for the National Marine Fisheries Service in Woods Hole, the Aquaculture Division Chief for the Connecticut Department of Agriculture, a clam farm owner from Connecticut, and a project leader from the Oregon Department of Fish and Wildlife. Three delegates — a shrimp-industry trade magazine owner from Louisiana, a technical manager for a large shrimp farm in Equador and a professor from the Department of Biology of Memphis State University — were all focused on shrimp, prawns or crayfish. Three were generalists with strong interests in aquaculture — an Associate Director of the Peace Corps in the Philippines, a researcher of production of aquatic foods in limited spaces and a graduate student. Five wives accompanied the group but I was the only woman delegate.

On the first day, we were assembled in front of the Ministry of Agriculture, Animal Husbandry and Fisheries building in Beijing, taking in the sights and sounds and smells. Off to the side of the walkway, a stone or cement sculpture really struck me. There were three figures, a man squatting down holding a rather large fish, a woman standing holding a basket of fish and another woman squatting whose activity was not clear. Both women were depicted with either cloth hats or the equivalent of bandanas on their heads; the man, who had a wispy goatee, had no hat. What struck me, though, was the smile on their faces that seemed to say, "We enjoy our work" but in a somewhat unnatural way. Those expressions continue to haunt me.

We were ushered into a large room with over-stuffed couches and chairs set in a large square along the walls with empty space in the middle. It was all very formal and impressive.

After requisite pleasantries of welcome and the response of how glad we were to be there, the real nuts and bolts began. The host gave statistics about their facilities and production and our leader gave a brief synopsis of aquaculture and wild fisheries in the U.S. and then we asked questions of each other. Everything had to be interpreted so there were delays in the conversation. But we asked many probing questions. There seemed to be fewer questions directed toward us but we fielded the questions to the best of our ability. Tony Provenzano, our leader, directed some of their questions to specific delegates whom he thought might best be able to answer, but at other times we simply provided information on our own. We were to learn that this meeting protocol would be fairly similar throughout the entire visit to China.

The meeting lasted a couple of hours but at that introductory meeting, we learned that there were state-owned shellfish farms as well as town-owned farms and individually owned farms. Individually owned farms in Communist China! This was certainly news to me. Our hosts explained that such a farm had to meet a state quota but if it exceeded that, the remainder was the proprietor's to sell on the open market. The Chinese officials talked about private enterprise being widespread and "profit incentives" being good.

I thought again about the sculpture outside. The smiles conveyed to me an idealized view of what I imagined socialism to be, but the information we had just received seemed to fly in the face of that ideal. It appeared that the state was still at the top of the production chain but that capitalism was making inroads. This was not my pre-conceived notion of China; the sculpture fit my pre-conceived notion. Was the sculpture there so that the government could still maintain a tight rein? Or was it just a sculpture with no "hidden meaning?" I didn't know. But I wanted to understand the 1987 China I was visiting.

At the end of the meeting, Tony conveyed our thanks for the opportunity to meet with our hosts. He said he recognized China's long history and advanced aquaculture techniques and hoped we could learn from China's experience. Then Tony discussed the issues facing the United States, including user conflicts, competing demands for coastal waters, and competition from recreational users. Our hosts seemed to have blank expressions when Tony talked about our problems. I had no idea why but I would see for myself a few days later.

Our hosts knew that Americans would want to see Tiananmen Square, the Emperor's Forbidden City and the Great Wall. They were right. We saw them all. In Tiananmen Square, we saw more sculptures and the same smiles were on all the people depicted on the sculpted walls. Everything in the square was fairly new, from the Great Hall of the People to the tomb of Chairman Mao, who died in 1976.

The new was sharply juxtaposed with the ancient, for across the street was the Forbidden City, home of China's emperors for thousands of years. The Forbidden City was amazing. Once through the main gate, a set of stairs leads down to an open-air square with a high wall on two sides. At the end of the square is a temple-like large building. The entrance leading up to the building has enormous stone carvings in the center and the stairs are on each side.

Inside the building, everything was ornate, many of the magnificent carvings were gilded. Thinking first that was it, we left the building at the opposite end and entered another courtyard and faced another large building. There were several such buildings, each seemingly more beautiful than the previous. Bronze statues of turtles and cranes and lions graced their entrances. For me, the symbolism, artwork, and beauty mixed with the realization that all the buildings were within a high wall, separated from all other aspects of Beijing. For thousands of years, emperors ruled the enormous country of China from within the confines of their own little world.

That kind of juxtaposition of ancient and new I saw repeatedly, and it symbolized for me two Chinas: It was at once an ancient country with ancient belief systems, and a revolutionary socialist nation with a completely different set of ideologies and expectations for the people.

We saw a seven-story building surrounded by scaffolding — made of lengths of bamboo lashed together. We saw every mode of transportation imaginable — including rototillers that had had the tines removed so that the Chinese could use them to pull wagons loaded with anything and everything. We saw a highway rotary being constructed — by manual labor with only a couple of machines in sight. I was fascinated.

Then we journeyed not far from Beijing to see the Great Wall. Again, there was the juxtaposition — the ancient wall and individual souvenir and T-shirt vendors and a building that said "Great Wall Souvenir Store" in English and in big red letters. Walking on the Great Wall of China was the most surreal experience I've ever had. Almost every one of us walked a bit alone and in silence, taking in the majesty, realizing that we were atop a centuries-old man-made structure half a world away from home, a wall so large it can be seen from space.

We left Beijing and headed for the coast. Our first stop was a meeting with representatives of the Dalian fisheries agencies and research institutions. At the meeting, one of our delegates asked our hosts what their main interests were, and one of the responses was that they wanted to learn about upweller systems. I had brought slides of most of Orleans' propagation efforts with me and was able to show our Chinese colleagues what upwellers looked like — finding it strange and slightly amusing that my home-made upwellers were the first ones they had seen — and I explained how they worked while a colleague photographed the moment.

The next morning, we headed to the Dalian Marine Fisheries Research Institute. All of a sudden, as our bus rounded a curve, we could see a huge bay to our left, full of long ropes and buoys and we knew we were looking at our first Chinese aquaculture operation, even though we didn't know what was being grown. The morning was misty, but we could plainly see that these ropes covered a tremendous area. We pleaded with our interpreter-guides to make an unscheduled stop. We were in our element now and wanted a bit of time to examine the scene.

Our guides complied and we piled out to look and photograph the scene. Small boats, anchored inshore of the buoys, appeared to be tenders for the operation, but there was no one visible anywhere on the water. Could these lines of buoys be holding pearl or lantern nets, compartmentalized gear used for growing scallops in layers through the water column? We were anxious to find out what was being cultured in the vast bay.

When we got to our destination, I didn't see a stockpile of pearl or lantern scallop nets, but I noticed huge piles of black plastic netting similar to the type we had used for bottom culture.

On our tour, the director showed us around the facility, which looked very different from any place I had seen. Large concrete tanks took the place of fiberglass ones used in the US and I did not see the same types of equipment that is usually present in a hatchery — no algae room, for instance. I saw scallops in a tank that looked an awful lot like *our* bay scallops although there are over 200 species of scallops world-wide. I asked for the generic (scientific Latin) name. The institute director didn't actually respond but gave me more of a questioning shrug. I happened to be wearing a necklace that had a small seed bay scallop glued to an oval metal backing and I pointed to my necklace, again trying to find out if it was the same animal. The answer I got was yes.

I later found out that a shipment of bay scallops had been sent from the US to China some years earlier. Some people say now they originated in Virginia and others point to Connecticut. Regardless, only a couple of dozen scallops made it to be used as parent stock. The Chinese were able to parlay that small number of survivors into a 6.8-million-metric-ton export product, 61% of the world supply of scallops. Most of them were being shipped to the United States.

The genetics of producing such an astounding number of animals from very few individuals had inevitably taken its toll and they were requesting additional shipments from the US to add to their bay scallop gene pool. However, by 1987, it was obvious that China was competing with the wild fishery in the US and obtaining more bay scallops became more difficult for the Chinese.

We had finally discovered that the long lines we had seen when we made our unscheduled stop were for scallops. Bay scallops. Our scallops. The site at Dalian was producing a portion of that 6.8 million metric tons of scallops that would be shipped back to the US. That was for me, a valuable lesson in the concept of "globalization." Their scallops were marketed in our local supermarkets as Chinese bay scallops. Locals back home on Cape Cod who revere the succulent native bay scallop would probably not buy them, but the less discerning consumer would and did, especially if they were a lower price then the native variety.

The set of long lines and buoys was my first lesson in Chinese shellfish aquaculture and opened my eyes to its vast scale. Machinery that made black plastic netting on-site was my second lesson. If the culture needs something, it is provided on-site rather than relying on a factory somewhere in the Chinese hinterland to manufacture it, making an aquaculture facility rather self-sustaining. The third lesson was that if the government said that a certain bay was to be used for aquaculture, the bay was used for aquaculture. Multiple-use problems, especially those involving recreational use, did not appear to be a problem.

No wonder our Chinese colleagues had had blank expressions when Tony had talked about user conflicts in the US. From what we could see, this bay was being used almost exclusively for aquaculture. It appeared that there was no such thing as recreational fishing there or sailboats or motorboats cruising up and down the bay. Cultural priorities seemed to be vastly different from those in our country.

While we were in Dalian, we also visited the Dalian Ocean Fishing Corporation. It was another eye-opener. Here on the industrialized site was a shipbuilding facility, unloading facility and freezer/processing facility. Everything needed for their vast off-shore fisheries was centralized at this one complex. It was phenomenal to see and to contemplate the wider implications of global fishing effort.

Later in the trip, in one of our meetings, the institute director talked about razor clams. The clam farm owner from Connecticut and I asked a couple of questions about how they were harvested in China. He responded that fishermen hooked them. "They hook them?" I asked incredulously. He looked at me, puzzled. "Of course." We asked, "How?" He responded that they take a bucket with a glass bottom and search for holes while wading around in water that is about three-feet deep. When the razor clam is feeding, its siphon is extended out of the hole and, he said, it is a simple matter to just hook them. We were amazed and so he then asked, "How do you harvest them?" Bill and I said almost together, "They dig them". "They dig them?" he asked in about the same tone we had used with his response. "Yes." Bill drew a picture of a clam hoe to show him. He couldn't believe it. Why would someone go through all the effort to dig a big hole when all you needed to do was to walk around with a line and a hook? If he didn't actually ask the question, his expression sure did. Neither of us knew where the process of digging razor clams had originated but it seemed to be one of those things that was just done that way "because it had always been done that way."

The last facilities we visited in China were an oyster farm and a pearl-oyster farm. At the oyster facility, near Guangzhou (formerly Canton), the scale of production was similar to the scallops, extremely high. We saw a pile of unshucked oysters approximately 20-feet-high. This farm was in southern China, near the tropics, and we did not see any evidence of ice or refrigeration. We had previously feasted on oysters from this farm for lunch and wondered if indulging in so many oysters had been a wise move. Luckily, none of us suffered any consequences from our actions. But it certainly made us think about sanitation issues.

The pearl oyster farm was incredible. It was located in a small rural village on a fairly large bay rimmed by mountains, a picturesque locale although not far from Hong Kong. When we talked to the pearl-farm director, it was clear just how capitalistic this area was.

The director of the farm had a surly expression when we met him. He told us about his facility, the number of pearls produced and their price and told us that he had a dual product — his oysters produced food too. He explained that we would be able to witness the procedure for creating the conditions in the oysters that would produce a pearl, but said pointedly that the procedure was proprietary and we could not photograph the process.

It was obvious that he was a private entrepreneur and had been in the business for several years. It was also obvious, from both his expression and from what he said, that he did not need or want any "help" from the American delegates. He was doing just fine, thank you.

We were led us to a building where about 10 women were processing oysters for pearls.

The first woman was using a knife to pry open oysters slightly and inserting wooden wedges into the oysters. At another table, two women took mantle tissue (the material that rims the inside of shells) from fresh water clams or mussels and cut them into thin strips about one-eighth of an inch wide with sharp Exacto-type knives. They put these strips into a purple solution and then cut the strips into tiny pieces. The tiny pieces were then given to a group of women sitting in a row at small tables, with a water trough of oysters behind them.

These women each had a dish of six identically-sized spherical pieces of shell — diameters about three-eighths of an inch each — taken from fresh-water bivalves. They stuck a piece of the purple "foreign" mantle material onto the sphere. With surgical or dental-type equipment, they pried open the oysters a bit more, cut a section of the oyster's mantle and inserted the sphere. They repeated the process so that each oyster had two pearls. They then removed the wedges and put the oysters in the water.

The oyster reacts to the foreign material by surrounding it with the nacreous substance — mother-of-pearl — that makes the pearls so lustrous and valuable. In nature, the foreign material might be a pebble that had lodged within the shell but the end result is often misshapen. The farm used perfect spheres to start the process.

The oysters were put in round pearl-nets and suspended in the water from floating rafts. They remained in the water for two to three years and when they were harvested, the pearls were a fairly uniform 7 mm (just shy of one-quarter inch), meaning the nacreous layer that produced the pearl was very thin.

The process was labor-intensive because the oysters had to be transferred periodically to clean nets and the fouled nets needed to be cleaned often. But the price quoted for the value of the pearls from this farm was staggering and the beauty of the pearls was outstanding.

To my mind, the beauty of the pearls was matched by the beauty of the farm setting, as the village and surrounding area had a special appeal.

Aquaculture in mainland China was big, big business and most of it was exported. We flew over massive shrimp farms but much to the discontent of the shrimp people in our group we never visited a shrimp farm in China. China, at the time, was the second largest exporter of shrimp in the world.

The small exchanges about how to harvest razor clams or the details of bay scallop culture and netting was, for me, what People to People was all about. The Chinese didn't really *need* us to be there. They've been practicing aquaculture and polyculture for thousands of years. Maybe they hadn't heard of upwellers yet and the slides I brought of our small facility were the first they had seen of the technique. But they had succeeded in importing fewer than 100 individual scallops from the United States from which only a handful survived and they were able to parlay that into a multi-million-metric-ton product. I have no doubt that we learned much more from them than they ever learned from us on this particular delegation.

In Taiwan we visited a clam hatchery where instead of bicycles there was a Mercedes parked outside. At that hatchery, they have to chill the water to get clams to spawn rather than raise the temperature like we had to do. As with our operation back home, it's the temperature shock that seems to do the trick. We also visited an eel farm where elvers (small eels) were grown for the Japanese market. And finally, to the delight of the shrimp people in the delegation, we went to a shrimp farm

As part of the cultural portion of the stay in Taiwan, we visited the National Museum. The museum can display only one-fifth of the treasures brought from the mainland by Nationalists during the Communist revolution. The remainder is stored in a secure mountain site and the museum displays are rotated. I was so taken by the place that when we had a few free hours, a colleague and I went back to the museum to take our time with the displays. I bought a book with many color plates so I could revisit the treasures at home.

Shortly after I arrived home, I put together a photo album of the trip, and when I got to the pictures of the sculptures I had seen in China, I labeled them "Propaganda Art." To my uneducated eyes, and admittedly after a mere three weeks visiting this vast and diverse country, I believed that the sentiment depicted in the sculpture was more related to the socialist revolutionary ideal than the 1980s reality, where a sort of state capitalism was emerging that in turn allowed the emergence of an entrepreneurial economy.

I also began giving slide presentations to any civic organization that gave me a call. It was the least I could do to show my gratitude to the people in town who had so generously sponsored my participation in the delegation. In my presentations, I did not stay completely with the technical aspects of the trip. There was so much more to it than that. If the country gets its act together, one-fifth of the world's population will be a global force to be reckoned with, the likes of which we have never seen.

I've never gotten the image of the Bohai Sea out of my mind. To see a bay with row after row of lines and buoys strung across the bay for as far as you can see, knowing that the buoys represent aquaculture on a grand scale, is a very impressive sight. I couldn't help contrast Bohai Sea with Cape Cod Bay or Pleasant Bay. I mentally compared their political system to ours. I imagined if Pleasant Bay was designated as an aquaculture area and no other activity could take place there — no sailing or rowing or paddling or motoring because of the mass of buoys and gear in the water. What would it be like with no motor boats cruising the bay for pleasure, in search of the elusive striped bass or bluefish or transporting fun-seekers to the beach? What would it be like without the kayaks, canoes, rowboats and sailboats that glide through the waters unimpeded by anything but maybe a sand bar?

I thought of what it takes to start with 24 animals and develop an industry that would eventually be worth billions of dollars. How much plankton in Pleasant Bay waters would it take to feed such a massive number of animals and what would be the effect on the rest of the ecology? What would it be like if shellfish were *the* most important resource of the bay, to the exclusion of almost any other activity with no multiple-use conflicts?

But then, what would Pleasant Bay be like if we really *needed* the food it produced? Would we be hunter-gatherers or farmers in the bay? Would people actually give up their recreational boats in favor of raising food? Would that be even remotely possible?

China was a world away. Globalization was at our doorstep.

Visiting China and Taiwan was the experience of a lifetime and a valuable lesson in recognizing opportunities when they arise. I sensed and discovered things that will stay with me as long as I live, not only in the research aspect I was sent there to learn about and contribute to, but in the culture and the people. I will be forever grateful to the citizens of Orleans who recognized the value of this journey and made it happen. People attending a meeting in the Selectmen's meeting room might wonder why a scroll, a piece of Chinese art, encased in a wood and glass case, is hanging in the Orleans Town Offices. A small brass plaque explains why.

Two years later the world was shocked to see the government crackdown on democracy at Tiananmen Square. Trips to China for any purpose would be on hold for years. But that wasn't the upheaval that concerned me then. When I arrived home, the town had changed dramatically.

Chapter 20

A Most Remarkable Year

New Year's Eve is a special time. It is a time of reflection on the year just passed and a time of anticipation mixed with hope that the coming year will be good. That night in 1986 was no different. I was anticipating the possibility of participating in a shellfish delegation to China. If it happened, surely that would be enough for the whole year. It did happen, but little did I know what else 1987 would bring.

No one had long to wait to see what kind of year it would be. Early in January, a northeast storm battered the coast. By most accounts, it was not an extraordinarily intense storm, but it happened at a time when celestial alignments were just right to produce higher than normal tides. With the added tide height of the storm, the ocean washed over Nauset Beach in Chatham and lowered the beach enough to create a small "v," a notch of sorts, a few feet wide. Huge consequences were to follow.

For several decades, Pleasant Bay had not been able to funnel all its water through the narrow channel between Nauset Beach and the mainland or, as it continued migrating south, between Nauset Beach and Monomoy. With the beach migrating further and further south and the already constricted channel getting ever narrower, the bay was holding its breath until the day it could exhale. In January 1987, it began to exhale on successive ebbing tides. Slowly at first and then very quickly, it released the pent-up energy by releasing more and more water through the "v," creating a new channel through the beach. It was a mile wide in a matter of weeks.

The pressure of a bottled-up Pleasant Bay had broken loose and nothing would be as it had been. Houses that had been protected by the barrier beach were suddenly threatened. Coastal banks that had been stable for many years succumbed to the effects of gravity when subsequent higher-than-usual tides took small bites of sand from the bottom of the banks, thus threatening the houses perched at the top. Navigating the new inlet meant learning the bay all over again because last year's channel was this year's sand bar. The new wide inlet meant more water poured into the bay on each incoming tide and more "old" water poured out on each ebb tide. One immediate result was dramatically improved water quality for the upper reaches of the bay, in the ponds and rivers where water flow had been so sluggish, we sometimes thought of them as nearly stagnant. We were cautiously elated because although emerging eutrophication problems in the upper bay had not been solved, the symptoms had been successfully treated, and the breakthrough had given the bay stewards a reprieve.

The natural upheaval of the Chatham Break was matched by political upheaval in Orleans.

In the three weeks I was gone, I had seen dramatic cultural shifts. The United States, China, Hong Kong and Taiwan were all very different from one another and I had spent considerable time half a world away from my culture in Orleans. When I returned, it was to a different world. Orleans was about to experience a cultural shift of its own through a fundamental change in the form of town government that had been in existence for nearly two centuries. This shift signaled a profound change in every aspect of life in the town.

Before I left for China, the town had been discussing the benefits and drawbacks of government reform. A charter committee had written a document, a municipal constitution really, that, if passed by the electorate, would change municipal government drastically. Gone would be a three-person salaried Board of Selectmen who spent a considerable part of each day working on town affairs. They would be replaced by a five-member, part-time, nominally paid ($1,000 per year) Board of Selectmen, who were expected to set policy and attend at least two meetings per week, while a well-compensated professional town manager would be hired to oversee the daily workings of the town. The town was split — many long-time residents favored having selectmen, as elected officials, running the town, and many newer residents favored the new method.

The charter vote was held a few days after I returned from China, and the new form of government was approved by a slim margin. The next day, all three selectmen resigned, setting the municipal boat adrift. An election was held and five people, only one of whom had formerly been a selectman, found themselves tentatively holding the rudder and mainsheet and hoping a fresh breeze would get the boat moving again.

Before I left for China, the town had received the large check from the out-of-court settlement with the supermarket for damages to the shellfish lab. The selectmen had promised the funds would be used to implement the plan they had approved for shellfish propagation. After the new selectmen took office, the money was not spent exclusively for shellfish propagation but rather to help offset the annual operating budget of the Shellfish Department.

Town government was in a state of chaos. There were five new selectmen, but no town administrator. A former selectmen's assistant was acting in the administrator's job until someone could be hired, and department managers were trying to bring the new selectmen up to speed even as a host of problems, old and new, demanded attention. Numerous projects and problems got lost in the cracks.

The Charter meant other changes as well. Some boards that had been elective office became appointive and the selectmen had to fill those positions. Problems were many and complex and demanded more of the selectmen's time than just two meetings per week. The learning curve was steep, especially with respect to environmental issues, and especially those related to development pressures that did not abate just because the government changed.

How could a town choose to send its government into chaos? To me, the answer lies in just a few words: sewers and a septage treatment plant. The wrangle over waste set the stage for the radical restructuring of government.

Prior to the early 1980s, houses in Orleans all had individual septic systems or cesspools that were pumped and emptied into septage lagoons at the town disposal area, universally known as "the dump". The lagoons were merely holes in the sandy ground. Orleans wasn't unusual — most Cape towns used septage lagoons.

The state Department of Environmental Quality Engineering or DEQE (now Department of Environmental Protection, DEP) mandated that the lagoons be closed within a very few years and Orleans was ordered to build a sewage treatment plant or find a plant that would accept the town's waste.

The consultant's analysis of groundwater flow in Orleans showed that the effluent from the lagoons was heading toward the Town Cove, along with effluent from the densely developed town center. Further, a new treatment plant could not be constructed at the dump because of the groundwater direction. A couple of other possible sites were suggested in the consultant's report, including one near an abandoned cranberry bog that flowed to Namskaket Marsh on the Cape Cod Bay side of town.

The options outlined for the town were limited. If the town followed the prescribed course of action laid out by the state, funds would be made available to the town for construction costs. If the town did not follow the state's "guidelines," the town would be liable to pay for the treatment plant entirely on its own. Because it would be a multi-million dollar project, many voters felt that the state had tied the town's hands and we had to comply. In addition, there wasn't much time to come up with plans. The state's clock started ticking and when it stopped ticking, not only would the lagoons be closed, but the construction funds would also evaporate.

But in order to have a sewage treatment facility, the town had to have sewers. The town balked.

After much wrangling and discussions of possible alternatives, the matter came down to a debate on sewering the downtown area only since the dense development there threatened the Town Cove nearby.

The town hired Woods Hole Oceanographic Institution to conduct a study to determine if sewers were necessary to protect the Cove. A secondary study objective was to determine what would happen if a treatment facility were built adjacent to a large salt marsh, a preferred site that had been identified for a treatment plant.

The study concluded that the Cove was not in imminent danger from the nutrients coming from the town center area, and that the salt marsh in question would change over time to a brackish marsh more quickly than it would if the treatment plant were not there.

The report was precise in describing the scientific methods used but the language was sufficiently vague enough to be interpreted many ways.

As the study was being conducted, the town split into factions. Committees formed.

One group was most concerned with how the sewers would be paid for. Since everything was still in the early planning stage and no decisions made, one of the options put forward was a betterment tax for town-center property owners on a per-foot basis of road frontage. One merchant, who owned a large segment of Main Street property for his retail operation and who had one or two bathrooms for his employees, was outraged at this idea and began organizing people to fight the idea of sewers. Another group in town said that the Town Cove should be protected at any cost and that we needed sewers to protect the Town Cove for the future.

Sewers were defeated at town meeting. That didn't really decide the problem, because the lagoons still had to be abandoned. The town now had quite a dilemma. Then the consulting engineering firm came up with a design for a septage-only facility, a new technology with an innovative system used by only one other approved facility in the state. That one plant had not been operational for long and so its track record was an unknown. People were very nervous to spend as much money as we were told it was going to cost for an unproven technology.

Without sewers, the septage-only plant could not run on Orleans' waste alone and so the selectmen began negotiations with the neighboring towns of Brewster and Eastham, since they had to close their lagoons and solve the same waste-management problem. But many Orleans residents asked why the plant had to be sited in Orleans at all, if we had to join our neighbors, since the options for locating it in Orleans were so limited. New committees sprang up to discuss the pros and cons of the new septage technology, siting, and of the idea of regionalizing septage treatment. Socially, the town was split apart.

The selectmen, two of whom were lifelong members of the community, were put through a wringer and were blamed for every decision. Every possible aspect of the problem of how to treat our waste became contentious — even decisions about how articles were to be worded for town meeting action were criticized. The selectmen took heat from some people even for new mandates coming from the state.

At about the same time, a municipal management consultant was making the rounds of Cape towns touting the benefits of a charter-style form of government rather than the system that had existed across New England since communities began incorporating.

Under the old system, the selectmen made numerous decisions in their meetings that were voted on in their office, not in a public meeting room, but were recorded in their publicly accessible log. The selectmen were available on a daily basis and knew the internal workings of the town and its people. But with a charter, the consultant suggested, the town would be a more business-like entity. Those in charge of governing would be more accountable to the public since all their meetings would be open to the public. The charter would spell out exactly which responsibilities were those of the selectmen, which the town manager should handle and which were in the domain of other elected and appointed officials. The town could make the charter as simple or as complex as it felt necessary, the consultant said, but the town would have its own "constitution" of sorts. He suggested that the selectmen, who would set policy only, would be paid a nominal fee and could only serve two terms so that they would not become career politicians. A professional town manager would be hired to run the town on a day-to-day basis.

A charter review committee formed. Many of those seeking to be on it came from the groups that had been opposed to sewers during that phase of the waste debate and/or those questioning the wisdom of a septage-only plant to be located near Namskaket Creek, along with those who voiced opposition to the handling of the whole septage issue. Rather than try to change the makeup of the Board of Selectmen through the electoral process, they advocated a whole new form of government.

The proposal for a charter form of government in Orleans passed by a majority of voters. And, after years of debate, Orleans entered into an agreement with Brewster and Eastham for a tri-town septage-only treatment plant to accept septage for the three towns in a facility to be located adjacent to Namskaket Creek, funded in part by state financing.

To my mind, the issue of sewers was the decisive factor in changing the form of government. The views and voting power of the newer residents in town began to outweigh the traditional Cape Codders, as by now, the latter group was outnumbered. No one anticipated that the then-incumbent selectmen would resign if the charter passed; they had not threatened to do so before the election although they had voiced their concerns with many of the charter's provisions and stated they were opposed to it. When they resigned en masse, they basically said that their views no longer matched the majority of the town who had voted in favor of the charter. They felt that the charter meant that the town would change from a small-town community, run like a traditional small town, to a more suburban-like town that was to be run more like an impersonal big business. In the '80s in particular, big business was not known as being especially people-friendly. To me, their resignations sent a clear, chilling message to the town.

During the town's bicentennial celebration in 1997, a new resident, who had not been a resident during the waste debates, volunteered his time to write a history of the town, focusing on relatively recent events that had not been documented well. Someone suggested that he talk to me. I prefaced my comments to him by saying that many people probably would not agree with my analysis about the waste-charter connection since people I had talked to thought they were very separate issues. But I told him the story anyway. He left my office with a look that said I was crazy to put sewers and the charter together.

After he had researched it further through newspaper clippings and records of town meeting actions of the time, identifying key players and turning-point decisions, he came back to see me and said he could not believe it but the story I had sketched for him checked out.

Sewers and septage — emblems of the cost of development. The obvious cost was the money needed to build a treatment plant. There were two less obvious costs. One was the toll the debate took on the social fabric of the town. And the other was the cost development was imposing on the water quality of the estuaries.

Meetinghouse Pond had been closed since 1982. Land use — increasing number of businesses, houses serviced by individual septic systems, and roads needed to interconnect the community — emerged as the reason for shellfish closures for bacterial contamination. It also became clear that getting the pond re-opened would require long-term commitment from disparate town departments, most of which did not give the estuaries a second thought as part of their own day-to-day responsibilities. I prepared and presented an article at town meeting that proposed creation of a Marine Water Quality Task Force to be comprised of representatives from the Shellfish, Highway, Planning, and Health departments in addition to a couple of "at-large" members. The article passed unanimously.

With the formation of the task force, the town had turned a critical corner in recognizing that we in the town were responsible for solving our water quality problems and could not rely on a higher level of government to do it for us.

Those of us in town government and those citizens who regularly paid close attention to environmental issues weren't the only ones recognizing that the waters were having problems. The shellfish closures had received a lot of local press coverage and all of Orleans' residents were getting concerned. They could see evidence of the water quality decline too — the odd-colored water, the seaweeds along the shore, the paucity of scallops. A community-based initiative seemed to many people to be a vital necessity, and a tool recently devised by state environmental watchdogs appeared to be a good objective for such an effort.

A year or two earlier, all of the marsh creeks along the coast of Cape Cod Bay had been nominated and approved for state designation as the Inner Cape Cod Bay Area of Critical Environmental Concern (ACEC). Through the designation process, the nominating towns selected the boundary to be drawn around critical areas, and within the boundary, state designation meant higher scrutiny for projects requiring state permits. The ACEC boundary was set at the contour line 10 feet above sea level. Rock Harbor was omitted from the designated area because it required maintenance dredging, a prohibited activity in an ACEC, but the adjacent marsh was included. And although the anticipated plume of the treatment plant would flow to another marsh adjacent to the plant, the plant itself was not located within the boundary.

On the other side of town, a group of people who lived on Pleasant Bay got together to discuss some of the changes they were seeing in the bay. They felt that the bay was such a precious body of water that it should be protected somehow. The group formalized their meetings with the creation of the Friends of Pleasant Bay in 1985 and before long, they had about 1000 members. Obtaining state designation as an Area of Critical Environmental Concern was their first priority. The young non-profit organization suggested to the selectmen of all four towns with frontage on Pleasant Bay that it should also be designated as an ACEC.

The selectmen from each town appointed a committee to move forward with the nomination process. The nominating committee set the boundary for Pleasant Bay as the 10-foot contour plus 100 additional linear feet, hoping that the greater boundary would result in greater protection. The group omitted Chatham Harbor from the boundary because of the volatility of the area and the maintenance dredging necessary for the commercial offshore fishing fleet to operate.

In order to be approved for designation, an area must have at least five of fourteen state-set criteria. Pleasant Bay had all fourteen. On March 20, 1987, the Secretary of Environmental Affairs approved the designation. In his supporting findings of the designation, Secretary James Hoyte noted the unique quality of the area and the fact that it contained all fourteen criteria. And he also noted that "the Bay is extremely important as an area of transition between two biogeographic provinces, areas which by virtue of their unique physical characteristics contain significantly different types of plants and animals.... Given that many of these animals and plants are living at the extremes of their ranges, they are somewhat more sensitive to changes in their environment, hence the need for greater protection of this unique resource."

Clearly, the people knew how special Pleasant Bay was. They also recognized, perhaps for the first time, that it was also vulnerable. They saw odd-colored water and rafts of seaweed that had not been there before. They saw new homes where trees had been. They saw the awesome power of the ocean to wash over and then create a "v' notch in a hundreds-yards-wide barrier beach that resulted in a new inlet. They knew that they could no longer be complacent in how they dealt with projects around the bay and they felt that the state designation would go a long way toward saving the bay.

But above all, they knew they had to be involved. The Friends of Pleasant Bay provided the mechanism for lots of people to get involved. The organization was the precursor of all the neighborhood groups that would form later, including the Friends of Meetinghouse Pond. It would take a while for residents to recognize the Bay's little sister, Nauset, in the same way.

Water had gotten people's attention. It was no longer just the fishermen and Shellfish Department talking to the new selectmen about issues. Other stakeholders — waterfront property owners and other residents, recreational fishermen, boaters of all kinds — all had a voice and were listening and learning and wanted to help, volunteering wherever they were needed. By establishing a water quality task force, the town agreed that "cleaning up our act" was in the best interest of the town's future and so paying attention to the estuaries became recognized as very important for the entire community.

As 1987 drew to a close, the road we had been on had taken a very sharp turn in terms of both natural and political events. On New Year's Eve, as 1987 closed, it struck me that it had been a most remarkable year.

Chapter 21

Shifting Gears

There was a magnificent piece of ivory sculpture on display at the national museum in Taiwan when I visited there. It was an intricately carved sphere freely moving within an intricately carved sphere, freely moving within an intricately carved freely moving sphere. In all, there were 21 concentric balls. It was an incredible piece of artwork.

By the end of the '80s, it was as if we, fishermen and managers alike, were somewhere in the middle of those spheres, spinning within our own little world while outside that world, events were spinning even faster and with greater influence. Discussions and petty internal bickering about how to manage shellfish resources paled in comparison to the larger issues we had begun to face in the late '70s and wrestled with through the next two decades.

Most of the towns of the Lower Cape grew tremendously during this period — the jump in retired-age people was enormous. Towns formed a raft of new committees to advise on every conceivable portion of town government, staffed by volunteers chosen from the ranks of the newly retired residents who wanted to do something useful and had the time to devote to town issues. All towns changed their form of government, putting professional managers in charge of operations to run the towns more like businesses. The role of the selectmen changed. No longer daily problem-solvers, the board set policy and gave marching orders to a town manager. Problems grew thornier and more complicated while solutions became more elusive.

In Orleans, town government grew in complexity as well. From my perspective it became impersonal, employees being pulled in many directions seemingly simultaneously — by directives from above to operate like a business, from liaisons with or membership on numerous committees set up to solve new problems, and from the demands of residents and visitors to act as a traditional small town assisting individuals. Somewhere in this tug and pull, the personal touch was lost in the shuffle at Town Hall. Laughter was scorned as an indication of un-businesslike behavior. Never again would we enjoy the frivolity of quahaug outhouses and nicknames painted on the door of a town truck. All town affairs became serious with no room for humor.

On the landscape, forests succumbed to subdivisions or house lots at a dizzying pace throughout the '80s. As the frenetic pace continued, marginal lots entered the real estate market — lots that had problems of slope or wetland issues. Land nobody wanted two decades earlier was sold easily. Marginal lots meant more oversight review by town boards such as health and conservation. Every year, more private roads were transferred to the town for upkeep, increasing the workload of the highway department while budgets were level-funded.

Building did not slow down until the recession that began in 1989, a three-year economic downturn that hit the Cape hard. Building contractors who had been given lots of money on speculation ended up being part of the fallout from the banking scandal that rocked the nation. Credit tightened dramatically. The second-largest industry on the Cape, homebuilding, declined for the first time in almost 20 years.

Out-of-work veterans of the building trades tried to go back to the sea but the sea could not support those already involved, let alone newcomers. Some tradesmen left altogether while others waited out the dark days until building once again gained king-of-the-mountain status in the '90s boom.

By far, most of the people moving into town were people who had fallen in love with the place. They wanted to learn about the environment in the area that they had chosen to live after retirement. When environmental problems began to show up, they stepped up to the plate to help in any way they could. Many of these people had tremendous experience and expertise in their former lives and became a huge asset to the town. Others spoke up at town meeting or voted with their pocketbooks for solutions to problems.

By the mid-'80s, however, we noticed not only an increase in the number but also an increase in the size of homes, the beginning of what looked like "one-upmanship". Along with the larger homes we noticed an attitude change in some of the newer residents, a change toward a degree of arrogance and big-city values heretofore pretty foreign to Cape people except in the summer. A number of summer tourists had always been mocked as having an attitude problem but now some of them were moving to the Cape.

Some of these new residents attempted to buy their way through the regulatory process in order to get what they wanted. Their money bought lawyers, consultants, engineers and other professionals to present slick presentations to the volunteer regulatory boards, clearly intending to overwhelm the board members. Town boards found they, too, had to hire outside help sometimes, and that was expensive.

What we were seeing with this relatively small but very demanding segment of society was, I think, a reflection of a huge social shift nationally. It was a time when company loyalty to employees and, in turn, employee loyalty to the company went out the window. It was a time of massive layoffs, when people who had worked for a company their entire lives were set adrift with no lifeboat. It was a time of stingy employee benefits, of profit-skimming company mergers and junk bonds. Those who had been doing the wheeling and dealing merely brought their values with them when they bought property for a second-home or moved to the Cape.

The importance of shellfish seemed to dwindle, both from lack of stocks and this new attitude, as fewer people wanted to see shellfishermen in front of their lovely homes. A shellfisherman represented a type of stigma on the picturesque landscape, marring the view. Shellfishermen weren't alone — in some cases, even walking in front of someone's house was no longer tolerated. But boating and other recreational uses of the estuaries increased with the influx of people and increased boating, especially motorboats, began to be implicated in decreased water quality. In fact, water quality became the overriding issue for two decades, and still is.

Our safe world was shattered when Meetinghouse Pond was closed to shellfishing because of bacterial contamination. Before the end of the decade, much more acreage was closed, including the entire Nauset estuary at one point. Pollution had come to our world.

Citizens questioned what was happening to the waters. They could see that the regulatory environment could not adequately protect the natural environment. They passed stronger and stronger regulations — zoning, health, conservation and wetlands. They tried to plug loopholes. They tried to come up with language that would slow things down but they couldn't stop what was happening.

Stopping development meant economic woes for those engaged in development and development was huge business that echoed throughout the community to just about every other business — merchants, restaurants, service stations, banks, real estate, accountants and law firms. Everyone's pocketbook benefited.

While the town was trying to solve problems, residents were searching for other ways to address the issues and formed grass-roots organizations. Property owners banded together and formed neighborhood groups starting with the Friends of Pleasant Bay, followed shortly by the Friends of Meetinghouse Pond. Quickly, membership expanded to include environmentally concerned residents who didn't own waterfront property but treasured the bay. Later, more pond groups were organized, each one focused on the water in their own back yard. And at present, coalitions of such groups are being talked about as a means to gain greater reach and clout.

All the Cape towns were struggling when this grassroots movement began. Changes were happening so fast that no one could keep up. The 1980s had enormous effects on the social fabric of the Cape not least because the ancient concept of local control was re-evaluated in response to the frenetic building booms.

Towns began questioning their ability to deal with problems as individual entities. Could the separate and very provincial towns individually address the concerns mushrooming throughout the peninsula or would they have to band together in an unprecedented manner? That was a question never asked before at such a sweeping level. A word, formerly used only in connection with schools and emergency response coverage, crept into the consciousness of the populace — regionalism. Could a regional planning and regulatory agency help solve the many problems caused by the accelerating Cape Cod development? If so, would the towns be giving up their coveted local control?

By the end of the decade, the state legislature passed the Cape Cod Commission Act, and Cape voters ratified it, birthing the Cape Cod Commission. For the first time, a regional agency would develop a regional policy plan that would require the support of the entire Cape population to be approved and implemented. The Commission went through growing pains and because the Cape Cod Commission was both a planning agency and a regulatory agency, the business community questioned just about everything in the plan which was advertised as having stringent environmental controls.

Not only was the Cape Cod Commission a new concept in land management, the state also had provided a new tool for environmental protection for the water — the Area of Critical Environmental Concern (ACEC). The Friends of Pleasant Bay convinced the selectmen not only of Orleans but of Chatham, Harwich and Brewster as well, that it was time to put aside at least some aspects of their traditional insularity. For the first time, the four towns worked together on a resource project of mutual concern — a multi-town approach to environmental protection.

By the end of the '80s, shellfish propagation became a low priority as the town grappled with the larger problems. State funding, a principal revenue source for the propagation program, including a portion of my salary, was eliminated in response to the statewide recession, and the town chose not to request funding from the residents. Instead, my position changed to Shellfish Biologist/Conservation Administrator. I began working with the Conservation Commission in 1990, administering and enforcing the Wetlands Protection Act and local Wetlands Bylaw.

The recession continued into the early '90s and gave us a little breather from the fast-paced '80s. It also gave us a second or two to reflect on what had happened. It did nothing to prepare us for what came later in the '90s when political and social upheaval was matched by natural events that continued to redefine the town.

Chapter 22

Lost Opportunity

The passage that leads from Lonnie's Pond to The River is usually calm and the ease of rowing depends on the tide. Going against the tide in that narrow, shallow, winding channel takes a bit of effort and concentration, while going with it seems almost like drifting — you just keep the boat steady with the oars.

On the left side of Lonnie's River going out — to my right as a backward-facing rower — is Kent's Point, and on the right — my left — is Mayflower Point. Mayflower Point, a peninsula of about forty-to-fifty acres, was developed mostly in the late '60s but the lots were large for an Orleans subdivision of that era, two or more acres per lot. Each lot had a 30-year conservation easement on the land that meant the land could not be further subdivided until the expiration of the easement. Most houses were built on the water, leaving the majority of the interior of the point in forest. A few years ago, in the late '90s, those easements expired. Many lots were further subdivided to the zoning minimum of one-acre lots. A building boom commenced on the point, with new construction echoing throughout the disappearing woods.

Kent's Point was a roughly 30-acre parcel, a peninsula with frontage on Frostfish Cove, The River and Lonnie's River and Lonnie's Pond. It had a single house that was built at the turn of the century near the point itself. The remainder of the property was wooded except for a single dirt driveway to the house, and two or three ramshackle outbuildings and a studio near the house. In the summer, Miss Charlotte Kent, a wonderful older woman — in her eighties in the 1980s — occupied the house. She revered the property, which had been in her family for several generations, and had myriad stories to tell about her happy times there on the point. As she thought about the future of the property after she was gone, she decided she wanted it to remain in its natural state, even though a subdivision plan had been approved and put on file years before. Had it become developed, it would certainly have become one of the most sought-after destinations for prospective homebuilders.

Miss Kent and her agents began negotiating with the town, and at the 1988 town meeting voters approved town purchase of the entire property. Given land values for waterfront property on the Lower Cape, it was an unbelievable deal at $1.8 million. She was allowed to live in the house for five years, a lease agreement that was renewed for another five years, in 1993, by which time she was in her nineties. At the time of purchase, the property was turned over to the Conservation Commission to manage.

I had thought that I was rolling along with the tide as far as the quahaug project was concerned. From 1976 on, we had planted at least 250,000 seed quahaugs annually, and after the devastating spill of 1985, we were producing a million seed per year. I also had lots of positive feedback from residents. Even with what I thought was success, though, I finally had to admit that I had been bucking the tide for years. By the time the town bought the Kent property, the focus of the quahaug program was changing dramatically. The changes were to have considerable impact on the town's long-term decision-making concerning Miss Kent's property.

Lonnie's Pond had been so successful for the rafts, dating back to the '70s, that our first choice for the shellfish lab site had been town-owned land on that pond. But residents of the area were adamantly opposed to the idea based on what appeared to be nothing more than fear of the unknown. Potential negative effects on the aesthetics of the pond shore seemed to be the most prominent comment. Faced with this opposition, we then decided that town-owned land in the business district of the Town Cove might be more appropriate for this purpose. Even though we thought there might be problems with siting a facility that required extremely clean water in such a busy area, at least we didn't get any negative comments about moving our building there. In hindsight, we probably should have fought harder for a better site from the beginning.

An odd twist of fate had occurred during the two years between the hydraulic fluid disaster and the receipt of the settlement check. Because of Town Counsel's "gag order," people in town knew that we had lost a million seed but they didn't know much else — we could not discuss the case any more than that. We lost a full growing season because we did not have the funds to retrofit the lab to get rid of the contaminated gear, and we could not replace the seed and realistically expect any return in terms of growth *if* the hatcheries had any left over anyway. To the public, it was simply a year of failure. People knew the town was suing the supermarket but very few people gave any credence to the possibility that an oil spill was what had caused total failure or that the loss had been completely out of our control. Talk began to circulate, especially from some in the commercial fishing community, that the whole quahaug program was a waste of time, effort and funds.

Those fishermen knew that the rafts represented a successful methodology and argued that we should have more of them, but I reasoned that if you could only put 25,000 seed on a raft, how many rafts would it take to really make a difference and where could they go? What body of water could hold enough rafts for a million seed and boats too? In addition, by then, the mid-'80s, bottom culture had "taken off" in neighboring towns.

A few fishermen were quick to point out that in Wellfleet, private growers were buying seed from the local supplier (Aquaculture Research Corp in nearby Dennis, Massachusetts), putting them in cages constructed of metal rebar and netting, and three years later — not five, six or seven — they were harvesting the stock. They talked about the town of Chatham planting *4 million* seed per year, not 1 million, using bottom culture and, very significantly, unpaid volunteer labor. Those fishermen felt Orleans should be doing the same thing because Chatham's approach was cheaper, more seed could be grown, and none of the complicated systems we used were needed. I knew that for three years, we had tried bottom culture at 20 separate locations and never found an area that was well suited to bottom culture. The talk was that it was my fault, that I just hadn't found the right place.

Aside from the basic disagreement on management techniques, there was another major roadblock keeping Orleans from following Chatham's path: Orleans wouldn't allow the use of volunteers on any project where there was the potential for injury. Volunteers, who had traditionally been counted on to help out when needed in Orleans, now, seemingly overnight, were considered an insurance liability. The town's volunteer insurance advisory committee suggested that if volunteers were working on a town project then the town, which was self-insured, would be liable and they didn't like that idea. Volunteers on committees continued to be the backbone of town government but volunteers on projects were discontinued.

Fishermen argued that they would be happy to help but Town Hall said they would still be volunteers and so essentially unwelcome.

That put us back where we had been, with what we saw as a successful seed-nursery program, but a program operating out of a less-than-ideal site.

By the time the settlement check arrived, we were growing a million seed per year at our small Town Cove nursery facility and had become successful using the upweller technique exclusively. But we knew that the busier the town landing next to our lab became, the higher the probability that we would run into more unforeseeable problems.

We searched for another site to move the building. The town had just purchased a property in South Orleans on Pleasant Bay and the selectmen encouraged us to put together a proposal for moving the building there. But as we were getting ready to present our proposal, news of the potential Kent's Point land purchase surfaced and we held off in hopes that Kent's Point might be the appropriate place for the shellfish propagation program.

I had been planting seed quahaugs along the shoreline of Kent's Point from the beginning. Old-timers I had listened to said that in the '40s, the area off Kent's Point was one of their favorite shellfishing spots. We had tracked the survival and growth rates of our plantings and knew that the seed had grown very well along those shores. I thought Kent's Point would be ideal for a shellfish facility.

I talked with Miss Kent numerous times when I was down there and she expressed strong support for the propagation program. I asked her if she thought it would be appropriate to have a shellfish propagation facility on her property and she very much liked the idea. By the time the deed and other official papers connected to the town purchase were drawn up, a shellfish propagation facility was the only structure to be allowed on the property except for the buildings that already existed. The article to purchase the land at town meeting also had contained language that a shellfish facility was to be the only other structure allowed.

Even with access issues inherent in the narrow dirt road that led to the land, the town endorsed the purchase by a wide majority and Kent's Point immediately became known as the jewel in the crown of the town's open space program.

When the new selectmen took office after the charter changes, they said, in effect, that the funds from the settlement would be spent for shellfish propagation if we could bring in a solid proposal. I put together estimates for a new facility on Kent's Point. They asked for more information. While I was putting together more information, the fishermen who were opposed to the lab told the selectmen that they wanted the town to use the settlement money to buy large seed. They said that the seed I was planting were too small and they wanted something they could see and get some benefit from quickly.

It didn't make sense to me. Why should we take a substantial amount of money, handed to us as recompense for a toxic spill at a successful propagation facility, and spend it on a one-shot deal? The better idea was to use the money to provide seed for years to come. To me the biblical admonition made the case — we could "give a man a fish" or "teach him to fish". Give them the seed once or provide a facility for continuous production.

Everyone tried to persuade the new selectmen to his or her way of thinking but there was no consensus. Gardy had long since retired by that time and even the new Shellfish Constable said he was having a hard time sorting out what the best route was. If I couldn't convince him or the folks who made their living from the water, it would be impossible to convince the selectmen.

Then the unbelievable happened. A woman came to me and said that she wanted to donate funds to build the building *and* endow its operation as a tribute to her husband who had recently passed away. I had a second conversation with another recent widow who said she too wanted to donate funds for a shellfish facility and would be waiting in the wings to pick up any financial slack.

I went to the selectmen with the funding proposals but to my consternation, they would not hear of it. They insisted that at some point, even with the donations and the settlement money, the town would be asked to contribute something and in any case they did not want to start any new programs. Thus, between the internal bickering and basic disagreement on the best route for shellfish propagation, the political condition of the town, and the fear of a potential money sink, the funds from the hydraulic oil spill went into the town's general fund to defray general Shellfish Department operating expenses, never to be spent specifically for shellfish propagation.

That decision proved to be fateful for me. Two years later, in 1990, state funding for propagation, monies that had paid a portion of my salary since 1975 and had paid for the operation of the shellfish lab, including a technician, was eliminated. Town officials decided not to ask the town, at the nadir of an economic recession, to fund the program out-of-pocket.

For years, the Conservation Commission had requested a full-time conservation administrator to help them with their workload, a workload that for unpaid volunteers dealing with major development issues was overwhelming. And so, rather than ask the town to fund the shellfish propagation program, town officials asked the voters to create a new position, Shellfish Biologist/Conservation Administrator and when the town approved, they offered me the position. It was made clear to me that if I did not take the position, I would no longer be employed by the town. If I chose to stay, I would be Department Manager for the new Conservation Department, administering and enforcing the state Wetlands Protection Act and the town wetland bylaw, working with a 10-member volunteer board, the Conservation Commission.

I was told that I would still be involved in shellfish propagation and that was why they kept "Shellfish Biologist" in the job title, but instinctively, I knew better. Once I was out of the Shellfish Department and forging a new department, shellfish propagation would be up to someone else. I was right.

I was devastated that the shellfish propagation program as it had evolved was being eliminated and that I would no longer work with shellfish. But I was also grateful that I still had a job with the town and the benefits that went along with that job. I thought back to the early days, marveling that the shellfish propagation program had lasted as long as it had, fifteen years, knowing the strong differences of opinion that had surfaced over the years and knowing that some people had always considered shellfish a luxury. I reasoned that I was lucky and that my career had just made a sharp turn and I needed to adjust to the new circumstances.

During the second five years of Miss Kent's tenancy, the Conservation Commission drew up a management plan for the property. By that time, the entire quahaug propagation program as we had developed it had ended, the shellfish lab had been razed (in 1993), the town was doing some bottom culture, and I had become Conservation Administrator. The Commission wanted walking trails on the property and said they'd deal with the house after Miss Kent vacated it.

The first draft of the new management plan included a section that stated that no new structures would be allowed on the property. I pointed out the language in both the deed and the article that had been voted on by the townspeople that specifically allowed a shellfish facility.

The second draft included the language but the commission included it reluctantly and stated that no such facility was being contemplated at that time. The commissioners cited as their primary reason for not endorsing a shellfish facility the basic philosophical differences of opinion about shellfish management they had read about in the local newspapers during the conversations about how to spend the settlement funds. Potential vandalism of a remote building also was cited and the Commission made it clear it truly did not relish the role or responsibility of property managers if the mission included managing buildings. The commissioners envisioned problems like potential vandalism and offered no ideas on how to deal with them, instead suggesting the problems made the whole idea untenable. The case was closed as far as the commission was concerned.

By 1996 or so, when Miss Kent moved out of the house to a nursing home, the house and all the outbuildings were torn down, leaving the site with land, walking trails, a handicapped-accessible walkway and steps up the bank from the water.

After 1993 when the lab was razed, I had chosen not to participate in public discussions on shellfish propagation or management. I rowed for too many years in choppy water.

But life is full of ironies. Twelve years after the last quahaugs were grown in Orleans upwellers in 1989, at least eleven out of fifteen Cape towns — including Chatham — use upwellers for municipal nursery culture to grow tens of millions of quahaugs, oysters and scallops. The die was cast long ago in Orleans — when the shellfish lab was razed. Orleans is not among them.

Kent's Point is a fantastic site to walk. But to me, Kent's Point it is missing a vital element, a true link to the water that surrounds it.

Chapter 23

Sand Worship

When I first started rowing for pleasure, my boat was moored in the Town Cove, not Lonnie's Pond or The River. I rowed around the Cove many times before I ventured out toward Nauset Harbor and the ocean, but one morning I finally felt strong enough to go the couple of miles from the head of the Cove to Fort Hill.

It was very early in the day, the tide was high, the ebb had just begun, and I could glide in the shallow channel between the mainland and Hopkins Island as I headed more or less northeast toward Fort Hill. A striped bass broke water chasing small prey and then another fish and another created concentric circles on the calm surface. When I got to Fort Hill, the powerful current helped carry me to the point where the channel breaks in three directions: southwest to the Town Cove, north to Salt Pond and the Coast Guard station, and south to Snow Shore and the Mill Pond.

I turned the boat around to face due east and although I'd seen this view hundreds of times, I looked around now and said out loud, "Oh wow!" The magnificence of this spot catches my breath every time but by stopping the boat and just drifting, I was able to pause and burn the moment in my brain.

The sun was just rising above the barrier beach, a solid line of sand broken only by Nauset Inlet, the vital force of this estuary. But between where I was and the beach, Nauset Marsh was a great green blanket stitched together with blue creeks. Fort Hill, with a small parking area at its summit, offered the only indication of a peopled world. The hillside itself was open fields, without one house, in utter contrast to the opposite shore, where big elaborate houses stood, protected from the sea by great granite boulder walls.

As I sat there drinking in the scene, my mind was flooded with thoughts of that barrier beach, a narrow strip of sand worshiped by so many various creatures.

The beach and inlet are among the very few barrier beach systems left in the United States where efforts to tame nature through engineered structures have proved unfeasible. The system has been allowed to behave in a natural manner. In 1967, the US Army Corps of Engineers concluded that the cost of constructing jetties and dredging the channel and the harbor entrance outweighed the benefit and such a program didn't make sense, even if it could work, which itself was an unrealistic assessment.

The inlet can't be tamed because it is a moving target. Historical records detailed in a 1982 technical report of the Woods Hole Oceanographic Institution show that the inlet has been most often located at the southern portion of the spit. Researchers Paul Speer and David Aubrey used historical charts dating from 1670 to 1978, and aerial photographs dating from 1938 to 1981 to draw their conclusions. Unfortunately, the photo from 1938 was taken after the great hurricane of the same year and there is no photographic record prior to the hurricane.

The barrier beach moves or migrates in two directions: north and west. The high banks along the ocean-facing Outer Beach of the Cape — the "back side" as it's called locally — provide sand to the miles of beaches below, but the sand doesn't stay there for long. Major ocean currents, called longshore currents, run parallel to the shore carrying sand up and down the coast. Wellfleet is the demarcation point between northerly trending currents and southerly currents. The northerly sand movement serves to build up the Provincelands portion of the Cape Cod National Seashore while the southerly currents build up the beaches all along Nauset from Eastham to Chatham and Monomoy Island.

With that scenario, Nauset Spit as it is known locally, should be migrating south, but the sand bars and marsh creek channels within Nauset Harbor conspire to drive the sand movement north on the ebbing tides. Oversimplified here, it is actually a very complex system where many conflicting forces act on the spit to refashion the sand in numerous configurations.

Under the normal every-day comings and goings of the tides, the sand moves in modest increments. But add the awesome power of a true northeaster and all bets are off as to what the beach will look like after such a storm has abated. It is the storms that have the most dramatic effects on the beach.

Beach grass on dunes is an important feature of the beach. Beach grass is effective against erosion because its rhizomes can grow down about 15 feet in the sand and spread laterally as well. With surf that is not severe, thick stands of beach grass are enough to hold a dune in place. But with a major storm, the grass is no more than a toothpick stuck in the sand, easily ripped out when the ferocious seas pound the shoreline for days. Twenty-foot high dunes can disappear in one storm — the Blizzard of 1978, the Perfect Storm of 1991 and the December 1992 storm all wreaked such havoc.

Interspersed with these giant storm events are the normal winter storms — two, three or four good ones most years. These storms are not destructive enough even to rate newsprint off-Cape, and yet they inexorably change the configuration of the beach.

In a northeaster, there is no such thing as a low tide. The wind and storm surge don't allow an ebb. The wind continually pushes water into the estuary, flooding the lowlands and then rising further, following the hydrologic path of least resistance. A whole lot of water can pile into an estuary during a storm event.

Where can a 20-foot sand dune go? If the wind and the waves are from the northeast, the sand ends up on the western shore of the barrier beach in what is called a washover. Clever name. The waves have washed over the beach. If the washover is pounded for long enough, a furrow can appear in the beach, and then the water flows over the beach even after the storm has passed. If that happens, then all the water piled up inside the estuary during the storm gushes back out to sea via the easiest location and the furrow becomes a new inlet.

In the meantime, all the sand from that 20-foot dune has been deposited on the western flank of the beach. The eastern edge of the beach has moved further west than it was before the storm and the whole spit has taken a hike toward the west.

How many bulldozers would it take to move that much sand and how long it would take? — Certainly not the couple of days that is all nature needs. For months afterward, the currents move the newly arrived sand within the harbor, often creating bars where there were channels, and decreasing the water depths in other places.

Throughout most of the history of the beach, most of the spit started at about the Coast Guard Station in Eastham and the inlet was deep into Orleans territory. The only way to get to the inlet from Eastham was to drive or walk from the Coast Guard station, about four miles or so to the inlet past Henry Beston's Outermost House. Beston chronicled a year spent living in a little two-room cottage on that beach, 1926-1927, in his classic book *The Outermost House*. Beston found that the sea's only constant was constant change, and the Blizzard of '78 —which hit ten years after he died — proved him right. His house, which he called the

Fo'castle, was swept off its foundation. The roof was found inside Nauset Harbor but I don't know the fate of rest of the cottage.

In the late 1960s, something odd had begun happening, a change in dynamics whose cause is still unclear (at least to me). The spit was no longer relatively stable and the inlet began moving north, decreasing the barrier beach north of the inlet and increasing the spit south of the inlet. It continued a slow march northward until 1978 when the northward migration speeded up. By 1990, the inlet and part of the southern portion of the narrow sand spit was between three-quarters-of-a-mile to a mile into Eastham. When the "No-Name" storm of 1991 hit (it's now known as The Perfect Storm thanks to author and sometime Truro resident Sebastian Junger), the inlet was at or near the most northern point in its history.

The storm broke through the beach and created a new inlet further south, leaving behind two distinct inlets that existed for several years. But the beach did not break through at the southern end as it had done many times previously. Instead, it broke in the middle, opposite a major channel through the marsh. After a few years, the northern-most inlet closed in, leaving the southern inlet as the only channel to the ocean. Currently, the inlet is moving north again.

With each successive washover, the deep cove at the southern end of Nauset Harbor began filling in with sand to the point where there was not much water left there. Until recently, a glacial erratic rock in the southern cove, which has a plaque affixed to it to mark the place where two Englishmen left for an epic row across the Atlantic in 1966, described in their book *A Fighting Chance*, was surrounded by water. After a storm, in March 2001, sand had piled up at least four feet deep around the rock and the cove was gone. Soon, the rock too will be covered. So too a channel that divided the beach from an island on the inside of the harbor — it has filled in so that very little water flows through there either. The island is not really an island any more and at low tide, it is connected to the beach.

The historical cycle of building north and breaking far to the south has changed. Now the cycle is for the beach to build north and break in the middle and then build north once again. The change means that Orleans residents have had up to two additional miles of beach to play on while Eastham residents have seen their portion shrink.

People have enjoyed this beach for decades. Generations have fished the shores of Nauset, and Nauset Inlet is a particularly hot spot. When the inlet was located to the south, Eastham residents accessed the beach by driving (or walking) south from the Coast Guard Station. After the Blizzard of 1978, Eastham Selectmen ordered that the beach be closed to vehicles. That action was ratified by a bylaw, passed by the voters at the following town meeting. If people from Eastham wanted to fish the inlet, they had to walk or access it by boat.

When the inlet started its march toward the north, residents from Orleans began driving out to the inlet. Even when the inlet migrated far enough north to be within Eastham's boundary, traveling on the Spit required residency in Orleans. The opposite was true when access to the beach was from Eastham and part of the beach was in Orleans. Regardless of the town boundary issue, Nauset Spit is within the jurisdictional boundary of the Cape Cod National Seashore. Long ago, Coast Guard and Nauset Light beaches were town beaches but Eastham gave up its rights to the National Seashore. Just recently, at the spring 2002 town meeting, residents started the process of creating a resident town beach between the two federal beaches. Orleans did not give up its rights to its traditional town-owned beach to the federal government and so, even though the beach is with the National Seashore boundary, Orleans owns and manages it.

The beach is an extremely important resource for the town and one of the town's major calling cards for its tourism industry. Used by thousands of beachgoers, fishermen, surfers, people exercising their dogs, and folks just strolling the beach at all times of the day and at all times of the year, Nauset Beach helps define the town. South of the spit, Orleans maintains a town beach with a thousand-car parking lot, lifeguard protection, and amenities such as bathrooms, showers, a snack shack and even a gazebo where free concerts were held on summer Monday evenings.

South of the town beach, a vehicle trail winds down among the dunes — with exits to the foreshore of the beach — to Chatham Inlet, a distance of over eight miles. Scattered along the trail are privately owned beach camps that have been on the beach for decades. Old-timers talk of a village of camps further offshore that are long gone, swallowed by the encroaching sea.

Beach buggy access has had a long history on this beach. Mooncussers — opportunistic residents who either took advantage of the misfortune of others who had been swept to shore or, as scurrilous legend would have it, actually lured boats to shore with lanterns — went to the beach with their horse-drawn wagons to strip stranded ships that foundered along the shore. People came in their Model A Fords when they came into vogue and people ever since have been coming to the beach in vehicles to beachcomb and fish.

Just as Nauset Inlet is a favored fishing location, so too is Chatham Inlet, as are guzzles that dot the outer beach — depressions at the tide's edge flanked by a higher sand bar a bit offshore — where the tide comes in faster than over the offshore bar. Fishermen traverse the beach looking for signs of fish.

In the '60s, a couple of enterprising young men started a surf shop in a former laundromat in Orleans. Nauset Beach didn't have the same caliber surf as places like Hawaii or California or even Florida, but there was enough surf a lot of the time to at least learn the sport and if a storm kicked up offshore, it often left pretty good surf rolling into the beach. Surfing took off in popularity, devotees searching the beach for the best waves.

As people bought more and more four-wheel-drive vehicles, the number of people accessing the beach by way of off-road-vehicle (ORV) increased dramatically. Anyone could access the beach if they were willing to pay a fee — nominal for residents and steeper for non-residents. In addition, people were getting to the beach by boat and the bayside of the beach near both inlets provided the preferred spots.

On a busy, sunny summer Sunday, the beach looked more like Coney Island to some than the Cape Cod National Seashore. For people who did not use the beach in this manner, many thought the use was a travesty and that the beach was being "ruined" by the number of people.

People started asking questions. Did the beach buggies, boats and people cause harm? If so, was that harm irreparable? Was there a finite number of ORVs that could use the beach without causing harm? How could the various resources be best protected? Was this just a case of aesthetics? Letters to the editor appeared in local newspapers; opinions were many and varied. The papers followed up with editorials.

Then, in 1989, an individual sued the town saying, in effect, that the town had acted improperly with its beach management program. The suit claimed that although the town managed the beach, it was still subject to the state Wetlands Protection Act. The plaintiff claimed that the town had not followed the state law especially with respect to the newly enacted Endangered Species Acts — state and federal statutes aimed at protecting endangered and threatened species. The town, through its Parks and Beaches Department, needed to file a Notice of Intent with the Conservation Commission, the body that administers the wetlands law, for a public hearing. I was in the process of being transferred to the new Conservation Department and was thrown into this controversy as trial-by-fire.

The hearing was continued several times, to accommodate the number of people who wished to comment and to obtain opinions from various experts who needed time to make their reports. Finally, the Conservation Commission issued an Order of Conditions that included a beach management plan. But to get to the point of acceptance took months of public hearings, studies, expert testimony and acrimonious debate.

To some people who testified at the hearings, ORVs were the enemy. This beach, they said, was a real jewel, a natural sand strip that should be left in its natural state. Others who testified said that this beach was a real jewel. A natural place where fish could be caught in the surf and you just had to find the right spot at the right time of day and tide to catch a whopper. To others, the beach was a real jewel. A natural place where sometimes the waves broke just right if you could get to them at just the right time. To others, this beach was a real jewel. A place where you could get a respite from the crowds, where you could distance yourself from your neighbor and the family could enjoy a day at the beach. To others, this beach was a real jewel. An economic boon to the town and a money-maker.

What they all agreed on was that the beach was a spectacular resource. What they strongly disagreed on was the best way to manage this resource, and to a resource manager, some of the popular activities were mutually exclusive.

The issues were many but top on the list was adhering to the federal and state Endangered Species Acts. Nauset Spit is home to several species that qualified — the area had piping plovers, a colony of 1000 least terns and several additional species of terns.

Tern nests contain 2-3 eggs that hatch in 20-25 days and they fledge in about 21 days. In 2001, Orleans had 150 least tern nests and 65 common tern nests. The terns nest on the spit but they also nest on an island inside the harbor adjacent to the spit, so the beach management plan did not include them per se, since there was not much human interaction on the island. The plover was a different story.

The plover is a small shorebird that nests on local beaches and flies to Florida, Louisiana, Texas and Mexico in the winter. Its nesting habitat is in direct conflict with human beach-going activities.

Both the bird and its eggs are well camouflaged in the sand — people often walk by and never see the nest. The suitable place to nest is an open stretch of beach, preferably with a little gravel mixed in with the sand, above the high-tide mark but often within storm tide areas. The female lays four eggs directly on the sand and if it is disturbed in the middle of laying all four eggs, it will abandon the nest and find another suitable location. The eggs hatch in about 25-30 days and the little fluff-balls start early on to travel on foot to the wrack line at the high-water mark where they feed. They, like the eggs, look like the sand and are difficult to see. During this period, they also can't fly. After about another 25-30 days, they "fledge" and can take flight when danger approaches.

The plover is a skittish bird that leaves the nest when disturbed and it will abandon a nest if disturbed too often. Dogs and people often disturb it while it is nesting. Among its natural predators are owls. Kites have been shown to frighten the birds also, perhaps looking like owls to them, so plovers leave the nest when kites fly overhead. Therefore people with dogs or kites are not compatible with nesting plovers.

But more often, their natural predators — foxes, coyotes, skunks, gulls and crows — cause plovers to abandon their nests. They will also abandon the nests if wind-driven sand covers the nest or high tides wash the nests away.

Plovers feed in the wrack line on either the ocean side or the bay side depending on the abundance of food, but on Nauset Beach, the majority feed on the ocean side and take infrequent forays to the bay side.

Because of their excellent camouflage, plovers are difficult enough to see when just walking the beach; they are almost impossible to see when traveling in an ORV. To a baby chick, which must walk over the beach to get its food, ORV ruts must be akin to a deep valley with steep mountains on each side and the chicks have to pass over the mountains to get to the water and their food. They can easily get stuck in the ruts.

According to the experts at the hearings, the only way to fully protect the birds was to shut down the beach to ORVs during the time they are vulnerable, rake over the ruts, prohibit pedestrian access near the nests with fencing and signs, and prohibit dogs and kites during the same time. All of those measures were included in the management plan.

The town hired a "Plover Monitor" each summer to traverse the beach searching for nests and document the bird's activity, also as part of the management plan. Plovers do not fledge until the end of July at the earliest. But if anything goes wrong — natural predation of the nests where half the eggs are gone, storm tide that wipes out the nest, poor hatch success for any of numerous other reasons — the birds will re-nest and their clock and the regulatory clock both start anew. They don't nurture two remaining eggs out of a clutch of four — they start all over again.

The management plan effectively closed the beach until the birds fledged, usually by the end of July, but if they had to re-nest, the beach could be restricted for beachgoers and closed to ORVs for another full month, well into August. With the protection measures, the plovers did well but a large portion of the Spit was closed to vehicles, especially since the end of the Spit was almost exclusively plover habitat. That meant the entire Spit and major segments of the south beach could be closed for nearly the entire summer.

The new plan calling for fencing, signage, monitoring, beach closures, and increased enforcement of beach regulations was put into effect both on the Spit and the larger section of barrier beach that protects Pleasant Bay and runs south to Chatham.

The Park and Beaches Department embarked on an education campaign directed to everyone seeking a sticker for the beach. They required that the person getting the sticker watch a slide show (later a video) about the birds and the proper and respectful manner to enjoy the beach, reinforcing the concept that it was a privilege. Failure to follow the regulations could result in loss of that privilege for the whole season. There had always been some "yahoos" driving out there who showed no respect for the magnificence of the beach or for enforcement, and the selectmen, who were also the park commissioners, hoped the educational campaign would curb the inappropriate behavior.

Concomitant with the beach closure was a drastic decrease in the number of vehicles that could be on the beach at any particular time. When the Spit was closed, residents who had used the Spit — a resident-only beach for which no amount of money could buy a sticker for a non-resident — had to share the public beach south toward Chatham with anyone who had bought a sticker for the privilege of driving there.

When the management plan was first put into effect, to say that tempers flared is a gross understatement. A bumper sticker that said "Piping plovers taste like chicken" appeared on ORVs all over town. The beach personnel were verbally abused. The beach monitor was ridiculed as being personally responsible for shutting down the beach. The cost to the town for the monitor, fencing, signage and all other costs associated with the management plan was substantial, about $20,000 per year. The Parks Superintendent, Paul Fulcher, took a lot of heat.

But there were also a lot of people who were glad to see the plovers protected and applauded the efforts of everyone involved in the management of the beach.

After several years, the monitoring reports showed that the management plan was working well. Initial nest success rate was good. But the fledge rate for re-nesting was dismal. Data analysis showed that wire-mesh exclosures — cages put around the nests to "protect" them from predators, did the opposite — they attracted natural predators. But the reports also showed that in the absence of summer storms that can wipe out the nests, the number of nests and the number of fledged chicks improved as a result of the conservation efforts.

In 2001, all 65 of the tern nests were lost in an August storm. Out of 14 plover nests on the Spit, 12 were successful, but not all the chicks made it through the entire process. Sixty-five eggs were laid, but only 46 hatched and merely 23 fledged, giving an average of 1.6 chicks per nest, the number needed to keep the population stable, not increase it. None of the eggs in a re-nest situation produced birds that fledged.

Some people are still very angry about yearly closures but they are more accepting that nothing they can say will change the situation. In reality, the major conflict occurs on 18-24 days per year, the summer weekends. The vulnerable birds have made a dramatic comeback but they are still listed as threatened and there has been no indication as to what the population should reach before they can be de-listed.

During the beach hearings, a second major issue surfaced concerning the natural migration patterns of the barrier beach. At the time, beach buggies were traveling on both the ocean side and the Nauset Harbor side of the Spit. Viewed along its peakline, a dune is usually a broad-based triangle where the ocean-facing side may be rather steep but the harbor side may be a gentler slope because the grass has trapped the wind-blown sand. We learned that driving on the harbor side prevented grasses from getting established on the harbor side, essentially preventing the dune from migrating slowly westward, and so driving on the inside was prohibited. Without the grass, the Spit would get narrower, and even though dunes would be higher, experts warned that the beach configuration would be very unstable. A high narrow sand dune is easier to topple than a lower and broader one. A high narrow dune actually affords less protection in most conditions than a lower and broader dune. In a really bad storm, it sometimes makes no difference.

Prior to the Blizzard of 1978, the beach had not experienced a really ferocious storm for a number of years. Dunes — built with the aid of beach grass planted by the Army Corps of Engineers in the mid-'70s — trapped sand, and had grown to 15-40 feet high. The Blizzard destroyed many of the dunes along the beach.

Afterward, the town planted beach grass along the Spit to build the dunes. The greater the size of the Spit in height and width, the greater the natural barrier from storm waves hitting the shore and the greater protection afforded the mainland. It takes time, often several years, for beach grass to get established in washover areas, and so each year the town would plant beach grass in washover areas to build up the dunes.

The storm of 1991 again wiped out the dunes. But by now, the beach management plan under the Order of Conditions was in place and the state Department of

Environmental Protection prohibited the town from planting beach grass because the washover areas were shown to be prime plover habitat. Dunes don't form easily on portions of a beach that are continual washover sites. So, although ORVs were prohibited from driving on the harbor side, dunes didn't form, and without the dunes, the beach continued to wash over frequently. In a summer storm, the plover nests in the washovers were wiped out too.

The beach had been advancing west at an accelerated rate compared with the rate prior to 1978. With no dunes, as the beach travels west the houses on Nauset Heights have become increasingly vulnerable. One section of the beach that is subject to frequent washovers happens to be closest to Nauset Heights.

The houses of Nauset Heights were built on a bluff about 50 feet above sea level. The bluff is a mixture of glacial material including sand, cobble and clay. Clay poses the greatest threat from erosion because if a chunk of clay lets go, it could be a huge chunk. Since part of the bluff is within the National Seashore boundary, the bank has no rock wall built around it and it is unlikely that residents will be able to build any form of protection any time soon. But watching the process, one cannot help but think that it won't be long geologically before the ocean waves lap or crash against the toe of the Nauset Heights bank and when that happens, the people will try to do what they have done elsewhere. They will try to protect their property.

This second issue caught the town between two competing goals that were mutually exclusive. The town needed to protect the plovers, but it also wanted to build up the dunes to gain more protection for the houses on the Heights. Other towns in Massachusetts that also had plovers had been able to move sand and plant beach grass to build dunes. Town officials wondered why Orleans was not able to follow suit. They have never gotten a satisfactory answer.

Nauset Beach and Nauset Spit are barrier beaches that are natural landforms going through a natural progression. They are not communities of dwellings with paved roads, gas stations and other examples of occupation as are most of the remaining barrier beaches on the East

Coast. They are used and have been used as recreational destinations for countless thousands of people for generations, whether that recreation is active as in surfing and fishing, or passive as in walking and nature viewing. There are sand roads and there are vehicles. There are self-contained campers whose owners must pay a special fee for the privilege of spending up to seventy-two consecutive hours on the beach followed by at least seventy-two consecutive hours off the beach before they can return. And yes, there are also some disrespectful idiots who use and abuse the beach.

The inlets at Nauset and Chatham migrate naturally and change on a daily basis. There are no rock or cement walls or jetties or other engineering marvels to tame the effect of the ocean waves or interrupt the flow of sand along the beach. The beach that looks torn up by ORV tracks after a busy summer day becomes smooth after the first storm that hits the beach.

Nauset Beach and Nauset Spit are not, however, sanctuaries or refuges either. Monomoy National Wildlife Refuge, a barrier island, lies south of the southern tip of Nauset Beach. Management policies on Monomoy are no less challenging then they are on the mainland. Refuge mangers angered Cape residents recently by poisoning gulls in favor of plovers and terns and more recently, by shooting coyote pups for the same reason.

Massachusetts has a high success fledge rate for piping plovers, and Nauset has one of the highest success rates in the state, in large part because of the requirements set forth in the management plan. And yet, regardless of the protections in place, the second-nest statistics that emerge when the birds have to re-nest, are dismal. While Orleans has this high success rate, the beach washes over year after year at the same location, the former site of the inlet prior to the 1960s. But this time, the inlet is a few hundred yards east of Nauset Heights and closing fast. The "Fighting Chance" rock that baby boomers water-skied around in the 1950s and '60s is now surrounded by sand.

Some ask if Orleans is being penalized for its success in nurturing plovers. Perhaps. Yet, what makes the place so darned attractive to the hordes of people who come to worship the sand every summer or choose to live here? It is the plovers, the dunes that get washed away when an angry ocean unleashes its fury, the lack of houses and paved roads on this sand spit, the fish that cruise along the surf zone searching for food, and the waves that break just right. It is all these things.

Conservation, protection and preservation are not always synonymous but they're not mutually exclusive either. Maybe, with the data in hand, a compromise could be achieved that protects the birds, preserves the species and conserves the beach. If a nest fails for natural causes, it fails. Re-nesting just does not produce healthy chicks, according to the monitoring conducted for over 10 years. As the birds continue to improve in their overall status, perhaps people may analyze the data from the plover monitors in Orleans in order to adjust the management plan slightly, giving a new look to the items dealing with re-nesting. It would be sensible to keep the protections very tight at the beginning of the season, encouraging the birds to lay down the three or four requisite eggs so that the birds can fledge early. That helps both them and us. It is what happens in the middle of the summer that may be the source of further discussion.

But then again, there would probably be some jerks who would try to get around new regulations merely to get the beach opened earlier. Then, we'd be back to where we were in the early '90s and I doubt that anyone wants that.

Some feel compromises have already been made. Those who do not want to see any ORVs on the beach have to live with them, while ORV owners who would like unrestricted use of the beach can't have that either and are restricted in numbers, time and legally accessible areas during the nesting season. Is there room for further compromise? Should there be further compromise? Or is this one more case of too many people loving the place? I don't know.

Two things seem obvious as the town wrestles with beach management.

First, the beach is incredibly important to the town and its import is the primary reason the town did not give up its rights to manage the beach to the Cape Cod National Seashore. As a government entity, it will maintain its obligation to manage the beach in accordance with the Endangered Species Act, but it will also maintain its obligations to its residents and visitors, thus continuing the juggling act between people and birds.

Second, the beach is constantly changing and no matter what we do, the shoreline is going to recede and the Atlantic will be closer to the land, day by day. If an inlet breaks through Nauset Spit where it had been historically, then so be it. Orleans residents will lose their right to drive on the beach. The houses on Nauset Heights will be endangered. Some day, we may even lose the town beach, or at least the parking lot, and the town should plan for that as well.

Orleans has been juggling the needs or desires of the various interest groups for a very long time. Ultimately, no group is entirely happy. But each group gets something they want.

When you look at the beach in the winter or spring, you have to wonder if all the people using the beach in the summer did irreparable harm. We know more than we did prior to the hearings in 1990. We know that even repeated foot traffic over a dune will wear it down and may result in a washover during a storm. So we may not use the same place every year to go from one side to the other. We close the beach if the tides are higher than normal and there isn't room to maneuver an ORV without impacting the toe of a dune. We restrict ORVs to the ocean side of the spit and in designated trails on the south portion. And we protect threatened species such as the plovers and terns.

Resource management is full of compromises. Managers walk a fine line every day, listening to perspectives on both sides of the line to draw their conclusions, which rarely turn out to be entirely agreeable to either side. They search for ways to allow people to use public natural resources while at the same time ensuring that the use does not cause irreparable harm. They are also searching for ways to ensure that the resources are sustainable, a concept that is even more important in setting policy, because a use may not cause irreparable harm but if it is increased in intensity or duration, it may render a resource unsustainable.

I drove to Fort Hill one day in the spring of 2002 and looked out over nature's patchwork quilt, thinking about the beach. It was a glorious day, the white sand of the beach in the distance in sharp contrast to the blue ocean, the more muted shade of blue of the creeks, and the new green of the marsh. Hawks flew over the hill along with other birds, all part of the natural world. I couldn't see them but I knew the plovers and terns had returned and were performing their nesting ritual. There was one vehicle at the inlet and I knew it wouldn't be long before there would be no vehicles at the inlet. The remainder of the beach was in its natural state. I drank in the incredible beauty of the spot.

And then I thought about the number of times I have gone to the inlet, driving or as a passenger in an ORV or by boat. I had not followed in the footsteps of some eloquent beach walkers — Henry David Thoreau, Henry Beston, John Hay, or Bob Finch. Was I doing something "wrong," talking the talk but not walking the walk as an environmentally conscious resource manager by going to the beach in a Jeep? I thought about parties on Father's Day, before the season really got rolling and Labor Day parties, signaling the close of a busy season. It was the Labor Day get-togethers that I cherished the most. Those were days when the residents of Orleans got together — friends and neighbors, people you hadn't seen for months because they had been too busy servicing the millions of tourists that came to town each year. Those were days for them to enjoy their beach for which they paid the taxes that protected the plovers. They came by boat and by ORV. They made ferry trips to bring people across. They played in the fast-moving current on the Nauset Harbor side or bodysurfed in the ocean or fished the inlet. They laughed and joked and took a deep breath now that the craziness of the summer season was over. Anyone who lives and works in a seasonal resort area knows the feeling.

I looked at the beach and thought of the times I had watched it during a storm. To me, it seems very unlikely that anything we do on the ocean side makes any difference at all when judged against the awesome power of the ocean that reworks the sand so easily, erasing all traces that any of us were even there.

The Cape's economy is its environment. That statement can't be said often enough. The economy and environment are intricately linked together, so that if the environment goes, the economy will too. Beaches and boating and fishing and property around these waters are the backbone of the economy because the water is what makes the Cape a very special place.

Resource management is a difficult juggling act. The resource manager is often a student of history who tries to predict the future based partly on the past and partly on incomplete information about the present. This sort of juggling is also what makes coastal resource management so incredibly challenging. You have to be kind of nuts to choose to get into the thick of it.

I smile knowingly looking back at the early days out in Pleasant Bay with my bull rake, thinking of the ecology courses and my youthful naivete — piece of cake, I thought — just plug in the appropriate resources. Yeah, right.

Chapter 24

Solid Ground

As I rowed up The River last summer, I looked at the land rising up from the riverbank. Most of the houses were slightly hidden behind a veil of green, the trees and bushes that help to keep the banks stable. A few houses stood out in stark contrast to those that remained in dappled shadow behind trees. I looked at one particular house and then another and then another, seeing the lush vegetation on the bank but thinking of them when they were not hidden behind the safety of greenery. Without the lush vegetation, these occasional gaps in the green may have provided the homeowners with wide-open views, but the houses stared out at the bay atop bare banks of sand, vulnerable to all the elements that shape this land.

I turned the corner at Namequoit Point and headed southwest through Little Pleasant Bay toward the Narrows but I looked at the point of land as I passed by it. Most of the steep bank was covered with grass and shrubs and I thought about how it had looked in the spring with the Scotch broom in full bloom, painting the bank in hues of gold and green. I saw that a portion was still mostly bare sand after all these years and remembered the letters I had written to the owners a decade earlier suggesting how they could help to save their bank through simple maintenance. If they would only remove the smothering grass clippings and brush that had been thrown over the bank, the bank would revegetate and would stabilize. They hadn't followed my advice.

As I rowed along, it seemed I had a memory about nearly every waterfront bank and house and about many of the homeowners. Their lives had intersected with mine during the late '80s and early

'90s when capricious nature caused public interest and private interest to slam together in controversies all over Orleans and Chatham. I thought about the couple several houses west of the Point who had been so nervous back then about what nature might do next.

Further near the entrance to Paw Wah Pond, I saw another house, my memory clicked and I got irritated at those property owners all over again. The events were long past but my feelings were still strong. Then I saw a group of houses perched on a bank, remembering the part they had played in the drama of the '90s, and next spied the bare rock wall that just couldn't be covered with sand and vegetation. It was all coming back to me.

I rowed through the Narrows and looked at the houses on the shore of Big Bay. The shift in the coastal landscape was palpable. These were not the soft vegetated banks I saw along The River and most of Little Bay but massive hard rock structures armoring the banks in an attempt to keep nature at bay. Only Sipson's Island looked as it had all those years ago.

What had happened that caused me to scrutinize the bay in this way? Storms. Or to be more precise, three storms: The storm that ripped through Nauset Beach in January 1987, creating a powerful new inlet from the Atlantic near the Chatham Light; the Perfect Storm of October 1991, famously chronicled in book and film; and the lesser-known but locally damaging storm of December 1992. These three storms all changed the bay in drastic ways, but perhaps their most lasting effect can be found in the changes they forced us to make in the way we look at coastal banks and erosion.

When you look at much of the Maine coastline and compare it to the Cape, one of the most striking features Down East is the rock. The Maine coast is not a jumble of boulders but rather unbroken masses of granite ledge. It looks sturdy and enduring, a natural fortress to buffer the forces of the ocean. The ocean waves crash against the rock, dissipating their energy in magnificent plumes of white foam. Wherever one builds a house along that shore, unless it is actually within reach of the stormy seas, chances are it is likely to stay in the same place for generations. The rock will protect the house and the lot it sits on, because the rock will shrug off the punishing force of the waves. Erosion occurs along the rock-bound coast, but at a rate barely perceptible in a millennium.

In contrast, Cape Cod was dumped in its present position by retreating glaciers. The land is composed of sand and gravel and clay topped by soil built up over hundreds of years by vegetative cover. There is no solid rock on this part of the Cape unless you dig down about four hundred feet to reach bedrock. When people build their houses high on a hill overlooking the water here, they may think they have nothing to worry about because they are on "solid" ground. And then the winter comes. Winter storms can give new meaning to the ancient wisdom that it is a foolish man who builds his house upon the sand.

In January 1987, a northeast storm battered the coastline. It was a typical storm of gale force winds and driving rain but by New England storm standards, it was not particularly ferocious. However, because of somewhat unusual celestial alignments, the storm was much more devastating than expected.

Courtesy Kelsey-Kennard

Tim Wood, editor of the Cape Cod Chronicle, Chatham's weekly newspaper, wrote a 100-page book about that storm and its aftermath. Now in its sixth edition (2002), it is called *Breakthrough: the Story of Chatham's North Beach*. Wood descibed the storm this way:

"There was snow early in the day of Friday, January 2. The air had turned bitter and winds whipped around from the northeast. All week the tides had been extremely high, due to a celestial phenomenon called syzygy, an alignment of the Earth, sun and moon that occurs every nine years. This year [there] was an added factor, a concurrent alignment of several planets, which happens once in every 35 years.

"Syzygy, along with a full moon tide, accounted for perhaps two to three feet in extra tidal height that day. But by early morning a full-fledged northeaster, packing sustained winds of 50 miles per hour (with gusts of 68 miles per hour recorded at the Chatham Weather Station on Morris Island), added a storm surge of eight to 12 feet.

"Breakers 10 to 12 feet high crashed over the narrow strip of North Beach opposite the lighthouse. High tide arrived at 1 p.m., and a crowd gathered at the overlook to watch as the Atlantic surged across the approximately 100-yard-wide beach and flowed into Chatham Harbor.

"Several other portions of the beach were similarly inundated by the January 2 storm. But at low tide the following day everyone in Chatham saw, for the first time in decades, a permanent channel linking the inner harbor with the Atlantic, isolating a three-and-a-half mile section of beach."

People living near the elbow of the Cape wondered if this was it, if this small flow-through area would become the new, permanent inlet, predicted by Dr. Graham Giese, one of the Cape's foremost coastal geologists, a decade earlier. The June 1, 1978 edition of the Cape Cod Chronicle had published a special supplement, "The Barrier Beaches of Chatham, Massachusetts, a report prepared by Dr. Giese for the Chatham Conservation Commission".

Dr. Giese wrote a compelling report that documented changes in the barrier beach system over a period of 200 years, using maps, and photographs where available, to create composite drawings of Nauset Beach in Chatham. The drawings indicated that in 1830, the beach had looked very similar to the way it looked in the 1970s. (See photo on page 68.) He showed that a breach had occurred in 1846 that widened to a great inlet. Eventually, the sandbars broke up on the inside of the harbor and migrated toward the land and finally the beach migrated south again. It was a cyclical phenomenon that likely had occurred many times since the barrier beach and bay behind it had been formed thousands of years ago, and it would occur again, Giese said. Giese indicated that each cycle lasts about 140-150 years. That meant, Giese predicted in 1978, that Chatham could expect a breach and a new inlet sometime between 1986 and 1996.

Giese wrote that there are two opposing forces in inlet dynamics: the force of water moving in and out every tidal cycle, and the longshore currents moving sand across the inlet trying to close it up. In the case of Pleasant Bay, if there were enough space between the barrier beach and the mainland to allow the bay's waters to flow with the tides in and out of Chatham Harbor to Nantucket Sound, off Chatham's southern coast, there might not be any inlet to the Atlantic through the east-facing Nauset barrier beach. Instead, there would be one very long barrier spit attaching to what is now Monomoy Island. But that was not the case.

Giese said that the Nauset barrier — called North Beach in Chatham — moves westward at about 5-10 feet per year. As the channel through Chatham Harbor becomes narrower and more constricted, somewhere in the barrier a breakthrough occurs. Pleasant Bay's waters then flow in and out of that channel through the beach to the ocean, rather than to Nantucket Sound.

Meanwhile, the littoral drifting of sand carried by longshore currents is intercepted at the inlet. Some sand gets carried to the inside and is deposited as a flood-tide delta, and some is carried outside the inlet and deposited as an ebb-tide delta. Between these two depositional processes, the beach south of the inlet gets starved of sand. It eventually breaks down and moves landward.

After many years, the inlet is not really an inlet any more, but rather just the southern end of the barrier spit. Without a true inlet, littoral drifting is free to continue south and sand gets deposited on the north side of Monomoy Island, eventually attaching the island to the mainland. The spit then continues to build southward and landward until the channel width decreases again, pressure builds in Pleasant Bay, and the cycle is ripe for another new inlet to form.

When talking with the Chatham Conservation Commission in 1978, Giese said that the barrier beach had migrated so far south and there was so little area for the bay to empty that he was relatively sure a breach would occur within a decade. He said that pressure had built up in Pleasant Bay and someday the water from the bay would find a weak place in the beach and rush out toward the ocean. He said he couldn't be sure where the breach would occur, but thought it might very well be east of Minister's Point at about the same site as the 1846 breakthough.

In January 1987, the beach did break through at a weak spot, about two miles south of Giese's "most likely" site and opposite the lighthouse, but from a predictive-model point of view, pretty darn close both in geography and in time.

On the morning after the breach in January 1987, Tim Wood rode down the beach with Lieutenant Wayne Love of the Chatham Police Department. Wood's book described the view and went on to recollect the events that took place shortly thereafter.

"... As we rode along the outer beach in the [Chatham Police] department's four-wheel drive pickup, he [Wayne Love] pointed out the various washovers and what had been high, solid-looking dunes torn apart by the storm. Arriving opposite the lighthouse, which still threw its warning beacon seaward against the cloud-shrouded early morning sky, we found a meandering stream in the center of a vast, football field sized washout. Approximately 18 feet wide, a foot or so deep, the channel seemed natural, nonthreatening, even beautiful in its undulating simplicity. Water flowed through it at a good clip, but it would not have been unthinkable for someone in waders to ford across....

"Within two weeks it was clear that the cut was rapidly establishing itself as an inlet and wasn't going to close up immediately, as some thought. Scouring had produced a 500-foot wide channel with respectable depths at both low and high tides, enough to allow the 42-foot fishing vessel *Asylum* to pass through at half tide....

"Through January and February the area was battered by two more northeast storms, with huge snowfalls and winds up to 80 miles per hour. At first the breach widened by as much as 1,000 feet in two weeks; but as it became more established and organized, the rate of growth slowed to perhaps 100 or so feet per week, as a mean average. In early March the breach was 1,710 feet wide with a main channel twenty feet deep. Dr. Giese, at the time, was guarded in his predictions about the fate of the cut-through, but left little doubt about where his attention was focused. 'We can't say at this moment for certain that this particular break is the one that will stay open,' he said. 'But we can say that the characteristics associated with this break indicate the conditions are right.'

The conditions were indeed right. Imagine the forces at work to create a hole in the entire breadth of beach, from ocean to bay, 500 feet wide and deep enough for a vessel to pass through at half tide in only 14 days or a mere 28 tidal cycles. Clearly, a new inlet had been born.

A coastal geologist can look at the sediment transport, measure the tidal amplitude, quantify other forces acting on the system, and predict the course of the physical environment. He does not predict the changes in the social or political environment that flow from the physical event. However, one can review the history of the area through the eyes of those who lived in long-ago times and get a sense of the type of havoc that changes in the physical environment can cause for people.

Wood researched the records and discussed what happened the last time the harbor had been so dramatically changed. In 1846 the inlet broke through across from Minister's Point, but in 1871, the location shifted southward, creating a great harbor.

"It would be several years before the people of Chatham realized the cost of this new, improved harbor," wrote Wood. "During the next decade, 'That Old Ocean' [would exact] a tribute that would include many acres of land, numerous homes and two lighthouses. . . .

"Henry Mitchell, in his 1874 report to the U.S. Harbor Commission, noted, however, that 'the upland has been but little disturbed during the past year, but attacks from the sea are so much apprehended, that buildings have been moved back from places where inroads threatened.' Chatham was preparing.

"Moving a house in those days wasn't the major event it is today. Especially those houses along the shore; they were for the most part smallish Capes and shacks, with nothing as an anchor except, in some cases, a dank Cape Cod cellar. There is no telling how many of the buildings were moved during the decade following the 1871 breach, but those familiar with the village claim that today, many of the houses along lower Main Street and the other avenues of the Old Village once sat much closer to the shore."

The homeowners of the late 20th century were enjoying their good fortune at having a house on or near Chatham Harbor when Giese's report was published. This was coveted real estate. But his report clearly showed that a dramatic change in the circumstances of shorefront property owners had happened before and would likely happen again.

Suddenly, in 1987, houses that had been close to the sheltered waters of Chatham Harbor no longer had the protection of the barrier beach. They now sat on oceanfront property. For a few months, it was exhilarating for the homeowners to see the ocean and watch the waves. But it soon became apparent that those same waves that were mesmerizing when looking out picture windows in the summer were tearing away the very ground that the houses were sitting on as the harsher fall weather set in.

The property owners and the town embarked on what would turn out to be a horrendous journey that involved engineers, lawyers, and government officials from the federal, state, county and local agencies. By the time the inlet had stabilized somewhat, the toll on Chatham property and pocketbooks was immense. Seven buildings were either lost to the sea or removed before the sea could claim them and 28 man-made erosion-control structures stretching along about a mile or more of shoreline had been built a cost of several million dollars.

Chatham was not the only area affected by the break in the beach. The changes in the rest of Pleasant Bay could not have been more sensational.

Scientists predict that sea level in the North Atlantic will rise about one foot in the next century. We saw a rise of one foot within *one year* in Pleasant Bay. The high-tide line was much further up the shore, leaving no place to walk at high tide.

"Mean high water", a phrase used extensively in wetland regulations to determine the approximate "normal" high-tide line, took on a whole new dimension and no longer meant the same thing as it had the year before. Bars and channels all over the bay were in different places. Tidal currents were much faster. It just wasn't the same body of water. Even the normal high tides nibbled away at the bottom or "toe" of the high banks. Storms did more than nibble at the toe; they took some hefty bites. The high-tide line was so much higher that at many places on the shore, there was no shore, there was no place to walk.

And then, in October 1991, a late-season hurricane named Grace sped up the coast and merged with a huge storm off Sable Island, Canada (Map 1, Frontispiece). A third big weather maker was a massive high-pressure area in Canada. Sebastian Junger, in his book *The Perfect Storm*, explained,

"The only good thing about such winter gales, as far as coastal residents are concerned, is that they tend to travel west-to-east offshore... The atmospheric movement is all west-to-east in the midlatitudes, and it's nearly impossible for a weather system to overcome that. Storms may wobble northeast or southeast for a while, but they never really buck the jet stream. It takes a freakish alignment of variables to permit that to happen, a third cog in the huge machinations of the sky.

"Generally speaking, it takes a hurricane.

"By October 30th, the Sable Island storm is firmly imbedded between the remnants of Hurricane Grace and the Canadian high. Like all large bodies, hurricanes have a hard time slowing down, and her counterclockwise circulation continues long after her internal structures have fallen apart. The Canadian high, in the meantime, is still spinning clockwise with dense, cold air. These two systems function like huge gears that catch the storm between their teeth and extrude it westward. This is called a retrograde; it's an act of meteorological defiance that might happen in a major storm only every hundred years or so. As early as October 27th, NOAA's Cray computers in Maryland were saying that the storm would retrograde back toward the coast; two days later Bob Case was in his office watching exactly that happen on GOES satellite imagery. Meteorologists see perfection in strange things, and the meshing of three completely independent weather systems to form a hundred-year event is one of them. My god, thought Case, this is the perfect storm."

When a really nasty northeast storm hits the Cape, it usually lasts for about three days. And this was a doozy. The barrier beaches were pummeled. Dunes were flattened and the sand that had been a dune ended up in the bays behind the barrier beach. Washovers between dunes were numerous everywhere along the beaches. And the ocean just kept forcing more and more water into Nauset and Pleasant Bay.

Low areas flooded first. Nauset Marsh was under several feet of water so that the fetch (a nautical term used to describe the distance winds or waves travel without being interrupted by land) was much greater than usual. The waves were not stopped by the beach or slowed by dunes or marsh as is normally the case. The waves roared in from the open ocean and crashed on the mainland at the first obstacle in their way, the coastal banks. The same held true for Pleasant Bay except that the barrier beach was higher and wider than Nauset Spit and the dunes in the Orleans portion of Pleasant Bay held firm. In the bay, however, the wind had enough fetch to build up huge waves from the swollen bay itself — already a foot higher than before the Chatham break. Those waves were hurtled against the banks.

High tide came at about 4 in the afternoon, during the height of the storm. It was late October and we had just set the clocks back to standard time, so sunset came just after 4:30. But because of the storm, it was dark, with limited visibility, well before then. I was a bit testy that the worst of the storm hit when I couldn't see what was going on.

I drove to several areas of town that I thought would be affected and what I could see dropped my jaw again and again. The height of the water was incredible, much higher than I had ever witnessed. Docks were under water — not just the walkways, but also the handrails. Low-lying roads were rivers. A 19th-century inn was flooded throughout the first floor and the Orleans Yacht Club, on Town Cove, miles from the open ocean, was filled with water. The road to Chatham was impassable. Every part of town had a story of flooding or some other storm-caused calamity. I wanted to be every-where at once.

The next morning, I began another tour of the town. Diehard sailors and fishermen abound in Orleans — in late October there were still lots of boats in the water. After the storm, there were lots of boats on land, way up on land. People had started to mark how high the water had reached on buildings and in yards. Everyone knew that this had been an extraordinary event.

Then I began to walk along the north-facing and east-facing shores that had been most vulnerable, those exposed to the wildest fury of the waves. What I saw again made my jaw drop open. Stairways on the banks, mangled, their posts in mid-air. Vegetation of all types, gone. Straight walls of sand and clay where there used to be angled slopes. Houses on top of the banks a lot closer to the edge than they had been before the storm. One building gone and three others off their foundations, floated up into the puckerbrush behind them. As far as structures were concerned, the town fared well but the psyche of homeowners had been shattered.

Almost immediately after the storm, residents began applying for permission for erosion control measures. The experience in Chatham was fresh in their minds and it was also fresh in the minds of the Orleans Conservation Commission. The Commissioners

desperately wanted some time to digest what had happened but they were not given that opportunity. They had to act within the time frame established by the state regulations. My job was to gather the information they needed to make informed decisions, knowing all the while that a lot of people in town weren't going to like those decisions. The next two years were to be among the most stressful in my 25-year career as a town employee.

Chapter 25

Private Rights?

Anyone who has watched a television newscast about a big Northeast storm — the wind-driven rain or snow buffeting the newscaster, waves crashing against the shore in the background — can marvel at the power of the ocean from their secure living room. Unless that living room is in a house on a coastal bank facing the storm — then it's not marvel but sheer terror.

For decades, people have been building houses close to the water, and at the dawn of the 21st century it doesn't seem that the trend will stop. If anything, as waterfront property values soar, it becomes more and more attractive to have a house on the water overlooking a beautiful calm bay. Seafaring captains of an earlier age wouldn't be caught dead building their houses near the sea — they knew its secrets — but we live in an age where faith in technology overrides a realistic evaluation of the potential dangers in our decisions. So some people build in harm's way.

Geologists and climatologists can talk about the formation of Cape Cod after the last ice age. They can introduce concepts such as subsidence where, once the ice sheet was lifted as the ice began to melt, the land, formed by the dumping of glacial debris at the edge of the ice, immediately began to sink as the water level rose because of melting ice. The fact that 15,000 years later, that process is still occurring is somewhat difficult to grasp. The greenhouse effect that we are creating in the atmosphere isn't helping any. The sea level is rising. If the sea level continues to rise, it will drown the land. It's that simple.

And yet, we keep thinking that we can tame the ocean somehow. We think all we have to do is build a small groin or a massive jetty perpendicular to the beach and we will keep the sand on the beach. But we forget that there are other forces at work, the longshore currents. They will serve to build up sand at one side of the jetty but the other side will be starved of sand and erosion will take place even faster, so we have to build another jetty and another and another and another until we end up with a scalloped shoreline. Or, instead of a barrier beach left alone to move the way it was meant to, we have paved roads and built whole communities on the barrier beach as if it were the mainland. Then, as a storm comes — it may be a hurricane instead of a northeaster — waves tear at the foundations of houses and they may fall into the sea. We wring our hands and say how awful and build a seawall, a vertical wall to protect the houses. The beach is gone in front of the wall after a short time but the houses are protected — for a while. The high plumes of salt water and spray as the waves hit the seawall in a storm make for spectacular footage for the newscast. But eventually, the sand is scoured at the base of the wall and it crumbles, leaving the houses vulnerable again.

No matter what man has devised in the way of erosion-control structures, it has proven to be no match for the ocean. But the belief in technology is hard to shake. For without a technological solution, what recourse is left?

Wallace Kaufman and Orrin Pilkey, Jr. wrote a book, *The Beaches Are Moving*, which describes both the nature of beaches and what happens to sand if beaches are stabilized by structural "solutions." Their overwhelming conclusion is that structures will not only fail to do the job they were meant to do at some point, but they will also cause unanticipated consequences that may be evident miles away from the structure. The authors explain the current methods of stabilization in this way:

"Over the past three thousand years shoreline engineers have worked toward the same goal — stabilization. With many variations in design and theory, they have tried to realize their goal in one of three ways: building structures perpendicular to the shoreline (groins and jetties) to trap sand in the longshore currents; building structures parallel to the shoreline designed to dampen wave energy before it reaches shore (breakwaters) or to absorb the impact of the breaking wave (seawalls, bulkheads, and revetments); replenishing or nourishing the beaches by pumping new sand onto the beach or into the longshore currents."

They discuss what happens to beaches when we use technology to stabilize them.

"Anything built on or near the beach usually increases the rate of erosion. Seawalls, bulkheads, groins and house foundations reduce the flexibility of the system to respond to changes in the dynamic equilibrium. If energy patterns and sea level change and the beach does not, residents will lose more beach than under the natural system.

"Once you start protecting the beach you can't stop. By destroying the beach, most protective measures eventually create peril for themselves and increased danger to the development they protect....

"In order to 'save' the beach, we destroy it. When we stop erosion it is not to save the beach, but the development behind the beach..."

The book discusses efforts on all US coasts to protect ocean-facing shorefront development. It does not go into detail on the effects of structures within estuaries but in a conversation with Dr. Pilkey, he told me that the general effect on beaches would be the same but on a reduced scale.

Loss of beaches is just one of the unintended consequences of an armored shoreline. Structures eliminate or severely limit wildlife habitat by replacing natural vegetation with structural materials. Loss of sand from eroding coastal banks may result in the gradual drowning of marshes and change or diminish shellfish habitat. Reduction in marshes, especially "fringe marshes" that would normally follow a bank inland as it erodes, would be blocked from such movement by a structure.

Once the beach is gone, the land is lowered, and when that happens, the lower land can be flooded, which destroys public access along the shore and reduces hunting, fishing and other recreational opportunities. While recreation on private property is not in the public domain, the rights to fishing, fowling and navigation along Massachusetts' shores are included in the Public Trust documents, the Colonial Ordinances of the 1640s.

A property owner is trying to protect his own property with a structure, but the structure has to end somewhere and beyond the point where it ends, increased erosion on neighboring property is likely to occur. If that happens, then it is more likely that the structure will fail from water getting behind it and eroding the land anyway, so not only is there danger to adjoining property, but the threat to the original property owner is not abated.

Finally, there is the question of aesthetics and public rights. A man-made structure reduces the beauty of a natural shoreline.

The importance of coastal banks is that they keep the system in what Pilkey calls "dynamic equilibrium." The banks supply material that nourishes marshes so that they can rise above the advancing sea-level rise. The marshes trap the material and act as a buffer to dissipate the wave energy. If the toe or bottom of the bank is stabilized, by a man-made structure, for example, the sediment movement from bank to the estuary is halted. The land may be temporarily protected, but the unintended consequences begin. The true effects may not be seen for years though, long after the structure has been permitted.

In Massachusetts, the local Conservation Commission administers the Wetlands Protection Act. The towns are also empowered to adopt their own wetland bylaw and promulgate their own regulations, which can be more stringent than the state standard but cannot be less stringent. In Orleans, a town that adopted its own local bylaw, public interests in natural systems were spelled out. They included storm damage protection, flood control, fisheries, prevention of pollution, shellfish and wildlife habitat, erosion and sediment control, recreation and aesthetics. Areas subject to enforcement of the law included banks, beaches, dunes, flats, land subject to flooding or inundation by tidal action, and land within one hundred feet of any resource that was listed. (There were other interests listed and other resource areas but the ones mentioned are most germane to the discussion of erosion.) The law stipulated that anyone who wanted to undertake a project in any of the resource areas where one or more of the public interests might be affected, must apply to the Conservation Commission for approval. For erosion control structures, an applicant also had to apply to the state for approval.

State regulators favored keeping banks as natural as possible. To do that, they recommended what were known as "soft" solutions to erosion problems. "Soft" meant sand bags, vegetation planting, or placing sand in front of an eroded bank to gain an angle where the sand would stay in place so that it could be planted. If none of those methods seemed to work, they recommended moving the house further back on the land to allow the bank to continue to function naturally.

Homeowners favored "hard" solutions to erosion problems. They included revetments (sloping rock walls), bulkheads (vertical wood, cement or steel walls), seawalls (vertical walls, usually cement and shorter than bulkheads), groins (rock fingers perpendicular to the shore) or gabions (rock-filled wire-mesh cages). Gabions could be used to build a wall akin to one using staggered bricks only on a much larger scale.

The difference in approach to erosion control was a test of wills between property owners and regulators on both the town and state level. It began in Chatham after the 1987 storm.

The biggest difference between the 1800s and the 1990s was that people just moved the houses out of harm's way in earlier times, while they wanted to build rock walls later to try to hold on to what they had. Where would they move to? A hundred years ago, there was plenty of land left where a house could be re-established. In 1988 and 1989, land was at a premium and few lots remained. Since the house couldn't be moved unless there was a large lot, and the people understandably wanted to save their expensive real estate, tremendous rancor developed when property owners and regulators clashed.

Tim Wood attended numerous meetings and wrote scores of articles on the erosion situation. He saw the conflict clearly in reviewing the extreme difficulties the town faced as erosion cut into the shoreline. Property owners needed to adhere to a regulatory bureaucracy that seemed to them intent on denying them protection; while the environmental protection regulatory community needed to adhere to a regulatory structure that did not seem to allow any flexibility. Tempers flared for months. Lawsuits were filed, some eventually going all the way to the US Supreme Court. Millions who watched the national news saw Chatham's distress when cameras caught one of the houses as it fell into the harbor.

It was a very difficult time for people in Chatham, and their plight was not lost on their neighbors in other towns who followed the accounts as the events unfolded. Most outside Chatham were glad that they were not part of such an emotional maelstrom.

Then, in 1991, The Perfect Storm hit. By mid-November, just weeks after the storm, the Orleans Conservation Commission received applications from homeowners on all three bodies of water wanting to do something to their eroded bank. Most of them had heard about "emergency regulations" enacted by the state that would allow people to put sand back on the bank and revegetate with minimum review. It appeared to many that the state had softened its approach toward regulating activities on coastal banks immediately after a major storm had stripped tons of soil and vegetation from the banks. Putting sand on a bank required heavy machinery that would alter the bank landscape. All of a sudden, the Orleans Conservation Commission had to hear cases of large-scale coastal bank manipulations with little oversight.

Applications came in for hard solutions also. The Commission responded to those by insisting that "soft" solutions — such as sand bags, revegetated sand replenishment, or a late entry among the soft solutions, fiber rolls (made of tightly woven biodegradable material) — must be tried first before they would allow any "hard" structures. The Commission took the stand that the soft solutions were inherently preferable. In essence their view was that reconfiguring the banks with sand and planting grasses and shrubs was better all around than replacing banks with a rock wall. The homeowners asked, "Would a soft solution hold in another big storm?" Commissioners said they didn't know for sure, engineers said no, and the regulations said there wasn't much choice. Hard solutions were not the way to go, according to the state.

How can you get a bank revegetated when it's turned into a vertical wall? There must be some angle to it or the sediment will fall to the ground. Technically, the term is the "angle of repose," the angle at which the sand will hold and vegetation can be planted to further hold the bank in place. A bank will end up over time at its natural angle of repose, but homeowners had no desire to wait for nature to do the work. Property owners wanted it done fast. Early November was only the start of the winter storm season. They reasoned, "What if another bad storm came and took more of the bank?" More houses would be endangered and those already threatened could be put in imminent peril.

The Commission said OK to "soft" proposals and allowed residents to rebuild their banks with sand and plant them. The Commission then had to wrestle with other issues that arose like having heavy equipment on the shore in front of the banks and potentially on the fringe marshes. How could such areas be protected? The Commission settled on prohibiting machines with tank-like tracks and allowing those with big tires. Heavy equipment appeared on the beaches. Tons of sand was dumped on the banks. Acres of grass were planted. What was the best type of vegetation? The easiest was beach grass but would it do well on coastal banks? The Commission didn't know. This was all new territory.

Some of the sand washed away during the winter but a lot of it stayed. The Commission had bought some time and worked feverishly on an erosion policy to handle the number of requests for help.

The Commissioners pored over the state regulations that they were empowered and required to enforce. They held meetings with state officials to find out more about the why's of the regulations. They contacted coastal geologists to learn about the function of coastal banks and how they contribute to the overall ecology of the estuary and to learn about the physics of waves and sediment transport. They learned about the effects of engineered structures on oceanside beaches; there were a lot of examples throughout the East Coast.

Yet, in all the research that the Commission did, they still could not find any document or person to tell them what would happen to the ecology of the estuary if the coastal banks on the *inside* were armored. Commissioners also wondered what would happen to all the sand that had been placed on the banks after the October storm — if another storm came and washed it away, would it smother shellfish along the shore or add to the formation of marshes? People like Dr. Graham Giese and Dr. Dave Aubrey, both of the Woods Hole Oceanographic Institution, said that the amount of sand added to the banks would not really make a significant difference in the function of the estuary and if there were an effect, it would not be adverse.

After months of anguish on the part of Commissioners and homeowners alike, the Commission adopted a policy regarding coastal-engineered structures or CES's. A policy did not have the force of the law that a regulation did, but the Commission needed to test their policy before they adopted it in their regulations.

The Commission took the approach that there were two equally important tenets:

Coastal banks serve a vital function and are significant to the interests protected under the state Wetlands Protection Act, such as storm damage prevention and flood control, erosion and sedimentation control, fisheries, shellfish habitat, wildlife habitat, recreation and aesthetics. Hence, they should remain in their natural state for as long as possible.

Owners of endangered houses should be allowed to protect their house even if the only reasonable method is a coastal-engineered structure, but such solutions can be used only when the house is relatively close to the top of the bank.

In the policy, they reiterated the purpose of the regulations and the public interests served. It was a delicate matter. It was all well and good to cite the public values of coastal banks that are private property but within the regulatory jurisdiction of the Conservation Commission. It was another issue entirely to develop regulations defining the circumstances a house on such a bank could be protected and when no "hard" protection would be allowed.

The first issue the policy took into account was when the house was built. For older houses, the first criterion was whether the house had been built prior to August 10, 1978, the date of the adoption of an amended state wetlands act. Even then, the Commission stated that while it had the discretion to permit a structure in such cases, it was not a guarantee to the homeowner that one would be permitted.

Houses built prior to 1978 caused the most headaches. In order even to apply for a revetment (or other "hard" structure) the applicant first had to answer several questions. Was there an alternative to the plan? Could the house be moved further back from the edge of the bank? Had the owner tried a soft solution?

The Commission looked next at the distance of the house from the top of the bank. They decided that if it were less than 40 feet, it could be endangered, depending on the circumstances of the particular bank. Houses close to the top of the bank on east or northeast-facing banks were in more danger than those with exposure to other quadrants.

Commissioners decided that they were most concerned about dwellings, not raw land. Early on, they decided that protecting vacant land was not an option unless the applicant could prove that by not protecting the land, erosion endangered the buildability of the land within a reasonable foreseeable future, or endangered existing buildings on adjoining properties.

The Commission settled on a policy, later codified into regulations that took into account new construction, raw land, and houses constructed prior to 1978. For new construction, the Commission said that they would allow a house to be built within 100 feet of a coastal bank but they would not approve a hard engineered structure to protect it in the future. They said that there was not much they could do about houses built prior to the promulgation of the state law. But if a current property owner chose to build in harm's way, he or she had to realize the potential consequences of building in a vulnerable area: The Commission was not going to allow erosion-control structures down the road if the house became threatened. The public was feeling bad for people who had lost their homes due to storms, but the public was also disturbed that in many areas people were being allowed to rebuild in the same vulnerable location and that federal funds were used to help them. The Orleans Conservation Commission had taken a bold step.

For older houses, the Commission reviewed the two separate types of erosion — storm-induced and the regular lunar-cycle tides affecting Pleasant Bay shores. They decided on two ways for an applicant to prove that a house was in jeopardy, and also decided on the cut-off for protection. If an applicant could show either that a dwelling was 40 feet or closer from the top of the bank, or if he or she could prove that within 20 years, based on the annual erosion rates, the house would be jeopardized, the Commission would listen to the proposal. If the house did not meet either of those criteria, the Commission would summarily deny the application.

The guidelines were complex but seemed to make sense for a complex situation. The Commissioners felt they had addressed the bulk of the issues brought to their attention. The policy allowed for the banks to continue to function naturally as long as possible to protect public interests under the law, yet it allowed homeowners to get some measure of protection if their house was truly endangered.

Unfortunately, even the policy was adopted a bit late. Many of the homeowners who had put sand on their banks and planted them with grasses watched in horror as another big storm hit in December 1992, just over 13 months after the Perfect Storm. Before the grass or other vegetation could get re-established, whammo! Another doozy of a storm hammered the Cape.

The Perfect Storm had been classified as a 100-year storm locally, meaning the chances were not great that another storm of the same magnitude would hit within 100 years. And yet, another mighty storm did hit, although when fully analyzed, experts countered that the December 1992 storm was merely a 75-year event. To those whose property was endangered, it did not matter how someone classified the storm. All they knew was that all the sand, grass and money disappeared from the banks and just washed away. The homeowners were understandably upset that they had spent thousands of dollars just to see it disappear the very next year. There was such fear voiced by residents of vulnerable areas that the pressure on the Commission to allow substantial structures was enormous.

The first major project to come before the Commission included four separate property owners on a stretch of shoreline in Nauset Harbor. One of the four houses was built earlier than 1978 and was the closest to the top of the bank, much less than 40 feet. The other houses were well back from the top of the bank, as much as 75 feet away and all were newer houses. The engineer suggested that if a structure were constructed only for the endangered house, the erosion on the adjacent properties would be accelerated. He prepared a plan that showed natural places where the land undulated somewhat and he proposed armoring the most seaward crenulation.

After months of hearings, plan revisions, getting to understand the new terminology, discussions with other professionals and soul searching on the part of the Commission, the plan was approved. The tide gate had been opened and a flood of applications for relief descended on the Commission.

Applicants quickly learned that if they banded together as neighbors, larger projects could be approved where an individual project might not. Each individual project required a "return," which was actually a curve in the structure set into the bank to deflect the waves inland and to prevent water from making an "end run" around the structure and eating away at the bank from behind the wall. But a return also caused accelerated erosion on neighboring properties. The Commission tried to protect neighbors and so required that a return be placed on an applicant's property, many feet from the lot line, so any adverse effect would be mostly on the applicant's property, and not his neighbor's. As applicants banded together, larger and longer walls could be built until the land itself curved so that waves could be deflected naturally.

But the Commission wondered where the end of all the new walls would be. Would the whole town or at least the most vulnerable areas eventually be walled in? Would the town lose all the fringe marshes that would not be able to migrate landward over time? Would these massive walls affect beaches a half mile or more away from the project because the beaches would be starved of sand? Would shellfish be impacted because of a loss of sediment from the banks? In a court case, the burden of proof was on the applicant. Could the applicant prove that their project was not going to cause adverse impacts? Could the Commission show that it would?

Local engineers became inundated by clients scared that they would lose their property, and the engineers developed lots of plans

for shoreline protection to bring before the Commission. Engineers researched new methods of protection (such as the fiber rolls), recognizing the regulatory framework that had been established by the Commission yet trying to give their clients the best protection possible.

Early projects sometimes placed the return too close to the lot line and erosion on neighboring properties did take place. In other cases, neighbors tried to get in on the action of protection when their property clearly did not require massive rock walls. The rock walls became a symbol of security for nervous waterfront property owners who were living in houses that were worth an enormous amount of money.

Applications came in for all bodies of water but primarily from Nauset Harbor and Pleasant Bay. The Commission watched in a state of resigned apprehension as what they had approved was built. Rock walls appeared on shorelines all over town. Few applicants would even consider "soft" solutions after they had watched their sand wash away. For most, it was rock, solid rock that they wanted.

The Commission rarely talked to the homeowners themselves; Commissioners were almost always dealing just with the engineers for the project. The Commission relayed messages to the engineer to bring back to the clients but from the responses the Commission never knew if the clients actually received the message or just refused to listen. The engineers might come back with minor modifications but usually not a change in overall structure or materials.

The term "structure" came into question in a different way as well. Could a boathouse be saved even if the main house was well beyond the reach of the waves? The Commission said yes in three cases. (In Chatham, the Commission said yes to a golf course where a green was endangered.)

By the time the policy had been adopted as a regulation in Orleans, over a mile and a half of shoreline had been stabilized by one method or another, essentially walled in against the onslaught of the waves in a storm. These structures gave the owners peace of mind but they also carried the potential to destroy the future shoreline for other public interests in the process.

As time went on, people who could not utilize "hard" protection tried other methods. Gabions were described as a "soft" solution primarily because it was thought that they could be covered with sand and revegetated. In some cases, gabions worked out well. They were viewed as being a compromise between rock revetments and sandbags and were thought to be less visually intrusive than revetments. If installed correctly, they seemed to do their job, but no one was about to suggest how long it would be before the wire broke down, the gabion fell apart, and the rocks alone wound up on the shore. Fiber rolls were used as a biodegradable option in several cases. They were said to last about 20 years and grasses could be planted in the rolls themselves.

In many instances, the Commission required that whatever erosion-control solution was used, it had to be covered with sand and planted, to at least try to preserve the visual appearance. But rock revetments in very high-energy areas just couldn't be covered easily. Most of those were impacted by each and every storm. Those that were not affected by each storm could be covered with sand and vegetation, but when that was the case, the applicant probably didn't need a rock wall in the first place.

Given time, nature heals itself. We tried to impress on nervous homeowners that they were reacting to a set of circumstances that was highly unusual and that the likelihood of damage to houses that were between 20 and 40 feet from the top of the bank or further probably was not great. We said that given time and some help in the form of planting, the banks would revegetate naturally and would continue to provide some protection. They didn't buy it. They had seen grasses, shrubs and trees ripped out, gone from view or strewn on the shore below. Vegetation was a colossal waste of time, effort and money in their eyes.

And yet, in my travels around the bay a decade later, some of the banks have indeed healed. Others appear to be naturally healed, although in reality they had been manipulated earlier with a structure and then covered with sand and planted. They look healthy and natural, and at least as important for the owners, a sturdy structure is underneath to protect them should another nasty storm hit the area.

Some people the Commission dealt with just would not take "no" for an answer. They applied for relief, had the application denied, reapplied, hired professionals, added more professionals, withstood the cost of hearing after hearing after hearing, expert after expert, minor revision after minor revision, wearing the Commission down or hoping the annual turnover of members would be in their favor. Several such individuals immediately come to mind and in no case was the house endangered according to the criteria established by the Commission. All houses were located way beyond the 40-foot criterion. All these individuals fought so that they would not lose even one foot of their property. None cared about the public's rights. All they cared about was their property. Finally they heard the word they had been waiting for. Approved. All now have structures at the toe of their banks, and all gave hope to other single-minded people with enough money to challenge the Commission.

Another couple living on the bay had been just plain scared, but their house was too far back from the top of the bank for them to be afforded any protection. Their neighbors' houses were far back too, so they couldn't join together as had been done in the earlier Nauset Harbor case. The couple and their neighbors all lost land in the storms but their houses have never been endangered. The couple said at the time that they were going to move but as things calmed down and several seasons produced no new horrendous storms, they must've reconsidered — they are still there, overlooking Pleasant Bay from the top of a high bank.

Route 28, the state highway that connects all the towns along Pleasant Bay, and provides panoramic scenic vistas of the Bay, is itself endangered. At one location, there is less than 10 feet between the roadway and the bank that is undermined. Prior to 1998, when I retired from the town, I fully expected state officials to come in with a plan for a revetment to save the highway. They did not. They still have not. My bet is they are working on crisis management rather than planning. It is a state highway after all, and when a storm hits and the road goes, then they'll come in for emergency action.

As I traveled around Big Bay 15 years after the Chatham break, I thought about its consequences and the changes that occurred as a result of the storms that followed. I knew Chatham had not adopted a policy or set of regulations similar to those in Orleans but I hadn't been following the revetment issue in Chatham when we were so swamped ourselves. I went down to the break and saw the massive rock walls of the properties fronting the harbor. I saw rock walls wherever a property faced the northeast all over the bay. The state had approved rock walls but only after houses were lost.

At high tide, I saw water on the rocks leaving no place to walk along the shore and around the walls except in the water. The public had lost some of its rights granted in the 17th century public trust doctrine. In Big Bay, small public beaches remain in all three towns. It seems the Orleans beach is shrinking, being replaced by cobble. Could this beach be showing what may happen when banks are "stabilized" with coastal-engineered structures? Could those structures be stopping normal sediment transport and starving this beach of sand? Are the private property owners in the area negatively impacting a public beach?

The beach in Chatham, on the other hand, seems to be increasing in size. Where is that sand coming from since there is so little of the shoreline remaining in Big Bay that does not have a rock wall? How long will it take before we can see the full ramifications of the actions taken during the last decade of the 20th century?

All of us involved in the battle of the banks learned a lot. We learned the technical jargon and the physics of waves. We learned that a plan shown two-dimensionally on a piece of paper might look quite different from the three-dimensional construction on the ground. We learned that engineers are not infallible. We learned that the estuary is actually quite forgiving. We learned that heavy machinery with oversize tires rather than tracks can still tear up a foreshore area during construction in winter, but if the machine operators leave the area in relatively decent shape before they depart, the vegetation will come back the following spring.

We learned that regardless of how impregnable the structure appeared to the homeowner and the engineer, all the work approved by the Commission will eventually fail and the water will go over, around or through the wall and use its force to tear the structure apart someday.

We learned that it is one thing to watch the power of the waves tear at a bank, leaving them denuded and vulnerable to collapse, and know that in time, they will become green again, looking as if nothing so intense had ever happened. It is quite another to own the land that has just been washed away and realize that each time that fury happens, less and less land survives, the dwelling gets closer and closer to destruction, and the land itself becomes a liability rather than a fantastically valuable asset.

Finally, we learned that it is difficult enough being a paid Conservation Administrator, presenting the Commission the information they need to make informed but likely unpopular decisions. It is excruciatingly difficult to be an unpaid volunteer who has to make the decision of whether a fellow citizen's property is less important than the beaches down the way or the marshes at the base of the bank.

All one has to do is stand on the bluff over Nauset Spit or at the Coast Guard Station in Chatham after a storm, or after several storms over a couple of years, to see the enormity of the changes that can take place over an incredibly short time. The Spit is moving west by hundreds of feet a decade. Stakes placed on the cove side one year, mark the high tide of the ocean side several years later. The beach now abuts the bank. As the beach continues to move west, it will eventually get thinner and thinner until the waves of the Atlantic crash against the bank itself.

For those not accustomed to seeing geologic changes take place in human lifetimes, the changes are awesome to witness. Cape Cod is disappearing right before our eyes. Deciding what we do in the face of the inevitable is the anguish that faces all of us. Stormwatch, as I like to call it, overlooking the fierce Atlantic Ocean in a winter storm that approaches hurricane strength, gives one a particularly good sense of the fragility of this sandbar we call Cape Cod.

In the end, the ocean will win. All any of us did was buy time.

Chapter 26

Succulent Morsels

I spend a lot of time in Little Bay and I've gotten to know well the intricate shoreline and some of the subtleties of the waters of that part of the larger bay. When I look at Little Bay, I see it as an estuary in all that that means — the interconnectedness of the salt water and fresh water creeks and ponds of the estuary, the plants and animals that dwell there, and all the watershed land around it that defines the nature of an estuary. But I have to admit, one of the animals that sometimes appears in the bay holds a particular charm above almost everything else — the bay scallop. With its beautiful, fluted, multi-hued shell and rim of blue eyes, and its exquisitely flavored adductor muscle that keeps the two halves of the shell together, this animal is the gold prize.

There is nothing quite like opening day of scallop season when bay scallops are abundant. November 1, 1983 was such a day. November weather can be tricky — relatively warm and sunny or gray cold and blustery or cold sunny and howling. I don't recall the weather that day but I remember vividly how my spirits were soaring. Since the previous summer, we had known that it was going to be a terrific year. Yet even the Shellfish Department did not know that while it would be the best year ever in the recorded history of scallop landings for Pleasant Bay, it would also be the last good harvest for nearly two decades — and counting.

Bay scallops seem to cause an irrational emotional reaction in people. They get worked up almost to a frenzy anticipating the scallop season, especially if there is a hint that there may a good year ahead. Locally it's called "scallop fever," and the condition afflicts countless people throughout the community. "The 'getting ready,' the anticipation, is as much fun as the activity itself" according to Cape Codder Dana Eldridge in his book *Once Upon Cape Cod*.

"In the planning, every scallop day is warm and windless, every weed bed is loaded with scallops, every drag comes in full. The fact that each year reality is considerably different does not dull the anticipation one whit....

"The drag is always heavy to haul in. It is cold work sorting out the shack, and if only two dozen scallops are garnered, it is hardly worth the effort. Scalloping is back-breaking work, but somehow it is fun, although I've never been quite able to figure out why. It's wet, it's cold, it's monotonous and it's expensive.... Why then, with all these negatives, does anyone look forward to scallop season? But we all do, and when next the scallops 'strike' in, my drag will be ready, the culling board freshly caulked. I'll be looking for someone to help pull in the drag and share the wet, cold joys of opening day. I can't explain the attraction, but it's there."

Bay scallops historically have exhibited a yo-yo syndrome in abundance — good one year and very poor for the next several years, and then an inexplicable peak in numbers. A good scalloping year gives an economic jolt to the fishing community that allows it to stay afloat during a time of the year, winter, when money is usually scarce. Everyone in town benefits from a good scallop season because there is a ripple effect from the fishermen to the people they hire to open (or shuck) the scallops, to the markets and restaurants and the businesses that supply them gear, and then all the way to the people they pay for past bills.

If a year looks promising, more commercial licenses are sold, and if the year turns out to be good, people who have a commercial license but also hold down another job will take vacation time in November to go scalloping and earn the extra money. Wives help their husbands and buy a commercial license too to double the family income. After a very good year, new trucks appear around town. Good scallop years are good for everybody. Everybody hopes for a good year.

Just as the quahaugs in Big Bay were recognizable in the markets as coming from Pleasant Bay, so too the scallops from Little Bay could often be identified because the shells were often quite large, as were the "meats" or the edible muscle that holds the two shells together and is the only part of the scallop that is eaten.

Scallops, like many bivalves, attach themselves to something else at least in the early portion of their lives. The mechanism for attachment for many species is a byssal thread, a strong and resilient strand of material that has a type of glue on the trailing end. The most obvious user of byssal threads is the blue mussel, which attaches to rocks, pebbles, sand and other mussels or abandoned shells and, once attached, can withstand the incredible force of waves and currents. Less obvious is the soft-shell clam that attaches to sand grains when the clam is very small (about one-quarter of an inch) but detaches soon thereafter.

The scallop attaches to blades of eelgrass or other plants, but eelgrass seems to be preferred. Attachment to the eelgrass appears to provide refuge from marauding crabs and other predators and the scallops remain attached until they are about one-inch-wide across the shell, at which point they detach. They remain on the bottom surface thereafter. When scallops were in the Bay, part of the reason was the vast eelgrass meadows in the shallow waters of Little Bay.

Bay scallops have a very short life cycle, only two years. State law mandates that they must have gone through a spawning cycle before they can be harvested, and because of a natural phenomenon, it is relatively simple to tell if they have spawned.

Scallops grow from May through December, at which time they go into a "dormant" state. When the water temperature rises in the spring and they begin to feed again, the new growth on their shell becomes a raised ridge that may be further marked by a definite color change as well. Known as a raised growth ring, it is the visual demarcation necessary for legal harvest. Any scallop that does not have a raised ridge is called a "seed" scallop because a seed scallop has not gone through its spawning cycle.

Generally, scallops spawn naturally in June or July but they can spawn as early as May and as late as late-September. When they spawn early or late, the enforcement of the raised ring law may be difficult because the shells may appear somewhat odd.

If scallops set early, in the first weeks of May, for example, they have a long time to grow before they go dormant for the winter and their shells can be quite large, but there is no raised growth ring present as required by law. At various times in Orleans history, fishermen have harvested these large scallops believing that they were "large enough" to harvest and that they would probably die before they could be harvested the next year.

On the other end of the spawning season, scallops that set in September or even early October have had difficult environmental conditions to deal with. Scallops, like other bivalves, spend up to two weeks floating with the currents as plankton, and by September, the water temperature is dropping steadily. Scallops don't feed in the winter and late-season scallops are still very small by the time the water temperature has dropped enough so that they won't feed. A second issue is that eelgrass dies off in the winter. By the time late-season scallops get through metamorphosis and need to attach to eelgrass, eelgrass is dying off naturally, floating on the bay until washed ashore in vast rafts. Many scallops end up on the shore too, and die.

However, if late-recruit scallops manage to live through the winter, they put on incredible growth during the summer. A raised growth ring first appears on the shell in the spring when they start to feed but the size of the ring is tiny, often less than the size of a pinky-fingernail. During the summer, they begin to get sexually mature, but only about fifty percent of them spawn during the summer.

If these unusual scallops live through another winter, they put on a second growth ring, when they begin to feed in the spring. They also put tremendous energy into the spawning process and have mammoth gonads to show for it. Set in late summer or early fall, they spawn in the summer, but unlike scallops born in the spring or early summer, the late-bloomers usually die after spawning, and are unlikely to live until November when the season opens.

This sequence is important for shellfish management. The appearance of a raised annual growth ring was the only criterion for harvesting. In one year, we saw both cases in Pleasant Bay — large scallops with no visible ring, and scallops that had a ring that was barely visible.

But in both situations, fishermen believed the scallops should be taken, thinking they would not live for another whole year and be there for harvest. Everybody involved in the fishery knew that anything could happen in a year — too much rain, too little rain, ice, too warm a summer, too cool a summer, too many predators or anything else any of them could think of to justify harvesting. It's better to get them now, they said — a bird in the hand sort of thing.

In the fall of 1979, the bay was full of large seed scallops. The season opened on November 1, as was the custom at the time. (State law says the season can open as early as October 1 but the quality of the meat is higher if the scallops are left in the water for that additional month.) In the harvest from early November, we were seeing large seed scallops with no annual growth ring mixed in with bona fide adults with a well-defined ring. When we, as shellfish officers, told fishermen that they could not harvest the large seed, they countered that they would not live a whole year if they weren't taken then. They said they wanted "proof" that they were seed if we were going to insist that they couldn't be taken. They requested a meeting with the selectmen and biologists from the Division of Marine Fisheries.

The Shellfish Advisory Committee agreed and called a meeting. The meeting began with the Shellfish Department identifying the problem. We estimated that the population of the bay consisted of about ninety percent scallops with no growth ring, nine percent of scallops with a ring at the hinge, and one percent bona fide adults with the raised ring.

Seed   *Adult*   *Ring-at-hinge*

The DMF biologists said they had seen this phenomenon before — large scallops that did not exhibit a growth ring — and they said that they believed the scallops were, in fact, seed. They said that not only had they seen it themselves, but Belding, who had written classic monographs of the life history of scallops, quahaugs, clams and oysters for the Commonwealth in the early 1900s, had also reported large seed. Belding had used Chatham as an example. The state biologists added that the only way to find out for sure was to hold them or recapture them during the spawning season and track their gonadal development microscopically.

The fishermen anticipated what was coming and suggested that the largest scallops would not make it through the winter to spawn the following summer and should therefore be harvested even if they were not adults. They suggested a size limit as a way of control and said that there were enough small ones that could be left in the bay to spawn.

The DMF could not sanction that suggestion of a size limit. It was illegal to do so because such a change would have to come from the State Legislature. And so the selectmen, upon recommendation by the Shellfish Department, chose to close the bay to scalloping in January, 1980 with the caveat that the Shellfish Department conduct a study to determine the life history of these scallops and their viability for later harvest. The fishermen wanted us hanged.

But if lynching wasn't an option, the fishermen were determined that this one study answer a lot of questions, a boatload of questions in fact.

There were a lot of scallops in the bay and the fishermen were looking at a huge loss of income in the winter when cash flow was otherwise slim. If they couldn't get them in the winter of 1980, they wanted to be damn sure they could get them in the fall of 1980 and winter of 1981, so the study had better answer more than just the question of the age and sexual maturity of the scallops. They wanted to know if they would survive the winter, spawn in the summer of 1980, and survive to be harvested in the fall. If they didn't live, they wanted to know why, and if the answer was predation, they wanted to know what the predators were.

Pleasant Bay is mostly shallow (except for much of Big Bay) but there are some deep pockets, "deep" meaning eight-to-twelve feet.

The fishermen wanted to know if there was a difference between the shallow and deep water as far as scallop survival was concerned.

They had seen a few scallops with a ring at the hinge and wondered how they fit into the scheme of things, both with survival and spawning.

Aside from the spawning issue, the fishermen wondered if there was any difference in size of the adductor muscle between the large seed (if they were seed, of course) and the adults. The bigger the muscle, the fewer scallop meats needed to make a pound and the more money to be made.

Finally, if the fishermen were right and the seed scallops didn't live to be harvested, was there any way to establish a size limit if this happened again so that they could get some benefit from the large seed?

That was a lot to find out about in a one-year study, but we knew that we had to make an attempt to answer all their questions. The DMF agreed to work with the town to help answer the questions, but they couldn't devote much of their resources for this project. The state would help track scallops in the deep water, but most of the responsibility would rest with the town. The town hired Northeastern University's Marine Sciences Institute to conduct the histological (microscopic) analysis. The rest was up to me.

We began collecting samples in January. Since the bay was frozen in February, preventing us from getting samples, we resumed sampling in March and continued until the following November. After June, we never saw scallops we had originally classified as adults. Apparently they had died naturally.

The samples from April and May were enlightening. There had been no change in either the size or appearance of the gonads between March and April — the sac was covered with a thin black coating that could be rubbed off — but in May, the sex organs changed dramatically. Scallops are hermaphroditic, which means each individual can produce both eggs and sperm. When they matured in May, the gonads enlarged, the black covering disappeared, the sperm sac turned a beige color and the ovary changed to bright orange. When they finished spawning, the gonads decreased in size and turned to a uniform beige color.

Also in May, new shell growth began to form the raised ridge, and the adductor muscle decreased in size. That made sense to us because the muscle is made mostly of glycogen, a sugar, which translates to energy. The scallops needed the energy for spawning and transferred the glycogen from the muscle to the gonad. We continued to weigh the muscle and measure shells for the remainder of the study.

In December 1980, just after the season opened again, we submitted our report. We had been able to answer all the questions to some degree. First and foremost, the scallops we had seen the previous fall, the large scallops with no growth ring, were, indeed, seed scallops. They had lived through the winter, spawned during the summer and were in the bay ready to harvest as adults. We found that they had spawned from May through September, an unexpected but welcome finding, since we thought they would only spawn in June, July or August. A longer spawning season meant the possibility of more scallops surviving to be harvested. They added a raised annual growth ring in May.

The survival rate was 70-80 percent overall. As we suspected, survival in deep water was higher than in the shallows where there was heavy predation from gulls, crabs and drills.

The decision to wait until November 1 for opening day in Pleasant Bay was a good one because the meats are definitely bigger in November than October. The scallop had transferred energy back to the muscle from the gonad after spawning and an unscientific taste test revealed that the scallops in November were sweeter than those of October — more glycogen in the muscle. And we also found that adult scallop meats were much larger than those of the seed scallops we had found the previous fall and winter.

We found that if a size limit of two and three-quarters of an inch were adopted, as suggested by the fishermen, 66 percent of the seed population would have been harvested prior to spawning. With the natural mortality rates factored in, there was no way to tell if the seed left —roughly one quarter of the original seed — would have been enough to repopulate the bay. We concluded that for natural reproduction and recruitment to the fishery, the state law should not be amended.

Prior to 1980, the highest recorded scallop harvest from Pleasant Bay had been 3,600 bushels, in 1977, a harvest that was followed by two very poor seasons. Then came the fall of 1979 when the large seed were observed.

Because the majority of the scallops found in January 1980 survived until November when the season opened, 1980 produced a record catch of 4,522 bushels with a wholesale value of $188,880. More importantly, we felt the moratorium on seed harvesting let them spawn, resulting in high harvests in 1981 and 1982 of 3,520 bushels and 4,235 bushels respectively.

But in 1983, the Bay produced a virtual bonanza. A whopping 37,500 bushels were harvested at a value of *$1,550,000*. This was, by far, the largest amount of scallops ever taken from Pleasant Bay. There were so many scallops that getting a daily limit took only a couple of hours rather than most of the day, which had normally been the case. Fishermen were quick to point out that in addition to the seed-harvesting moratorium, their transplanting about 200 bushels of seed scallops in 1981 from the Town Cove to Pleasant Bay was a likely factor, contributing to the parent stock in the Bay. Regardless of how it happened, everywhere you looked that winter, people were happy — everyone was making money for a change. By season's end, new pick-up trucks could be spotted all around town, thanks to the previous winter's windfall.

Ironically, with the tremendous number of adults in the bay in 1983, there were remarkably few seed and in fact, there has not been a "good" crop of scallops (generally considered greater than 2,500 bushels) since that time. The town has seeded the bay with hatchery stock since 1987 to no avail. But Orleans is not alone.

In 1999, Barnstable County Cooperative Extension and the Southeast Massachusetts Aquaculture Center hired me — by then an independent consultant — to execute a study to determine the health of the scallop industry. At some point in the mid-1980s, from 1983-1987, all towns in Southeast Massachusetts reported severely depressed scallop landings, even such towns as Nantucket and Edgartown that had been the standard-bearers for the industry. To date, there is no broad explanation for the decline over such a wide geographic area but there are a lot of suspected causes.

One suspicion for the dearth of scallops was a bloom of a very small planktonic species, *Aureococcus anaphagefferens*, commonly known as the "Brown Tide," that has severely affected scallop harvests in Peconic Bay, Long Island, NY. This microscopic plankton species is tiny even for plankton and it may actually clog the scallop's gills so that the animal starves.

Another factor may be the introduction of MBTE, an alternative to lead, as a gasoline additive, spewed directly from outboard motors and washed off roadways into the estuaries. Fertilizers, pesticides and nutrient loading from the increased shoreline development were also suspected causes for the decline. Whatever it was, it again reminded us of how fragile these animals are and how susceptible they are to environmental changes.

My study showed that without town aquaculture programs — where seed either was collected in spat collectors or planted from hatchery-reared seed — the scallop picture remained dismal throughout the region. One thing was clear: You need adults to have babies to have more adults ... and without the parent stock, the population will crumble.

The County and the Aquaculture Center took the project a step further and began a scallop restoration program for Cape communities. They purchased seed, put them in plastic mesh bags for the winter and then planted them in the towns the following fall. Concurrently, they developed scallop spat collectors which they deployed near the seed to attract natural seed production through gregarious setting. Spat collectors are mesh bags filled with netting to act like eelgrass for baby scallops looking for something to attach to. In areas were there isn't any eelgrass, spat collectors have been pretty successful in "catching a set" of scallops. The two agencies are currently monitoring the entire project and are considering adding eelgrass restoration as well in areas where eelgrass has diminished.

Fishermen, residents and shellfish officers of the Pleasant Bay region have been greatly disappointed that the breakthrough in Chatham in 1987 has not increased scallop productivity in the bay as we all had hoped. The eelgrass cleaned up as a result of better water quality, and seed was planted in the bay, but nothing seemed to work. There has not been a good scallop crop since the bonanza of 1983.

There have been some years with significant numbers of late-spawned individuals present in the bay, but they have been harvested.

It may be just a ring-at-the-hinge, but they do have a ring. I still think such scallops should be left for parent stock, but when they are the only scallops available, and they won't live to be harvested the next year, it's difficult to convince fishermen that they should remain just for spawning stock. But then again, you have to have adults to have babies to have adults.

There is still hope that someday scallops will return to the bay. It would be nice to have the yo-yo return and move upward for a change — it has been "walking the dog" for a very long time and it's time to start a new trick. Unlocking the secrets of scallops in order to produce abundant and consistent crops would help the community maintain its economic ties to the water and to the shellfish that live within the bay.

I look forward to another November 1 when I can go to a vantage point overlooking the bay at dawn and see dozens of boats dragging for the succulent morsels. And when the season is over, I like to see the new trucks.

Chapter 27

Gunning Camps to Mansions

The Bay is home for many sailing craft, but is especially renowned for catboats, those graceful, shallow-draft, beamy boats that were born to glide across the Cape's shallow waters.

What a magnificent sight to see an array of gaff-rigged cats plying the Bay waters in the annual catboat regatta organized by Tony Davis, a man who purchased a boat yard in Arey's Pond a few years ago because he wanted to build boats and he wanted to honor the sailing tradition of this particular bay. The regatta ensures that at least once a year I get a vivid flashback memory of the races that were held when the summer sailing camps were still camps.

Although kids continue learning to sail on the Bay, and Namequoit Sailing Association still teaches sailing and holds races, it's not the same as when the camps were in business. The camps almost defined the Bay for the decades they were in operation. The daily sailing and the races were a glorious sight in the summer. Sailing is still popular, and there are many lovely boats out there, but motor boats seem to have outpaced the more serene and gentler craft by quite a bit.

I see the houses on the sloping upland where the summer sailing camps, Quanset and Pleasant Bay, used to be and I remember the sadness when the town learned that the camps would close their doors and the hillside would be developed, as an upscale residential subdivision named East Egg.

The loss of the camps and their fleets, replaced by developments and motors, says a lot about the changing nature of the land around the Bay.

The elbow of Cape Cod was beginning to be defined by its real estate value, not by its natural resources, although without the natural resources, there would be no booming real estate market. Subdivision names tell the story. East Egg, Namequoit Estates, Quanset Harbor Club, Snow Point Association — these and many other Estates and Associations all engendered a sense of exclusivity. The very words helped drive up the price of the lots. At least the developers, real estate brokers and homeowners wanting to sell sure hoped so. However it went, prices began rising fast and haven't stopped rising since.

It was a wrenching change, and relative to the Cape's previous 350 years of history as a hardscrabble-poor place where cash money was hard to come by, it was also a sudden change.

Pleasant Bay had always had some substantial houses; families that have lived along its shores for generations always had nice properties. But the beautiful "mansions" of the sailing captains and wealthier merchants were located near the town center, not on the water. The last thing a blue-water captain wanted was to have his house endangered by the sea, whose force he knew better than anyone.

The shoreline, well into the 20th century, was reserved for sea shanties, buildings to hold gear needed for fishing; for boathouses, buildings to keep boats safe when they were hauled for repairs or for the season; and for gunning camps. The gunning camps were small, rustic buildings that dotted the shore and housed people who came to the Cape to go waterfowling, one of the public rights on Massachusetts waterways that has endured since first stated in the Colonial Ordinances of the 1640s.

Somewhere along the line, probably as the tourist industry "took off" in the early 1950s, waterfront property became a huge drawing card. The shanties disappeared. The gunning camps were made into cottages or traditional "Capes," houses with four or five rooms downstairs and a finished second-floor with a dormer. A few boathouses remained, but not many.

Next the cottages and the traditional Capes began disappearing, being torn down so much bigger houses could be built, including a few monuments to wealth that can only be called "trophy houses," the new term for mansions.

Two of the biggest changes in the Bay as a whole have been, first, actual development of the waterfront for year-round residential use, and then the increased scale of the newer waterfront and water-view houses, many now commanding prices of $1 million or more.

Most homes constructed along the Bay during this period, or along any of the waterways in the state, fell under the jurisdiction of the local Conservation Commissions because of wetland protection laws passed in the 1970s. No longer could people do whatever they wanted on their land. Each commission's purview extended 100 feet inland from the edge of any resource area defined by law. Many of the homes built between 1970 and 2000 fell into this category, and the sheer volume inundated and overwhelmed the local commissions. Human nature being what it is, most owners wanted their house as close as possible to the water, and they wanted a totally clear view of the water from every vantage point in the house. Both desires were in conflict with environmental protection.

Hailed by many as one of the nation's most comprehensive environmental protection laws, the Massachusetts Wetlands Protection Act, originally passed in 1973, goes a long way in protecting wetlands from direct, immediate effects of development. The law defined wetland resources exhaustively, and included marsh, pond, coastal bank, beach, dune, creek or any other similar area. The law also stated that the land adjacent to the wetlands, called "buffer zones," were important in order for the wetlands to function properly.

The authors of the law and its regulations set the boundary of a buffer zone 100 feet from the edge of the wetland resource and required that any work proposed to take place within that zone, must be permitted by the local Conservation Commission. That means that since 1973, any owner planning a new house, an addition or renovation to an existing dwelling, or any other project, including tree removal and "vista pruning," that is slated to take place within 100 feet of a resource area, has been required to come before the local commission to obtain an "Order of Conditions."

The Order specifies what the owner can and cannot do within that zone.

By the time I became the Conservation Administrator in 1990 — the salaried technical adviser and information gatherer for the volunteer Orleans Conservation Commission — it had become obvious to many that the state law was not strict enough to protect buffer zones. The law was good on wetlands, but there were no "performance standards" specified for the buffer zones as there were for the defined resource areas themselves. Yes, the law noted that the buffer zone was important, but there was nothing in the language that said what was allowed and what was not allowed within that zone. The only way for a town to improve the environmental situation was to have a local bylaw and regulations that were better defined and more strict than the state's — a course that the state left open to the municipalities.

Why wasn't the law strict enough? Why did the act stop short of setting requirements for the important buffer zones? Was it the vigor of New England's traditional deference to individual property rights? The political clout of the state's "home rule" tradition? (For centuries "home rule" has meant that individual Massachusetts towns have the power to make many significant policy decisions, power that most areas of the nation expect to see exercised only at the county level of government or above.) Was it pressure from the real estate, building and banking lobbies? Or the tendency for the General Court, the Massachusetts term for state legislature, to seek common ground on contentious issues by adopting a plan that outrages the smallest number of people — in a word, politics?

All of the above likely played a part. The upshot was there was no legislative or regulatory mandate. The issue of the types of projects that could be approved or denied in the buffer zones was left open to interpretation by each local Conservation Commission.

The way the system works is as follows. Someone applies to the commission for a project. If it approves, the commission issues an Order of Conditions, a legal document that specifies how the project is to proceed. If the commission denies the applicant's request, the commission issues an Order of Conditions that states the reason(s) for the denial. If the applicant doesn't like that outcome, he or she can appeal to the state Department of Environmental Protection. DEP can issue a Superseding Order of Conditions approving the project under certain conditions, or it can uphold the town and deny the project. If denied at this level and still willing to do battle, the applicant can take the case to the courts.

Towns don't like litigation as a route to solve problems, and all the Orleans committees were reminded regularly to do what was necessary to avoid expensive court battles. So, at the Conservation Commission, if an applicant wanted to build a structure within the buffer zone, even as close as 10 feet from the edge of a wetland, the commissioners knew they would be running the risk of litigation if they denied the application. If the commission denied the application anyway, on the ground that the structure would impair the function of the wetland, the owner could appeal to the state and go on to the courts. Many would likely win eventually because of the state law's lack of performance standards for the buffer zone.

In practice, it rarely went that far. Either the town or the state would realize that there was little choice except to approve because the wetland itself was not being damaged and it was difficult to prove that an individual project in the buffer zone would adversely affect the wetland. In the law, the burden of proof was on the applicant to show that a project would cause no damage to the wetland. But in practice, when a project went to the appeals process, the local commission had to prove that the project would cause damage.

Local commissions were not getting many applications for work in the wetlands themselves; they were getting buried by applications for work in the buffer zones, adjacent to the wetlands. The buffer zone was where all the action was taking place, especially in areas with intense development pressures such as Cape Cod. Finally some towns, including Orleans, decided to try to plug the regulatory hole by adopting local wetland protection bylaws, more stringent than the state's, with sections inserted that regulated buffer zones.

Most towns that took this route created a minimum setback distance for new construction at somewhere between 25 and 50 feet from the edge of the wetland. Although the commissions had jurisdiction up to 100 feet from the edge, they did not extend the minimum setback for the entire distance for fear that such a bylaw just couldn't be passed at Town Meeting. Any setback regulation would increase the amount of land that would become "unbuildable," and the greater the setback, the greater the presumed loss in real estate property values that would follow for many townspeople. Commissions statewide felt that 100 feet would be political suicide.

In Orleans, the commission agonized over the buffer zone issue. A large percentage of existing homes near wetlands were about 50 feet from the edge, but many were closer than that. The Cape Cod Commission could not dictate to the towns, but it recommended the full 100 feet be established for new houses. However the local commission recognized the political backlash that would follow if it suddenly made more than a few lots completely unbuildable because of the setback distance. The commission finally compromised and established a 50-foot buffer zone. It established guidelines for work within the 50-foot mark that essentially allowed only vegetative work — tree removal and pruning. But for new construction, including septic systems, there was a minimum 50-foot setback.

With the adoption of new regulations in 1995, consulting engineers and lawyers entered the picture in a big way. These professionals were hired to secure as many of their clients' wishes as they could. We dealt mainly with them — not with the owners themselves. If we were lucky, an applicant would do some of their own homework and stop into the office to ask some questions. At that point, we were able to explain why the regulations were necessary and to explain a bit about the ecology of the area where they wanted to build.

Face-to-face discussions with applicants were very fruitful. If they wanted something in particular, we could tell them why it might not be appropriate for the area. If there was a coastal bank issue, for example, we could tell them about storms and erosion and why, in the long run, it was in their best interest to locate further from the edge of the bank. If it was a vista issue, we could suggest that they cut a few trees, not an entire swath, and live with it for a while, maybe noticing the shade in summer, or the value of a windblock in winter, or the aesthetics of a water scene framed by native trees and shrubs. Attitudes about projects sometimes changed as a result of these conversations.

But if applicants stood back and let their hired representatives handle the whole project, we never got to talk to them. The educational opportunity was lost and the commission found that its suggestions were a much more difficult "sell." Often the applicants would dig in their heels and go through the entire legal system to get what they wanted without ever talking directly to us, their fellow townspeople. That approach, it must be said, often prevailed, often to the environment's loss. Courts have been reluctant to decide buffer zone issues in strict accordance with town bylaws and cases often were settled in favor of the landowner despite clear conflict with local public wishes.

In the 1990s, there were an average of 200 residential property turn-overs in Orleans annually, excluding condominiums. Out of the total number of properties in town, that might seem to be of relatively small consequence. But it meant that there was a possibility of 400 new people per year (assuming two adults per house) who might not have a clue about the history of the land they were moving to, or the environmental integrity of that land, or the functional requirements of the estuaries adjacent to the land. It also meant that the educational component of the job was not just important, but never-ending.

The incredible and rapid rise in value in boom times makes property, especially Cape waterfront and water-view property, a good investment for those who want to make a fast and substantial profit. People who buy a property strictly for investment, who plan to own it for only a year or two and then sell it at a huge jump in price, often have no personal stake in the area. With no emotional commitment to the land, to the estuary adjacent to the land, or to the community as a whole, the attitude of such a property owner toward environmental values is sometimes, "So what? — I won't be here long enough to care what happens." That has never been the Cape Cod ethic and such a seismic shift in philosophy is extremely difficult to counteract. Such people reason that if their investment calls for manicured lawns and exotic landscaping to increase the value, and that in turn means irrigation and fertilizer in large quantities, and fertilizer means excessive nutrient enrichment that may some day choke waterways — well, they say to themselves, so be it. Or they may never even bother to learn about the consequences of their actions at all.

Local tradesman who have spent time working on Nantucket all have stories now of people buying two-million-dollar houses, tearing them down, and building five-million-dollar houses. The seeds of that island practice have been planted on the peninsular Cape. We see houses torn down all the time, replaced by newer and bigger homes. The estimated cost of renovating an existing older building is typically double that of tearing down and starting anew, in part because of the strict building codes in existence now that make renovation projects difficult and expensive. The cottages like the one I grew up in are long gone, a distant memory of a time when just being on the Cape was what mattered most. And as the 20th century closed, the "modest" Cape house along the waterfront was also fast becoming a thing of the past, being replaced by huge extravagances. The first $1,000,000 sale brought gasps around town not very long ago. Now $3,000,000 doesn't seem that outrageous.

But from the perspective of natural resources, prices like that are frightening. When a house on a half-acre or acre of land is worth that much money, what chance does a fragile and priceless estuary have?

At the other end of the real estate spectrum are the folks who move here to stay out of a deep love for the Cape, a love that likely grew over years of vacations and getaway weekends. It's a dream for them, and when they have finally bought a piece of land or a house to retire to, they are already invested in the town and its exquisite environment. Many have had careers in some professional or management capacity somewhere, and some of them decide to offer their expertise and some of their free time to help their adopted home towns.

Orleans is a town run to a large extent by volunteer committees. Such committees influence every conceivable aspect of municipal government, so there are plenty of slots to fill. The finance committee scrutinizes every dollar of the annual municipal budget proposal in order to make recommendations to the voters at Town Meeting. The insurance advisory committee determines how best to keep the town secure from liability claims. The Old King's Highway Historical District Committee reviews projects to ensure that they are in keeping with the traditional style of the region. These committees, and many more, all have responsibilities for determining how the town functions and what it looks like.

But no matter how careful individual committees are to stay true to Orleans' traditions, the members can't help but bring to the table, along with their experience and expertise, a sense of how things were done wherever they came from. Longtime Cape Codders are outnumbered now by people who came only recently "from away," and their historical perspective often is not heard. Without such perspective, any town, in all its aspects, will change rapidly.

A common thread in newcomers' views of local government is that property taxes should be kept low, an argument made most vociferously by those on "fixed income" (regardless of the amount of that income). No matter what the property taxes were in whatever community they came from, they feel taxes should be far lower where they've retired to because of their reduced income. And yet they also expect high levels of service from town government. The contradiction is a big issue in any community with a sizeable retirement community, but it is a huge issue at the elbow of the Cape. Orleans and Chatham are the oldest towns in Massachusetts — ranked one-two among the 351 cities and towns in the state in the average age of residents. The seven other Lower Cape towns, from Dennis to Provincetown, are also among the 20-oldest communities in Massachusetts. And the Cape continues to be the fastest-growing retirement region in New England.

The demographics work out in interesting ways. Retired people who may complain about state or national government often feel there is nothing much that they can do. But they definitely feel they can do something about local government, especially with the old Yankee traditions of volunteer committees and town meetings firmly in place. Anyone can speak his or her mind about government on the floor of Town Meeting — and many do! Anyone who works for the town, especially in a decision-making position such as program or department manager, quickly learns how the dynamics work. Employees are reminded constantly that they work for the taxpayers, and every dollar counts.

The flip side of that coin is that in debates about the cost of a service that is highly desired by a large sector of the population, the people often approve the project regardless of the budget recommendations of the Finance Committee. If the Fire Department can demonstrate the need for a state-of-the-art ambulance, for example, or for several new employees because of increased trips to the regional hospital in Hyannis, a voting population dominated by people who can imagine needing such services sometime soon is almost sure to approve regardless of the cost. If a proposed new wing to the Senior Center can't get grant funding because the state's formula says the Cape town is too wealthy, the people frequently say, "OK, we'll pay for it ourselves." Even schools get generous support from such voters because the population as a whole is well-educated and recognizes the value of a good public education system.

As we have seen, if they can be shown that it's in their best interest to spend a good deal of money to fix drainage systems to help preserve water quality in the bays, they will say, "Well, OK, we'll pay for that out-of-pocket too." But if the cost is large enough and the potential benefit isn't perceived as accruing to everyone in equal measure, they may well bring out the "fixed income" arguments at Town Meeting and vote "No." That's how it went when sewering downtown was proposed.

The irony of the sewering debate and its aftermath is that multiple-family housing increased markedly between 1987 and the present in the center of town, where it was a permitted use in the zoning bylaws. It was precisely the effluent from a higher-density downtown, permitted but not fully constructed when the debate took place, that sewering was supposed to address.

However, public awareness of nutrient enrichment issues has increased in recent years, beginning in the mid-'90s I would say. Comprehensive wastewater plans are in the works for both Orleans and Chatham. The Orleans effort will be designing a wastewater and nutrient management plan for the entire town. Sewering the center of town is again becoming a focal point of discussion. Treating effluent before it reaches the town's coastal waters may yet become a reality. Many residents on the new wastewater committee in Orleans, and many town employees concerned with such matters, were not here or did not have a government role to play during the original debate. The entrenched opinions and longstanding animosities that fired the last debate may not carry the same weight this time. The outcome this time may prove again that the turnover rate in the population is an increasingly important aspect of how Orleans functions.

Currently, the town is discussing the "Village Center" and how it should plan for the future of that area. The Cape Cod

Commission is pushing towns to continue to refine Local Comprehensive Plans so haphazard growth is discouraged. A build-out analysis — which shows what an area would look like if current zoning were utilized to the fullest possible extent — showed some scary statistics for the center of Orleans. Some critics say they doubt any such full build-out will ever occur. But if Cape Cod history is any teacher, the Planning Board should plan for the worst-case scenario. They can always give a sigh of relief if time proves that just this once development will not be pressed to the legal maximum.

Not all the recent history is negative. Preserving land as open space has been shown to be cost-effective for municipalities in the long run. Massachusetts voters, and the Cape and Islands towns in particular, have prudently but decisively moved in that direction. The town established an Open Space Committee to assess undeveloped lands and prioritize them with respect to public benefits. Among the public benefit considerations that might spur a town purchase of land are wellhead protection for drinking water supplies; the environmental integrity of coastal ponds and freshwater lakes; transit corridors for wildlife; the beauty or special habitat of a parcel that would be lost were it not kept in its natural state; and the need for public recreation facilities to be sited on suitable land. The committee produced a report, the Conservation, Recreation and Open Space Plan, to summarize its assessment. It met the state's requirements and enables Orleans to compete for state funding from a dedicated fund for land purchases.

Land of course is a commodity first and foremost in our culture, before it is considered as a resource. It can be sold at any time, whereas raising the funds for municipal purchase requires action by Town Meeting — held just once a year. Open space advocates lobbied prospective sellers to come to the town first, but it didn't always work out that way. Sometimes the sellers felt they couldn't wait for the outcome of a town meeting debate, put their property on the open market, and sold it promptly. Many desirable, high-priority parcels "got away" that way.

Even so, the Open Space Committee has been able to bring some extraordinary pieces of property to the town for purchase, and private conservation trusts have also made a big difference. According to the 1999 Open Space report, 29 percent of the total land area of the town, 2635 acres, has been set aside through a variety of land preservation efforts, including the municipal program. Much of this protected land is waterfront or marshland. Surrounding towns have done likewise for open space.

Bearing in mind that waterfront acreage is the backbone of assessed valuation and hence yields a relatively greater portion of tax revenues than any other kind of property, it is remarkable that the Open Space Committee has been able to persuade voters that public ownership of such land is in the best long-term interest of the town. Two significant purchases on Pleasant Bay were a parcel of six-plus acres that borders both Paw Wah Pond and Little Bay, and Kent's Point, the 30-acre peninsula that extends from Lonnie's Pond to The River. Both have public walking trails to and along the waterfront. Several other parcels are located on the Town Cove, including a six-acre former farm. Another piece adjoins conservation land in neighboring Brewster, which in turn abuts Nickerson State Park. So the Orleans purchase helps protect a much larger chunk of land and its ecosystems, including a large freshwater lake.

Land in conservation was not a new concept for the town. An established private organization, the Orleans Conservation Trust, has long accepted land donations and managed the properties. The gift of the land, or its development rights, provides a tax break under state law. Chatham and the other towns with shorefront on the estuaries also have private conservation trusts. Trusts control most of Strong Island in Chatham, and all of Little Sipson's Island in Orleans, both in Pleasant Bay. Hopkins Island in the Town Cove is another property that belongs to the Orleans Conservation Trust. In all, some 575 acres in and on Orleans waterways have been protected by trusts.

A third mechanism for land conservation is a public-private partnership between the Cape Cod National Seashore and the Pochet Island Family Trust. Under that agreement, 360 acres of island land are set aside in perpetuity for conservation purposes, although managed by the trust, which retains ownership. Because those islands remain in their natural state, they are revered by many as exemplars of what Pleasant Bay is all about.

East of the islands — "behind the islands" in local language — lies the great Nauset barrier beach, 8 miles long, some 1500 acres of unbroken sand dunes and marsh guarding the mainland from the mighty ocean beyond and protected by the federal government. Except for one town-owned asphalt parking lot, a few "grandfathered" dune shacks, and a pathway for off-road vehicles, it too remains in its natural state. To row or paddle or sail or motor in the relatively remote waters between the islands and the barrier beach is to experience a sense of peace and natural order in which the cares of the world seem to vanish. It is to the winding creek between Sampson Island and Hog Island that ospreys have returned, after nearly being extirpated by the effects of DDT and other pesticides. It is on the island marshes that egrets congregate. It is in these waters that the greatest concentration of egg laying horseshoe crabs in the Bay can be found. It is the waters east of Strong Island that striped bass favor most.

So, even though land-use patterns have changed dramatically in recent years around the estuaries, there is hope for the elbow of Cape Cod. The people who live here are the final arbiters of how the town develops, and they have shown that they know the true value of places like Pleasant Bay, the Nauset system, Nauset Beach and Cape Cod Bay. I don't refer to monetary value — although people do know that! — but to that intrinsic value that these places have to transform the lives of those who choose to see and listen. Getting a proposal to Town Meeting may be a cumbersome, sometimes quarrelsome process, but when voters are asked to step up to the plate, they have shown that they will. The proposals have to make sense economically, because there is respect for frugality even in a generally well-to-do enclave like Orleans. But most of all, the proposals have to make sense spiritually, because the residents are determined to protect what is most dear in their hearts.

At least for the quarter-century that I was involved in town government, there was nothing more dear to the people than water, the water they drink and the water that surrounds them and nurtures them in other ways. I certainly hope that the 400 new people coming in each year don't lose that resolve in the future.

Chapter 28

Drop of Rain

It's very possible that the lack of scallops for the past two decades is a direct result of increased development on land and increased motorboating on the water since scallops, as well as other marine life, are very sensitive creatures. In the early '80s, we had gotten our wake-up call, but as the years advanced, the problems kept mounting.

Shellfish closures were a countywide problem. The county Shellfish Advisory Committee knew that shellfish officers saw the problem at the end of the pipe, in the estuaries, and that we could not solve the problems alone. We met with the County Commissioners and requested that the county form a Marine Water Quality Task Force, and they agreed. The Task Force represented planning, health, highway or DPW, conservation or natural resource departments from all over the Cape. The Task Force identified the extent of the pollution problem on a town-by-town basis and documented the ability of towns to deal with the problem in terms of professionals on staff. It also suggested remedial actions, including the creation of town water quality groups. The Task Force noted that an essential ingredient in any possible resolution of the problems was collaboration among people and departments that normally did not function collaboratively. The County Commissioners did their part by adding a new position at the Cape Cod Commission, a marine resources specialist, who worked with the Task Force.

The county committee was instrumental in appealing to the state to fix their highway drainage system and in alerting legislators of the seriousness of the problem so that funding could be secured. But the individual towns still had to solve local drainage issues. Most of the problems had to be solved within the individual towns.

Orleans was one of the first towns to create its own local water quality task force in 1987 and when I introduced the article at Town Meeting, I cited the weirdly colored water in Town Cove as well as the expansive seaweeds to make the case for approving the motion. The discussions with other shellfish officers plus the degrading water quality made me painfully aware that it didn't matter how many quahaugs I could grow if the town was closed to shellfishing because of pollution and people couldn't harvest whatever I produced. I said that at Town Meeting too.

Once the task force was approved, the group immediately set to work. For the inaugural meeting, I drew up an outline of the issues the task force would need to address. Road drainage was the first one. The group created a map of the town that showed every drain and where the water went after it went into the drain. Of particular concern were those pipes that emptied into the salt water. But also of concern were roads where a slope or launching ramp allowed water to run directly into the estuaries.

The next step was to sample the water in all the areas where the pipes emptied directly into the bays. I created a town water quality laboratory to test the water for fecal coliform bacteria. Using our own lab, we could analyze samples ourselves, especially after rain events, and not be constrained by the requirement that we adhere to the county schedule for testing. The lab was not "certified" and the results could not be used to reopen areas for shellfishing that had been closed, but the samples allowed us to discover drains that were particularly important because of their contribution to the overall problem. From those samples, we learned where the worst offenders were with respect to water quality. We chose the top five drains to retrofit under a drainage remediation program.

We went to the 1988 Town Meeting requesting funds for engineering to see what, if anything, could be done to address the five drains. I advised the residents that if they approved the article, we would be coming back for additional funds for engineering design work and then we'd be back a third time for construction funds. We would seek funding from other sources but due to the economic situation of the state, it did not appear likely that state funding would be available. I said we had created this problem with our road drainage system and we would have to fix it, given our new knowledge. To my amazement, the town funded all three articles, including construction, at the deepest point of the 1990 recession. A proposed state transportation bond issue that was being touted by legislators as an important source of money for drainage remediation projects, never saw the light of day, and we could find no comparable funding.

In all, the town spent over $400,000 to "fix" five drains. Three of those fed the Town Cove and two led into Meetinghouse Pond, the area that had been closed originally in 1982. For one of those drains, the Friends of Meetinghouse Pond paid, out of pocket, for the design phase. A corporation funded construction of one of the Town Cove drains (they were a major contributor to the problem) where the only solution was an innovative one that had to be constructed on their property because there was no suitable town land available.

For each of the big drainage systems (except the innovative one), the engineers used the same basic components and each system was based on the same basic principles. They mapped the existing drainage system, determined how much water was flowing, and then determined what was needed to retrofit the system in order to handle or "treat" a one-inch rain event. They chose one inch of rain because studies had shown that most coliform bacteria washes off the roads in that first inch of rain. After that, there's minimum benefit in terms of treatment at an exorbitant cost. Any system designed to take care of one-inch events would take care of most of the contamination. We needed to find town-owned land large enough and high enough to install a treatment system designed by the engineers.

In four out of five new systems, the existing drainage pipes led to mammoth containers called gross particle separators. From the huge chambers, the water would flow to the leach fields. These chambers were designed to catch sand and debris before the water flowed to leach fields — similar to those used for septic systems — with the capacity to treat the volume of a one-inch event. As with septic systems, the bacteria would be killed as the water filtered through the gravel in the leach fields and then through the ground.

As the water percolated through the ground, it eventually merged with the groundwater flowing toward the estuary. Nutrients still would be in the water as it reached the estuary but it would not be a major jolt, rather would get there over a longer period of time. The water would diffuse into the estuary. It would not be a torrent laden with contaminants and nutrients spewing out of the pipe. If the rainfall was greater than normal in a particular storm, a diversion pipe allowed the excess water, relatively bacteria-free, to drain freely to the bay or cove.

The fifth system was the innovative system and it turned out to be problematic. The drainage system happened to be the pipe that discharged water from the lagoon behind the supermarket, across the street from the shellfish lab. The lagoon was the last vestige of Jeremiah's Gutter. Not only did the natural drainage from the surrounding wetlands and the supermarket's parking-lot drainage system feed the lagoon, but the state highway also drained into it. In addition, there was no town-owned land high enough or near enough to install the leach field. Instead, the engineers designed a filter dam in the lagoon under the theory that the water could flow through gravel in the dam and seep underground to a pool before it flowed to the Cove via the pipe. It was never projected to remove as much bacteria as the other systems. Whenever the filter media have been replaced, it works relatively well. But the system clogs easily from a biological process that coats the gravel and stones with a red film, making sample determinations for bacteria counts difficult and making the whole place look horrendous. To have the system operate effectively, the media would have to be replaced often, a costly proposition. There has been no satisfactory resolution to the problem.

In addition to overseeing the drainage system design and installation, the Task Force formed a group of volunteers (mostly from the Friends of Meetinghouse Pond) to take water samples at the five sites. I met with them several times to teach them the appropriate sampling techniques. They took samples before the projects were completed and many times after they were in place to get a before and after picture of how the systems were working. Simultaneously, the highway department increased their street sweeping schedule to prevent clogging of the new systems. Once the pipes had been retrofitted, the state resumed official testing in areas that had been closed to shellfishing, including Meetinghouse Pond.

Finally, in December 1995, Meetinghouse Pond reopened for the harvest of shellfish after twelve long years. The Friends of Meetinghouse Pond held a celebration on the shore and treated all of us who had worked to solve the problem to a festive luncheon. It was a great day.

The Task Force submitted a grant proposal and was funded by the state Department of Environmental Protection to retrofit five more drains that were a high priority. This time the improvements were leaching catch basins along hilly roads and at the bottom of the hills to reduce the amount of stormwater that eventually entered the estuaries. Three were designed to help the Town Cove/Nauset estuary and two benefited Pleasant Bay. The town partnered with the Cape Cod Conservation District and although the time between grant award and construction was lengthy and frustrating, the partnership was a good match.

From 1993 to 2000, ten major drainage systems were retrofitted. A few small drainage systems remain but in September 2001, one of the last remaining high-priority drains for the Town Cove/Nauset system on the Orleans side was retrofitted with the addition of many catch basins. I may have been the only one smiling when traffic was stopped on the busy road for periods during construction or when driving over the uneven pavement while the ground settled after they were done putting in the basins. It was one more major drain fixed.

The town has come a long way from 1982 when Meetinghouse Pond was closed. Shellfish closures from bacterial contamination have not occurred in either Meetinghouse Pond or Town Cove since the drains were fixed. Stormwater remediation even became a specific standard operating procedure for the town to follow into the future, identified in the town's Comprehensive Plan as essential to obtain the goal of protecting water quality.

We were to learn, however, that fixing drains was the easy solution. A much more difficult problem was identified as well.

Chapter 29

Insidious Silent Partner

Bacterial contamination was not the only manifestation of trouble in the water, although we didn't know how to read the other signs for a long time.

We had been working on the quahaug program for about five years and had gotten to the point that the rafts were steadily producing quahaugs to a plantable size each summer. We were in great shape as long as we could buy large enough stock to begin the season and got them early enough so that they would have plenty of time to grow before they had to be transplanted. But smaller seed meant that the rafts had to stay in the water longer each year. The fouling on the rafts (seaweeds that attached to the wire mesh on top of the rafts or sat on the surface of the sand where the quahaugs were) seemed to be increasing over the years and had to be removed more often. Each year it was more work but I wasn't making any other connections.

Meetinghouse Pond had been closed to shellfishing in 1982 because of bacterial contamination, a result of the stormwater runoff. The drainage remediation program took care of the bacteria and to a large degree, other toxic contaminants, but it did not address another important issue, the high amounts of nutrients entering the water.

As the '80s progressed, there were more and more signs of water-quality degradation in Orleans waters. I saw odd colors of water, more and more seaweeds along the shore, and heavier fouling on the quahaug rafts, but all of these were in the upper reaches of Pleasant Bay or at the head of the Town Cove, where the flushing was poorest and the currents relatively sluggish. By 1985 and 1986,

I was also noticing that the eelgrass beds in the major portion of Little Bay were different as well. The individual blades of grass had growing quantities of other plants and animals attached to them, the eelgrass was very long, and there were seaweeds on the bay bottom among the eelgrass stems.

The day that I got the phone call asking about the color of water in the Town Cove, added to my own observations of the water color and explosion of seaweeds in Pleasant Bay, made something click. It suggested an even more insidious threat was present. This threat wasn't just to the water quality but in the long run could be a threat to the quality of life enjoyed in Orleans. The seaweeds piling up along the shore and floating in the ponds and the blood red water in the River finally made sense to me. I had just been in a long state of denial. I was beginning to see what it really meant to love something to death.

I had been hearing more and more about the process of nutrient enrichment (the technical term was eutrophication) at scientific meetings. The problem was being studied intensively on all coasts of the United States and was recognized as a serious problem globally. Finally, with that phone call, I emerged from my personal state of denial and realized that our bays were in trouble because of nutrient enrichment. What I was seeing were the early signs of eutrophication, a long, slow process that had begun years earlier but did not manifest itself until the resilience of our waters had finally been broken.

Eutrophication. It means "good food." It's an elegant word camouflaging a potential horror show! Scientists use it to describe a natural process. But when that process is accelerated by man's activities, it results in the utter disintegration of ecological, physical and aesthetic values of these magnificent bodies of water, the estuaries. The terms eutrophication and nutrient loading or nutrient enrichment do not, in any way, convey the sense that the problem is extremely serious and calls for prompt action. Once the effects of eutrophication are seen, in fresh water ponds as well as estuaries, correcting the situation is a monumental job. But in our world of "seeing is believing," trying to get action before the effects are seen is almost impossible.

To most of us, estuaries are somewhat mysterious. We know the basics. First and foremost, they are beautiful bodies of water to look at, often dotted with vegetated islands and fringed by wetlands of salt-tolerant plants. Often they are adjacent to dunes and barrier beaches. They are home to myriad fish and shellfish, creatures we know and can recognize, but they also are home to the birds flying overhead or wading along the shore, as well as lesser known and usually smaller plants and animals. Estuaries are also delicately balanced. Add something or take something away and major changes can occur, resulting in a system very different from the prior one. But their inherent resilience is difficult to unhinge and sometimes the major changes we finally see in estuaries can be the result of decades of insult hurled at them until they can no longer function in the same way as they did before the crucial addition or deletion.

The biota (the plants and animals) require certain chemical and physical attributes in order to function properly, and they play key roles in many of the processes that cycle some elements such as nitrogen, carbon, oxygen and sulfur through the estuarine system. Plants and animals also require certain nutrients to survive, but an overabundance can upset the natural estuarine system.

One nutrient that has become too abundant is nitrogen. It's hard to believe that there can be too much nitrogen since our planet's atmosphere is 78 percent nitrogen. In salt water, nitrogen controls the amount of plant growth or primary productivity that can take place. When more and more nitrogen is added to salt water, plant life, both plankton and seaweeds (or macrophytes), can explode in abundance. As the plants mature, they use oxygen in respiration, and when they die in the late summer, the decay process uses ever more oxygen. Just as we landlubbers require oxygen to survive, so the animals of the sea also require oxygen.

The depletion of oxygen by a plant explosion can cause fish kills and create "dead" zones in the water that are called "anoxic" or without oxygen. When the decay process is exhausted each year, it creates a muddy sediment that is left on the bottom, in a process similar to that which builds soil on land. As the mud builds up, the water depth of the estuary decreases and it begins to fill in. Over time, the estuary changes to a shallow lagoon and finally to upland. The eutrophication process is natural, and in nature takes a long time — decades or even centuries. But the nutrients man adds can radically shorten the time it takes an estuary to "fill in".

Where does the nitrogen come from? In a natural system, much of it comes from rain or is brought in from the ocean by the tides. If these were the only sources, we wouldn't have to worry much about eutrophication. But nitrogen is cycled through estuaries in a complex process that yields nitrogen compounds and pathways that intensify its effects. Moreover, we make ever-increasing additions of nitrogen compounds through our own waste products and the fertilizers we use.

Each and every septic system, whether it is a brand new Title 5 system, the current state standard, or an old cesspool, adds nutrients (mostly nitrogen and phosphorus compounds) to the groundwater. As the material from the septic system percolates through the soil that is supposed to cleanse it, the bacteria die but a large percentage of the nutrients remain.

Just as nitrogen and phosphorus are the most important nutrients in fertilizers for the garden, they are also the most important nutrients in aquatic systems. Nitrogen is the most important factor to monitor for salt water, and phosphorus is the most important one for lakes and ponds. Recent research has found that a septic system removes only about 25 percent of the nitrogen that we excrete (it was thought to remove much less or none). The remainder filters through the soil until it reaches the groundwater.

Groundwater is the Cape's only source of drinking water, so it is tapped for community drinking supplies as well as for individual wells. High concentrations of nitrogen in drinking water supplies can pose a direct health hazard. Houses on small lots where there is no central water system risk pumping a neighbor's filtered effluent from their septic system into the well.

Once the nitrogen from a septic system reaches the groundwater, it mixes with the effluent from everyone else's septic system and travels to the estuaries. Scientists have found that it takes far less nitrogen to make an impact on the estuaries than the amount necessary to impact the drinking water supplies. Thus, if a management policy were to target the nitrogen concentration low enough to prevent changes in the estuary from groundwater flow, drinking water would also be protected, at least for nitrogen. Researchers have been struggling for years to develop methodologies to compute acceptable levels of nitrogen and translate these findings into workable land use planning initiatives to protect the estuaries.

The nutrients can take years to reach the estuary from individual septic systems. With our predominantly sandy soil, the groundwater travels at about a foot per day. If a septic system is a hundred feet from the water, it will take about a hundred days for the effluent to reach the estuary, and if it is 350 feet, it will take about a year to reach the estuary. If the house is a mile from the water, it will take almost fifteen years for the effluent to reach the water. If the house is two miles, it will take about thirty years.

Think about what this means on Cape Cod. It means that the effluent from houses built a mile from the shore in the building boom of the mid-1970s began to enter the estuary at the beginning of the 1990s. The building boom of the '80s is beginning to enter the bays now. And the effects of the massive amount of building that took place in the '90s hasn't hit yet. But it will.

Land use maps of Cape Cod show that the "interior" regions of the Cape have been among the fastest growing areas in recent years because land closer to the water has already been developed. The effluent from these "interior" homes has recently been added to the groundwater flow. The implications are enormous, since some towns, Orleans being one of them, are approaching build-out, where every lot that can be built upon will be built upon.

Until a building is no longer used and the lot reverts back to open land, nutrients will continue to flow to the estuaries. Moreover, whatever is in the groundwater at the time a septic system is discontinued will continue to flow at about a foot per day until the waste-stream has been halted. This means that it can take years after a building is no longer in use for its nitrogen to be purged from the groundwater.

Think about it. It will take 15 or 20 or 30 years — depending on how far the house is from the water — to reach the estuary from the time the effluent from the bathroom starts flowing. Then, even if the waste stream has stopped, it will still take 15 or 20 or 30 more years for the flow to stop going into the estuary. If we magically stopped using individual septic systems tomorrow and halted all development until much more efficient wastewater systems were in place, it would still take a generation or more to rid the groundwater of the nitrogen.

Aside from the folks living around the small ponds, most people did not catch the significance of increased seaweeds along the shore. But it was becoming obvious to scientists that the substantial increase in development and the increased human usage of Pleasant Bay meant that Pleasant Bay needed protection.

The National Park Service has been researching the nutrients in groundwater for several areas, including Nauset, for years. As part of their research, the feds used a sophisticated tool called thermal imagery to visually depict the groundwater flow into the estuary.

In early August, the differential between the warm salt water and the cooler fresh groundwater is at the maximum. The National Seashore contracted to have a plane fly overhead on an ebbing tide one early August evening in the mid-'90s, when the salt water would be at its warmest point. The plane was equipped with a thermal-imaging camera that took aerial photos. The plane made several passes over the estuary for roughly three hours from about 5-8 p.m.

The resulting black and white photographs were incredible. Groundwater seeping into the Town Cove showed up as virtually a second shoreline, a dark-gray wavy line that delineated the edge between fresh and salt water. Since salt water is heavier than fresh, the fresh groundwater floated on the surface, before it mixed with the salt water. If one looked closely, one could see the fresh water flowing around objects such as boats. The photo hung in the

Conservation Department office through the late '90s and was the source of numerous opportunities for us to discuss groundwater with residents. It was a powerful educational tool.

There are two basic reasons that knowledge of the amount of water and how it travels through the ground beneath us is important. First, towns need to know where there is enough high-quality water to sustain a well for drinking water, keeping in mind that all of the Cape's drinking water comes from the groundwater below us. Second, the groundwater moves toward the estuaries. In order to address the issue of nutrient loading to the estuaries, and to protect municipal drinking water supplies from contamination, we need a lot more definitive information about the direction of groundwater flow.

On land, a river collects water from hills on both sides of the river. At the top of the hills on one side of the river, there is usually a ridgeline where the water flows toward the river or to the other side of the hills. That line is called a divide. The same thing occurs with groundwater. For a peninsula like Cape Cod, we could assume that somewhere in the spine of the Cape, there was a groundwater divide that would determine if water flowed toward Cape Cod Bay or toward Nantucket Sound. But we didn't know where that divide was and it wasn't really much help to make assumptions. We needed more information.

But how do researchers gain knowledge about groundwater, something unseen, something underground and something as elusive as water among sand grains? Hydrologists use wells and from the wells, they can tell how far below the land surface the groundwater is and they can also determine the depth of the groundwater.

The Cape Cod Commission, with assistance from the U.S. Geologic Survey, mapped the majority of the groundwater on the Cape in the early '90s using existing wells whenever possible. Prior to widespread municipal water systems, houses obtained water from private wells and some of them were still in the ground and could be used to obtain data. The researchers plotted the data points on a map and connected the dots. If they found too many gaps in the data, they installed additional wells. The finished product was a map with contours similar to a topographic map. The closer to the shoreline, the less distance to groundwater and as the land sloped up from the shore, the groundwater was found at greater depths below the surface.

Groundwater travels at right angles to the contours so once the maps were drawn, the direction of flow and groundwater divides could be determined. When they had the contours and divides, the researchers could then delineate watersheds to estuaries — groundwater flowing into each estuary from the land surrounding it. All the water flowing into Cape Cod Bay or Nantucket Sound comprised major watersheds. But each estuary had its own watershed. With the number of estuaries, the Cape's groundwater picture became rather complicated.

When the Cape maps were completed, the hydrologists discovered several distinct "lenses" of water that were segregated from one another by the topographical landscape. A major feature such as Bass River, a salt river, divided the groundwater into separate "lenses" on either side of the river. Just as squeezing a gel pack in the middle creates two separate pouches of gel material, as the ground surface dips toward sea level, it squeezes the fresh water flowing below the ground.

The hydrologists determined that there was a major groundwater divide at the eastern edge of what was named the Monomoy Lens, east of Bass River to Orleans. Another lens was identified in Eastham, dubbed the Nauset Lens. In between those two lenses was the Town of Orleans and there was no information regarding the groundwater flow for the town except for the tiny portion that was located at the eastern edge of the Monomoy Lens. The estuaries Orleans was blessed with made Orleans too complex for the budget of the Cape-wide mapping project.

Once again, if the town was going to solve its problems, it needed to dig deep to pay for another project out of pocket. The town Water Quality Task Force petitioned the town with an article at town meeting to have our own groundwater mapped since county and federal funds were unavailable. And once again, the residents came through and paid for the mapping project.

When the map was completed, we were astounded to discover that there were *ten* distinct watersheds within the town but even they could be further subdivided (Map 6).

We instantly recognized the importance of this information. We were able to overlay the groundwater map on the zoning map (Map 6) and the land use map and the flood zone map or any other configuration we wanted. For instance, the zoning map shows where particular activities are allowed, such as commercial, general business, limited business and so forth. The overlay shows where the groundwater will flow from activities on the land in, say the business area, critical information if there is a problem such as a toxic spill of some kind. Likewise, the density of housing is spelled out in the residential districts map and the overlay allows the flow of effluent from those houses to be traced to its end point in the estuaries. Similarly, the actual land use shows what types of activities are already present in given areas and the land use map can show the density of particular uses, such as multiple-family residences, for example, and where the effluents from them will flow. When the overlay is added to the flood zone map, it shows areas that are likely to be impacted by waves in a nasty storm and those areas subject to flooding.

It is the land use maps that are the critical element to show directly how activities that take place on land could impact the estuary of a particular watershed when things go wrong.

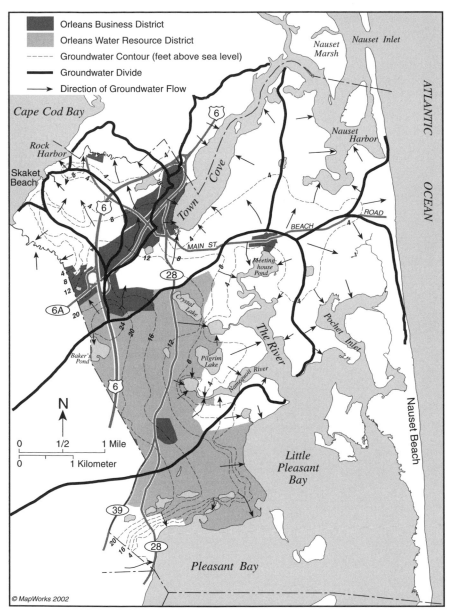

MAP 6 *Watersheds of Orleans and Zoning Districts*

Finally, we were beginning to have the technical information we needed to combat what had been happening. We had some tools to help us address what was already taking place and to plan for the future. But we needed a whole lot more.

Chapter 30

The People Speak

Wide expanses of beautiful white sand beaches. Large salt marshes that change color with every season. Acres of trails to walk in many different types of environments. Sand flats to explore that extend over a mile from the shore. Shellfish that can be harvested by the family on an outing to the shore and later eaten with cocktails or cooked to have a mess of steamers. Quiet rivers and ponds begging for that kayak or canoe trip. Beautiful vistas at the end of roads that all seem to lead to the sea. Sunrises over the water. Sunsets over the water. Moon rises over the water. Fishing opportunities by foot, by ORV, and by boat, in fresh water and in salt water. Recreational opportunities in every town. This is the Cape Cod of the early 21st century.

The fastest growing county in Massachusetts. The highest growth in retirement-age people in New England. Thousands of acres Cape-wide closed to shellfishing from bacterial contamination. Land as a good investment because of rising values. Relatively low tax rates. Dwindling numbers of people who make a living from the sea. Walled-in shorelines to keep out the sea. Loss of beaches from walled-in shorelines. Signs of eutrophication in all the estuaries. Drinking water threatened and wells abandoned because of contamination. Congested harbors and waiting lists for moorings. Beach parking lots full by 10 a.m. on sunny summer days. Huge gaps between the haves and have-nots. Mythical affordable housing for the labor force. Total reliance on personal automobiles because of very limited reliable mass transportation. Traffic gridlock. Strip malls. Summer labor force imported, increasingly from overseas. A peninsula bursting at the seams. This is also the Cape Cod of the early 21st century.

Sure, Cape Cod's beauty is still there in its natural environment and there still are pockets, saved from the bulldozer, that are reminiscent of a less crowded place where time has stood still. Those places, though, are becoming more and more rare, and preserving that precious landscape becomes increasingly difficult as people continue to flock to the Cape in search of fun in the sun and a respite from city life.

The Cape Cod Commission, seen by some as the enemy and by others as the savior, required towns to produce a Local Comprehensive Plan for future growth and development, in order to receive funds and the Commission's technical support. Rather than hire consultants, Orleans chose to do it all in-house in the mid-1990s, using guidelines from the Commission. An important concept agreed to early on, was that the plan would be resource-based, a huge departure from earlier town plans that had been economically based. It was an extremely long and tortuous process filled with intrigue, animosity, angst, mixed agendas and lots of hard work by many dedicated people.

One of the first actions of the planning committee was to mail out a town-wide survey that encompassed many aspects of local life and asked residents to assess their relative importance. The response was excellent. Water resources — drinking water as well as marine and fresh water ponds — were listed as among the most important resources to the people.

Based on those results, a second survey was distributed regarding marine resources specifically, as we explored the knowledge and desires of both year-round and seasonal people in order to write the coastal resources chapter of the final plan.

With so much water to choose from, we wanted to know where people were participating in certain activities and so we designed a matrix that listed activities such as shellfishing, boating, fishing, swimming, and beach-walking across one axis, and listed places along the other axis. People could just check off all that applied. It proved to be a space-saving way to obtain a wealth of information and demonstrated that many people used more than one body of water, a factor we had surmised but could not previously document.

Then we got down to the nitty-gritty. We wanted to know how people felt about the marine issues such as nutrient loading, the connection of fertilizer use and nutrients, knowledge of alternative septic system designs, and the connection between shellfish and water quality. Another important aspect of the survey was determining what residents felt about how funds should be used regarding such issues.

We asked questions about activities designed to protect the natural resources or improve water quality. We asked respondents to simply answer whether they agreed or disagreed with such efforts, with no gradations of how strongly they agreed or disagreed. A simple yes or no was all we asked.

The results were remarkable. First, the response rate town-wide was over 20 percent — even though it was the second survey sent within a year. Second, the information culled from the survey indicated that the people felt very strongly that the town's marine resources were incredibly important and efforts should be continued to protect them by whatever means was feasible, including the expensive drainage remediation program.

Shellfish proved to be important to respondents. Eighty percent said that they would like to see the shellfish seed program expanded, almost 70 percent said they supported a shellfish grow-out facility, and over 60 percent said they supported a marine education facility. About half responded that they supported private aquaculture but not if it meant decreased boating accessibility. Almost 70 percent did not support reducing the number of moorings but over 60 percent supported increasing the number and size of no-wake zones. These results indicated that both shellfishing and boating were important and where shellfishing and boating might cross swords, there was no firm agreement on whether one should yield to the other.

Meanwhile, over 60 percent said they favored encouraging "green tourism" activities, but they did not support rezoning for marine business or using public docks for private business or expanding parking at town landings or increasing the number of launching ramps. Support was strong in the abstract, but when it came to particular actions that might advance "green tourism," the respondents saw them as undesirable.

The results were quite revealing when we asked about expenditures. Nearly 60 percent said they would pay more for shellfish licenses, pay for shellfish seeding, and pay for more enforcement. Roughly 65 percent also said they would reduce or eliminate fertilizer use on their property, would eliminate or reduce surface runoff on their own property, and would use a boat pump-out facility if available. But only a slight majority said they would install a nutrient- reducing septic system. It seemed the higher the personal ticket item, the more cautious the reply. Perhaps they just needed proof that the added expense would be justified by results.

The survey not only told us what activities were taking place where, it also gave a clear mandate to continue to do the best we could to protect the marine resources. We were heartened that the course we had set decades earlier seemed appropriate to the people.

During the same time period, the state had amended its regulations pertaining to activities on the water that required a state permit, including erosion control structures such as bulkheads and revetments as well as private docks. Called the Chapter 91 regulations, they required all property owners who had private docks to get them properly licensed if they had not already done so and established an amnesty period for licensing. They also placed a moratorium on all new docks in an Area of Critical Environmental Concern, as Pleasant Bay was designated, until the town developed a state-approved Resource Management Plan.

Private docks had always been considered rather benign structures by permitting authorities at all levels of government. However, evidence was mounting that the structures themselves, and their use, might not be as benign as once thought. Concern about docks in shallow embayments centered on vegetation loss from shading, shellfish habitat loss, impacts to eelgrass, chemical leacheates from treated wood, construction impacts, fragmentation of beach habitats, sediment resuspension from boat propellers, boat paints, chemicals used in marine sanitation devices, and petroleum and petroleum byproducts.

The Commission inventoried the existing docks and photographed each one from the water to have a permanent record of the number and location of all of them. Prior to the moratorium, the Conservation Commission had been inundated with requests for new docks. As waterfront property changed hands, the new owners would come into the Conservation office requesting permission for a new dock. Although the burden of proof was on the applicant to show no adverse effect from the dock, in practice, it was nearly impossible to deny a dock, especially if there was an existing dock on neighboring property.

The county Shellfish Advisory Committee had been concerned about the proliferation of private docks for years and saw the adverse effects that docks had on shellfish resources. In Orleans, we could easily picture most property owners wanting docks, not only because a dock made boating easily accessible, but it could also add as much as $50,000-$100,000 to the value of the property. The Conservation Commission welcomed the moratorium but not the deluge of applications for licensing of existing docks. Between the erosion control measures coming in after the storms of 1991 and 1992 and the dock licensing, the Commission was frazzled.

The moratorium on new docks was the impetus for developing a bay-wide resource management plan that could be approved by the state. With our marine survey results in hand, the Conservation, Planning and Harbormaster/Shellfish departments attempted to draw up a management plan for the Orleans section of Pleasant Bay, but we recognized that a plan developed and agreed to by all the towns bordering on the bay would be preferable.

After several false starts, the Friends of Pleasant Bay entered the picture. They pledged $30,000 to get the planning effort off the ground, if the four towns would agree to a regional management plan effort. The Executive Office of Environmental Affairs pledged another $25,000. In-kind contributions from the Cape Cod Commission were authorized (through staff time and development of digital maps).

Finally, the towns agreed, provided additional funding, and began the process of developing a Pleasant Bay Resource Management Plan, the first time the four towns had embarked on such a cooperative venture for management. It was one thing to get a committee together from the towns to nominate the Bay as an ACEC; it was quite another story to get them together to agree on how they would conduct their business together.

A steering committee of four members, one from each town, took responsibility for administering the planning process. Town staff from the Planning, Shellfish, Harbormaster, and Conservation departments or other similar entities were asked to served on a technical advisory committee that also included state, county and federal resource management professionals.

The steering committee hired a professional coordinator to keep track of committee actions, synthesize information being generated and accumulated, keep everyone on target, and write the final plan. Public participation was a vital component in developing the plan; more than a thousand people responded to a survey sent to residents throughout the region.

Once the process began, early discussions focused on the study area for the plan. The ACEC boundary did not include the entire bay since Chatham Harbor had been deleted because of concern about future dredging for this important fishing port. ACEC regulations do not allow dredging for navigation purposes only. But the source of ocean water for the entire bay was through Chatham Inlet. It seemed inadvisable to follow the ACEC boundary and not include Chatham Harbor in the planning process. Furthermore, the ACEC boundary included only those lands seaward of the 10-foot contour and the issue of nutrient loading alone suggested that the watershed of the Bay be included in the study area.

The final planning area did include the entire bay and its watershed. While Chatham Inlet and Chatham Harbor were suggested to be added to the ACEC by an amendment to the boundary, the watershed, although integral to the functioning of the Bay, was not recommended to be an extension of the ACEC boundary. The existing regulatory requirements for the watershed areas would continue. With more than 9,000 acres of saltwater surface area, 458 acres of fresh water surface area, 71 miles of shoreline and over 21,000 acres of watershed, and with some parts of all categories located in four municipalities, Pleasant Bay was a large and complex area for a resource management plan.

The plan development progressed swiftly with the cooperative effort. The planning team met regularly for over two years to review technical data that had been compiled; to determine trends, current conditions and gaps in the data; and to assess issues and investigate management options. Every effort was made to utilize existing documentation within the four towns, but experience from similar planning projects across the country was also taken into account. Finally, five management topics — biodiversity, boating safety and navigation, public access, shellfish/aquaculture and shoreline structures — emerged as the most critical components of the plan. The Steering Committee sponsored a series of workshops that took place over a three-month period and focused public attention on the five management topics. Hundreds of people participated in numerous public meetings that winnowed out long lists of issues to identify those for which management options seemed the most appropriate.

The workshops were a remarkable exercise in the democratic process. Many, many people lent their voices to the shaping of the final plan. Members of the technical advisory committee (TAC) were asked to participate in one of more of the groups. Attending all the meetings for all the groups kept some people extremely busy. I chose another route: I decided to focus on two subjects, shellfish/aquaculture and structures.

All the workgroups needed to produce maps identifying where the resources were located as a necessary first step. In some cases, doing so was a daunting challenge. Take shellfish for example. Many people define shellfish areas as those that have shellfish. That seems obvious. But shellfish species can be short-lived as with scallops, and they can set one year and not the next, so defining shellfish *habitat* became more important than identifying areas that have shellfish at any particular moment of time.

How can you define shellfish habitat? After meetings with people involved with shellfishing, including fishermen, aquaculturists, town shellfish officers, recreational shellfish permit holders and other professionals, we decided on how we could identify the areas. We focused not only on currently productive areas but also those areas that historically had had shellfish. We added a category for areas that were likely to support shellfish at some time, and included areas that had been seeded through municipal propagation programs. With base maps prepared by the Cape Cod Commission, we used crayons to literally color in areas appropriately.

The shellfish group meetings were fascinating because fireworks were expected in discussions among individuals who routinely didn't talk to one another, or, if they did, usually didn't agree with one another. But the fireworks didn't happen. Everyone present talked together about where they had seen shellfish. The resulting map, a compilation of expertise from a wide array of experience on the water, was probably more accurate than it would have been using any other conceivable method.

The shellfish working group focused on two issues. First, what research, resources and management actions are needed to help ensure the sustainability of the Bay's fisheries resources, and how should they be conducted or administered? Second, how does private aquaculture affect the Bay's natural resources, and how should requests for additional area for private aquaculture be managed?

The group identified a long list of possible reasons for declining shellfish stocks, including over-fishing, use of poor harvesting techniques, juvenile mortality, predation, environmental stress resulting from the Chatham break, non-point source pollution, natural species-dependent growth cycles, and habitat loss. It was fairly obvious from the list that bay-wide shellfish management was difficult, required cooperative effort and additional assessments of the resources. For example, the last comprehensive resource assessment for Pleasant Bay was conducted in 1967 by the Massachusetts Division of Marine Fisheries. Another "snapshot" of the bay's resources was sorely needed.

The group agreed that bay-wide propagation efforts should be enhanced and believed such an effort to be crucial to the sustainability of the resources. The participants recognized that funds would be needed and they also recognized that there should be guidelines for measuring success of the propagation efforts.

Private shellfish aquaculture was another area of serious discussion. When the grant area in Orleans had been set aside in 1986, the state criterion for allowing a private shellfish grant in public waters was that the grant could not adversely affect the town's shellfish resources. The statute changed in the mid-'90s so that a grant area could not adversely affect the town's natural resources. This was a subtle but incredibly important change in the law because now, in order to obtain a shellfish grant, the grant activity could not adversely affect any other resource in the Bay.

Two principal resources that seemed likely to be most affected were birds and horseshoe crabs, both known to be present in the grant area. On the other hand, shellfish aquaculture was suggested to be beneficial to overall resource integrity because of natural spawning from the dense plantings, and because water quality enhancement could be expected because of the filtering capacity of shellfish. The plan recommendation was to determine the potential for aquaculture and develop guidelines for grant siting and administration. This recommendation meant that the moratorium on expansion of existing grants and on enlarging the grant area to accommodate additional farmers should be maintained until studies were completed.

The structures issue presented a special challenge. First, it was the very subject that had led to the resource management planning process, because the dock moratorium was the trigger. Second, most people who attended the structures workshop were initially thinking only of the traditional way of handling them, on a lot-by-lot basis. The technical advisory committee members knew that way hadn't worked. It became obvious in the first couple of meetings that management options for the structures group were going to be elusive and so members of the technical advisory committee began to search for other ways of handling the issue.

After many meetings, we came up with a completely new methodology for assessing the environmental consequences of private docks in public waters. We decided to take a holistic approach to the problem and look at the bay as a system.

We developed the methodology in a step-wise progression. The first step was to look at the bay as a whole and think about the different areas — the ponds and rivers, Little Bay and Big Bay, and Chatham Harbor. Intuitively we knew that there were differences among the areas and we asked ourselves if we could describe the differences. We decided we could describe the differences and we concluded by dividing the bay into 26 areas or component parts.

The second step was to describe the attributes of each subsection with respect to biological, physical and human use factors. For instance, did the area support shellfish? Did the area have eelgrass and/or fringe salt marsh? What was the depth of water 200 feet from the edge of the marsh or from the mean low water mark, whichever applied? Was the area open water, a river, or a semi-enclosed pond? What was the ratio of docks to parcels without docks within the subsection? Was there a navigational channel within 500 feet of shore? We used such questions because in total the answers would give us a sense of the area and what the potential impacts of a dock would probably be.

Because aesthetic values are subjective and extremely difficult to quantify, we asked ourselves, what was it about a dock that may produce a negative reaction when looking at one? The answer to us was that docks make a natural shoreline look man-made. We judged natural shorelines to be pleasing and man-made structures to be less desirable aesthetically. We said that the greater the number of docks within a visual path and the higher the docks were, the less aesthetically pleasing the scene was. Thus we were able to address the aesthetic issue by using the ratio of parcels with docks to those parcels without them.

From the discussion of the attributes of each area, we analyzed our descriptions and found that there were nine major parameters. We evaluated each parameter for each subsection using a quantitative scale. We defined our terms to eliminate ambiguity.

When we were finished, we had created a sensitivity index of the bay with respect to private docks. Treating docks in this manner had never been done before — we were really thinking outside the box! The beauty of the sensitivity index was that it took docks out of the lot-by-lot morass that had been in effect earlier. It also treated discrete areas of the bay independently from one another based on the resources.

We then mapped the data analysis and determine a cut-off point. We determined that the most sensitive areas should not have new docks and the moratorium imposed by the state prior to adoption of the plan should remain.

The final step was to present the methodology to the public.

We anticipated a huge backlash when back-water areas were shown on the maps as being particularly sensitive areas where the moratorium would continue, but it did not happen. The moratorium meant that those wishing to use docks would have to try to use existing ones that belonged to friends and neighbors. They would all have to sort out the legal and insurance issues privately and those not willing to share their dock were certainly within their rights. It seemed that once property owners were given a definitive answer based on a non-capricious set of criteria, they accepted it. When the plan was approved by the towns, the methodology was part of the package and was accepted almost unanimously at town meetings.

The methodology was later added to the bylaws and regulations of the local Conservation Commissions to give it the force of law. Further criteria for construction of docks in the non-moratorium areas were developed and also added to the local regulations.

The other work groups tackled their specific issues. Other natural resources were mapped in a similar manner, either from personal knowledge or a compilation of personal knowledge and existing data. The extent of eelgrass was one of the resources that needed to be mapped. The Friends of Pleasant Bay had contracted with Dr. Fred Short of the University of New Hampshire to determine the health status of the eelgrass in the bay. His report, in addition to "local knowledge" and older documents, indicated that the eelgrass distribution had remained fairly constant over a 30-year period but Short indicated that the eelgrass now faced serious threats from disease and pollution.

At public meetings, the maps from all the work groups were displayed for comment and correction. As I recall, very few corrections were needed after the initial process.

With all the work by the various workgroups completed, Carole Ridley, the coordinator, wrote the plan, which was then reviewed by the technical advisory committee. The resulting document was applauded by county, state and federal agencies as a model that could be used in other areas.

A section of the introduction to the Pleasant Bay Resource Management Plan sums up the reverence many people have for the bay:

"An estuary left alone will nurture and care for itself with no help of human hands. It is only when human activities interfere with natural processes that the bay responds by showing signs of stress, damage and disease. This stewardship plan for Pleasant Bay is intended to provide a practical framework for the towns of Orleans, Chatham, Harwich and Brewster to work together to sustain the Bay's natural resources, and to promote a degree of use and enjoyment of those resources consistent with long-term sustainability. Accomplishing this will require residents, visitors, and businesses alike to place the long-term health of the Bay above individual interests. It will require change and sacrifice, and an on-going commitment to preserving the health, beauty, and tranquility of Pleasant Bay for future generations."

Members of the Steering Committee asked members of the TAC to comment on the plan at our respective town meetings. Prior to the string of meetings, the Friends of Pleasant Bay had sent a mailing to their members urging each to attend their town's town meeting. As

I looked at the assemblage of Orleans residents, I noted that many of them were members of the Friends. It was clear that in the decade between designation as an ACEC and the town meeting that night, the Friends of Pleasant Bay had become an influential group.

I don't like reading a prepared statement at such a gathering but in this case, I felt it was important enough to prepare my comments. I said that it was a pleasure to speak on behalf of a plan to protect a bay that means so much to so many of us. Further, I said,

"During my tenure with the town, I witnessed many changes in Pleasant Bay, some of them as a result of spectacular natural forces and some of them at our own hand. If we never venture forth on those waters again, the bay would continue to change; the barrier beach would still migrate, the bay would gradually fill in as the beach migrates westward as well as south. Fish and shellfish would spawn and populate the bay; predators would stalk their prey and competition for food and space would continue.

"But we will continue to use the bay. And we will continue to use it in ever-increasing numbers. And we will use it mostly during the summer when all the marine life is in full progression to repopulate their species; when a tiny clam seed that you never notice unless you're specifically looking for them, gets easily dislodged from its home just under the surface because of some disturbance by us; when nutrients tied up in the sediment get resuspended and become available for an abnormal bloom of plankton or seaweed mats that decay and stink along the shores. Those nutrients are coming into the bay from Brewster, picking up effluent from all our septic systems along the way that are within the Pleasant Bay watershed. We plow through the eelgrass cursing its presence because it slows us down and then curse in bitter disappointment because there are no scallops that need the eelgrass to set.

"The pressures on the natural production are enormous. What we do on the land and on the water can have a monumental effect on the productivity of the bay. We have finally come to realize that the bay knows no political boundaries. It has taken us a long time but we have developed a plan that, for the first time, recognizes that the total is greater than the sum of the parts, that each town has a stake in the whole and that we are all in this together. A plan that takes into consideration the natural complexities but also the need for us to continue to use the bay in a responsible manner. It was not done in a vacuum but with the help of hundreds of people and with lots of compromises along the way. Not everyone likes all of it. But we think it is a document we can work with. Now is the time for us to step up to the plate and support this plan, not only by our vote tonight but in the coming years as well when we will have to pay for the privilege of our stewardship. What better legacy can we leave for future generations than the knowledge that we took the hard way, not the easy way, but the right way before it was too late?"

When the meeting had ended I saw the Orleans representative to the Steering Committee and asked him if that was what he had been looking for. He just grinned.

The overwhelming adoption of the plan by the towns (except Brewster which has much of the watershed but almost none of the bay itself within its boundary) indicated a willingness to do what needed to be done to protect the bay.

Finally, the majority of the people who loved the place for its intrinsic value, not necessarily its economic value, were starting to "get it".

Chapter 31

Resolving Issues

When the Bay Plan was approved, it signaled, for many, that we had turned the corner. Environmental protection of the water was important to the vast majority of the people. The Bay Plan had been approved by the voters of three towns, a joint action of a kind that had never been taken before in these particular towns. It was not approved in Brewster, the fourth town, because many in Brewster did not feel they had a personal stake in the future of the Bay — even though much of the groundwater flowing into the bay originates from Brewster — since they owned only 40 feet of shoreline. Perhaps someday, they too will join in the effort.

It had taken a long time to get a plan together that would be acceptable to the towns. But we knew that just getting it approved wasn't the end by any stretch.

We had accumulated many pieces of information to develop the plan but we found major holes in our knowledge as well. The only biological assessment had been done in 1967 by the Division of Marine Fisheries and no updating had been done since that time. We knew the direction of groundwater flow and could identify discrete watersheds, but we had no real good hydrographic data — bathymetry (water depth) or current velocity and direction. We had information on tide heights from several studies of barrier beach dynamics in which tide gauges had been placed at the Fish Pier in Chatham and in Meetinghouse Pond. But they were old data and most of the reports were pre-1987, the year of the break, and so the data were nearly useless given the changed conditions after 1987.

We knew that tides bring in new oceanic water that mixes with the bay water but we had no information on how long it took for water to be exchanged or renewed, especially in the more remote portions of the bay. This was an important gap in knowledge because water, especially in the ponds, had a high nutrient content from the groundwater. How long would it take to "flush" that water out of the system? How much nitrogen was brought into the pond from the tides? How much nitrogen was flowing into the ponds from groundwater? How far "over the top" were the nitrogen levels in the ponds and how could we begin to address the issue? How was the remainder of the bay faring with respect to nutrients?

In order to get a full picture of how nutrients affect the estuaries, we needed to know how much was coming in from where, and in what forms, and how fast it was going out. This was the simplified version because to get a "true" picture, we would have to know how the nitrogen was being "used" while it was in the estuary, which would require multi-disciplinary studies more in keeping with major universities, not Cape Cod communities.

The Cape Cod Commission proposed to conduct a nutrient loading analysis for the Bay, to get at the questions of how much nitrogen was coming into the estuaries and where it was coming from. Included in the analysis was an estimate of the amount of nitrogen coming into the Bay from the groundwater and from other inputs such as fertilizers washed directly off the land; nitrogen levels in precipitation; nitrogen drained off roads; and the amount brought into the bay with the tides. We felt the lack of information on the flushing rate — how fast it was going out — was important enough for us to contract with a consulting firm to determine the flushing rate for each part of the bay. When both phases of the project were completed — the nutrient loading analysis and the flushing study — we would have a good idea, watershed by watershed, of the nitrogen amount and the likely fate of specific areas throughout the bay.

The Commission was trying to calculate the maximum amount of nitrogen that each different segment of the bay could handle before it shifted toward eutrophication. The researchers needed the volumetric calculations presented in the flushing study to determine the nutrient loading capacity throughout the bay. For planning purposes, both these studies were crucial to get a handle on nutrient loading in order to plan for the future.

The flushing study analyzed the Bay in segments similar to the segments used by the structures work group for the dock analysis. We suspected the ponds might flush slowly because they are deep kettle holes where the water volume can't be exchanged in a single tidal cycle or even a few cycles. The results showed our assumption proved to be depressingly accurate.

Not only are the ponds like Meetinghouse, Lonnie's and Arey's deep kettle-holes, but they are also ten or more miles from the oceanic inlet. The tide comes in and the tide goes out, but not all the water goes out. A lot of water stays and mixes with the incoming tide so every day, twice a day, the outgoing water mixes with the incoming water. Once the water gets into The River, it still has to travel at least 8 miles to get to Chatham Inlet. One step forward to inch closer to the inlet, two steps back toward the ponds.

When the data were analyzed, we were shocked to learn that the flushing rate of Lonnie's Pond was 443 days, well over a year. In Arey's Pond, it was 1045 or over two-and-a-half years for water in the pond to get to the ocean! And all the water that stays in the pond is loaded with nitrogen from the various inputs identified in the nutrient loading study. That's a lot of time for the nitrogen to remain in the ponds.

The nitrogen coming into the ponds from all sources is reactive — the more there is, the more seaweed or plankton there is going to be. The longer it stays in one place, the longer it has to grow the plants. Thus, when the summer wind is calm and the plant growth is at its greatest, the plants don't move much just from the force of the tide. They merely rise and fall or stay on the sediment surface in the shallows. There may be slight movement of seaweeds around the ponds from the tidal current but it is not much in the larger scheme of things.

Many days are calm so there isn't much mixing with the deeper water in the pond. If only the top water gets exchanged on a tidal cycle, and plants decay on the bottom, the nutrients stay in the pond in the sediment unless that sediment is brought to the surface. Motor boats churn the water, bringing nitrogen-laden sediment closer to the surface where you might suspect it could be flushed out. A percentage does. But water that is not flushed out is more turbid because of the motor boats and the nitrogen becomes available for yet more plant growth. When the plants die, they're still in the pond, where they decompose, their nutrients bound in the sediment. So the nutrients stay there in the pond, for months or years, building up in the sediment after each annual growing cycle of the plants.

We, on the technical advisory committee, knew about nutrient loading and knew that the majority of nutrients came from the groundwater, which in turn came primarily from septic systems. We had the groundwater maps that delineated the watersheds, a flushing study that indicated how long it takes the water from the ponds to reach the ocean, and a nitrogen loading study based on the results of the other two. Now the planning process could go to the next and more difficult level of trying to address the effects of eutrophication.

Many people and labs have been testing the nutrient content of various bodies of water within the region and several groups developed ways to interpret the data. One of the most "user friendly" methods was developed by Dr. Joe Costa of the Buzzards Bay Program who sums factors to yield what is called "a pollution index". The index includes particular water quality parameters such as water clarity, dissolved oxygen, pH (acidity), salinity, nitrogen compounds, phosphate, and chlorophyll *a*. For each parameter, there is a range of values in the model from unimpacted to eutrophic.

Because of the variability of each of the Pleasant Bay segments, water quality from one area to another can be quite different. In an effort to refine our understanding of the bay, citizen water quality monitors have been invaluable assets to obtain the water samples.

Orleans has been using citizen water quality monitors for years, ever since the Friends of Meetinghouse Pond began taking water samples to identify sources of bacterial contamination. That effort was expanded through the Water Quality Task Force to monitor the drainage remediation program. They expanded the program to include several other water quality parameters and nutrient analysis. The volunteers not only learned how to take the samples, but they also learned how to analyze them (except for some complex nutrient analysis that was performed at a research laboratory) and they were the impetus behind developing a new water quality laboratory in town, staffed entirely by volunteers. The Orleans group found that the upper ponds were showing signs of declining water quality the first year they performed the tests in the late 1990s. When the numbers for the pollution index were applied for Pleasant Bay samples, the upper ponds were eutrophic. While they were anxious to get the information to the public, they recognized that it was the first year of such an effort by the volunteers and they felt the results needed review by independent authorities. Meanwhile, they planned for the next year.

Chatham had its own certified water quality laboratory. In Chatham, the testing was performed by Bob Duncanson, the Director of the Water Quality Laboratory, a specialist in this field. But Chatham, Harwich and Brewster also had people willing to participate in a water quality-monitoring program. The stage was set for the Pleasant Bay Alliance (the name for the implementation group under the plan) to embark on a bay-wide monitoring effort in 2000.

The Technical Advisory Committee of the Pleasant Bay Alliance recognized that coordination of testing was necessary. They wanted to get a snapshot of the entire bay during successive summers beginning in the summer of 2000 and sent out a call for volunteers. The response was tremendous. Boats, boat operators and volunteers answered the call. The Alliance set up 16 stations in Pleasant Bay for the project and added four stations in July 2002. Orleans had an additional 13 stations monitored by the town and Chatham has additional stations monitored by volunteers. Some of the town sampling is conducted more frequently than the Alliance monitoring program.

The monitors obtained the samples which were then brought to local, county and private research labs for analysis. The results were inserted into the pollution index model of each parameter for each body of water to determine how much the water had been impacted.

The pollution index proved to be a useful tool. Preliminary results from early years of data both from the Orleans group and the Alliance were not encouraging — the upper Bay and Chatham Muddy Creek and Frostfish Creek were showing signs of trouble. Now the information was coming from several sources: the flushing analysis and the water quality monitoring.

We could no longer ignore the fact that the water quality reprieve we had received as a result of the Chatham break in 1987 was no longer in effect. In a mere decade, the awesome changes we had witnessed just after the break were countered by nutrient loading. The costs of development had caught up with us. The news is a difficult adjustment for many of us to make but the signs have been there for several years. The numbers just confirmed our own suspicions.

Although the water quality news has been distressing, a positive aspect has been seen as well. The number of people involved in the monitoring effort served to heighten awareness of the problems facing the Bay.

This heightened awareness led to the formation of citizen groups. As mentioned earlier, the Friends of Pleasant Bay was formed in 1985 and Friends of Meetinghouse Pond was formed shortly thereafter.

Pam Herrick, a life-long resident of Lonnie's Pond, had a meeting of neighbors in the early 1990s, and asked me to attend and talk about the problems that were significant to that area. Lonnie's was special because two fresh water lakes flow directly into it. After a couple of years, the Friends of Lonnie's Pond was formed, along with a separate friends group for each lake. Then, in the late 1990s, Ken and Gussie McKusick formed the Friends of Arey's Pond. Several fresh-water ponds within the Pleasant Bay watershed also have a "friends" group.

Many members of the small pond groups are also members of the Friends of Pleasant Bay. A proposal to form a coalition of groups, while also maintaining individual identities, is under consideration in 2002. People who live near a small pond have a proprietary affection for the water in their back yard. As the seaweeds build up in the ponds, the residents are more and more anxious to have someone do *something* to alleviate the situation.

Unfortunately, there is no comparable group in the Nauset estuary except for the Mill Pond Association. Grand View Estates and Nauset Heights have neighborhood associations but Nauset, as a whole, does not enjoy the benefits of an organized group on both sides of the town line such as the Friends of Pleasant Bay.

The problems facing Pleasant Bay and all the other estuaries are overwhelming and "fixes" are elusive. Watershed management is extremely difficult because of the vast area of a watershed and the political difficulties involved in getting people to accept responsibility for harming a resource that may seem to them to "belong" to somebody else. It doesn't matter whether the watershed is a riverine system, where all the water from the surrounding highlands flows downhill into the river, or a groundwater watershed, where all the water in the ground eventually flows to the estuaries. Watersheds cross political boundaries and sources of a problem may be miles away from where the problem is seen.

The heartening aspect of the struggle we have been waging is the support we have had from the people in our quest to find solutions. The more people who are involved through testing, who become members of neighborhood associations, or embrace membership in larger regional groups like the Friends of Pleasant Bay, the more people there are who are willing to learn about the problems and gain an understanding of the complexities of the estuaries. It goes back to the tremendous number of people who have an emotional attachment to the area and are willing to do what they can to maintain its viability.

The Friends of Pleasant Bay awards grants each year to two local schools for programs about Pleasant Bay. The teachers who apply may have proposed curriculum that introduces young students to the wonders of Pleasant Bay, or developed year-long programs for older students to enhance their knowledge of the Bay. Each year, at the annual meeting, the students give a presentation of their program. These kids are the future and their insights are just wonderful. The resourcefulness of the teachers is tremendous and the audience has walked away on many a night grateful for the innovative projects the kids have undertaken.

And so, as I row around the Bay, I am depressed when I see floating seaweeds and muck along the shores and dwindling numbers of shellfish. I look at the eelgrass during the summer, hoping I will not see the weeds in among the eelgrass beds and epiphytes on the grass blades, but I do see both. I look longingly for scallops attached to the grass in the late summer, and find none. I look for clam holes and quahaugs and hope that some day I will see more in the Bay.

And then I go out on a particular early morning and see a small boat anchored near a small buoy and I row over and talk to the people in the skiff. They are taking water samples. Ordinary folks from all walks of life and diverse backgrounds who share a love of this place and who are willing to take time out of their lives to take classes and then use scientific equipment to take the samples. They laugh, saying they haven't handled such equipment since high school chemistry many, many years ago and wonder if they still remember anything. I laugh with them and tell them they are doing just fine and I'm so glad they are willing to do this. They tell me that they like coming out. It makes them feel needed, helpful, and just plain good that they are doing something worthwhile for the Bay.

There is a very long road ahead. But at this point, the people are willing to do whatever they can. The people themselves are one of the most important resources the towns have — and one of the greatest detractors because of sheer numbers. We know there are too many people, too many boats, too many septic systems, too much fertilizer and not enough land or water or shellfish to support us all. Now we have to fix what we have done by wanting to be here. We can only hope that new people moving to the Cape will quickly gain an appreciation for these magnificent coastal gems and join in the process to help protect them.

I may be depressed by what I see but I am also hopeful because of what I see. I hope generations down the road will be able to row around the Bay and gain the enjoyment I have been lucky enough to have. Giving up now is not an option.

Chapter 32

A New Day, New Hope

The Bay Plan and all the associated studies produced some very depressing information with respect to water quality issues. But the plan and its implementation have also fostered hope for the future. The fact that nutrient-laden groundwater takes 15-30 years to reach the estuary from houses built one to two miles from the shore, and that water takes one to two-and-a-half years to be flushed out from the ponds to the ocean, are causes for real concern. The water quality monitoring taking place all over the Bay is cementing that picture that all is definitely not well.

We are forced to conclude that the reprieve we received in water quality after the Chatham break in 1987 has ended, and we are now looking at a bay at nearly the same place it was before the break — a bay that was showing serious signs of eutrophication.

We are seeing the increasingly detrimental effects of this enriched groundwater entering the estuaries. Hefty research has taken place nationally over the past couple of decades to look at eutrophication, and comprehensive research locally over the past decade has focused on the problems of nutrient enrichment too. The numbers represent what is going into the ground now and consequently, what is going into the estuaries from the land. Although some effort has been aimed at planning for future growth and development, it is difficult to predict what will happen, though researchers are busy analyzing build-out models. But we know that what is entering the estuaries now is beyond the amount they can handle.

To make matters worse, what is in the ground now and flowing toward the estuaries can't be stopped, even if we stopped the flow of nitrogen from the land *today*. Since that is not likely to happen any time soon, now that we understand more about the mechanisms involved in nutrient loading and the effects on the estuaries, many people are trying to figure out how to work around this black cloud.

One way is to work from the land and address the nutrient loading from the source, our septic systems. Even though it will take a generation or more to see a difference, without addressing the nutrients at their source, the estuaries as we know them today are doomed.

As a prelude to action, the towns of Chatham, Orleans and Eastham and the Pleasant Bay Alliance have embarked on a massive sampling regimen to document the nutrient loading to the estuaries. This information, in concert with the groundwater mapping, the flushing analyses, and the nutrient loading models that will identify the critical nutrient loading or the maximum amount of nitrogen that can flow into the estuaries to maintain sustainability, will be used to develop comprehensive wastewater management plans in Orleans and Chatham.

Chatham is ahead of Orleans in this endeavor but "ahead" is a relative term. Already two years behind their original schedule, Chatham officials estimate ten more years for implementation before the entire program is in the ground and operational. The Chatham Board of Health is currently investigating interim regulations to address nutrient loading while the wastewater program continues, and part of their investigation has centered on existing development rather than the easier-to-deal-with new construction. Several options are currently being explored, ranging from a requirement that homeowners significantly reduce their contribution of nitrogen, to a less stringent proviso that would at least maintain the status quo with no net gain of nitrogen for any new project. Chatham is also examining trigger methods for the review process, including building and conservation commission permits.

The implications of such a review of existing development with respect to nitrogen loading for the entire town, based on building permits or conservation projects, are immense. As could be expected, those involved in land development have already stepped up to the public comment plate, very shortly after a newspaper review of the issue appeared in the local press.

The Orleans Board of Health is carefully watching Chatham's efforts as Orleans forges ahead with its own wastewater management plan. Although too early to tell, it is surmised that each watershed may have specific recommendations to implement and that the implementation measures may differ markedly from one to another.

As seen in Chatham, this approach will take years to develop and decades to prove fruitful. But it is a very positive and an essential step in the process.

There are other hopeful signs for the future of our estuaries as well, some coming from partnerships thought to be unlikely a mere decade ago. Two new regional groups have sprung up, both of which provide a forum for an exchange of radically different ideas.

One of those groups is the Cape Cod Center for Sustainability. Its council members hail from social, environmental and economic groups or businesses on the Cape.

The Sustainability Center developed a set of sustainability indicators from all three lenses — social, environmental and economic — based on the assets of each lens. Their premise is that it takes the positive overlapping of all three lenses for the region to be truly sustainable. Then the Center took the "pulse" of the Cape in accordance with the indicators. Their results have been publicized in newspaper articles and they have solicited public input from their "snapshot" glimpse of the Cape. In taking all three lenses into consideration, they can focus on those indicators that appear to need the most attention. With a set of indicators, they can track progress or slippage in any sector and suggest corrective actions. It is a useful tool that hopefully will continue.

Another group is the Business Round Table of the Association for the Preservation of Cape Cod the major Cape-wide environmental advocacy group. Comprised of environmental advocates and "well-known pillars of the Cape business community" according to the fortnightly Cape Cod Voice, the group meets to address major issues facing the Cape. The Round Table is a forum where participants "acknowledge the surprising number of issues on which there is common agreement." In the past, the two groups have more often been political adversaries, but the Voice reports that the business community is beginning to "mouth the slogan, 'The environment is the economy of Cape Cod'" and environmentalists have learned that "in order to live here, people need jobs and business need to grow". How both premises can be compatible is the subject for discussion. The group is perceived at this point as being in the political center, the only place where coalitions can be fruitful.

Together these two groups give hope that problems that cross social, economic and environmental boundaries might find common solutions, reached by consensus of all groups dedicated to preserving a sense of what the Cape is all about.

The second approach to solve the nutrient loading problem is to start from the water and work back upstream. Several new directions give me hope for the first time in years that we can begin to turn the situation in the estuaries around. The irony is that to do this, we need to look to shellfish.

Shellfish are filter feeders. They take in plankton in the water, convert it to energy so they can grow, and excrete waste products in the form of fine particles that get added to the sediment. These particles are acted upon by other organisms that de-nitrify — or change the composition — of the nitrogen so that it can exit the system more easily. In addition, when shellfish are harvested, the nitrogen in the shellfish is also removed. Of course, it's really part of the larger cycle — we eat shellfish locally and a portion enters our waste products that go into the septic system and back to the estuaries. But in the smaller view, shellfish can be a critical agent in obtaining water clarity through their filter-feeding ability, especially if there are lots of them.

In my conversations with colleagues about eutrophication, I pose many questions to gain a better understanding of how the systems work. At the latest international conference of the Estuarine Research Federation, the number of presentations dealing with eutrophication in some manner struck me as being remarkable. As I listened to the presentations, I thought of Lonnie's Pond, a small pond that had an explosion of macrophytes in the summer of 2001.

The water clarity in Lonnie's had been terrible as well that

summer and after I returned from the conference, I began to wonder: If seaweeds drive the system in the pond, what would happen if
the seaweeds were "harvested," and physically removed from the
system? Could it be done effectively? Would they grow back quickly
after they had been harvested? How often would the seaweeds have
to be removed? Would removing the "sink" of nitrogen make any
difference for the next year or would the nitrogen coming from the
land just continue to produce seaweeds regardless of the amount of
seaweeds removed? Could a program be designed to test these
questions? If it worked experimentally, could it work on a larger
scale in a pond perhaps? If the seaweeds were removed, would the
pond switch to a phytoplankton community? If it switched, could
shellfish be added to take up the plankton to clarify the water?

A grant proposal to address some of these questions, submitted
by colleagues from the University of Rhode Island, was not funded,
but the reviewers made some very helpful suggestions for grant
proposal improvements.

Even though that grant wasn't funded, my thought process has
continued. What if you just added shellfish in huge numbers? Would
that be enough to change the system somehow? In a plankton-
dominated system, if the phytoplankton is so thick that it causes the
water to change color, then if we add shellfish to the estuary in
sufficient numbers, will the shellfish filter enough water to keep the
system in a sort of balance? Do we know how much shellfish it will
take to make a difference? We do know how much nitrogen shellfish can remove from a system through their pumping activity, and
therefore, theoretically, is it possible to let the shellfish do the job?

Shellfish as clean-up organisms are being tried in several areas
around the world. Mussels, a species notorious for its pumping
ability, have been used in Europe to filter seriously eutrophic waters
with good success. But the biomass of the mussels has been tremendous. Mussels don't grow in the upper part of the Bay. But what
about oysters? They are also great at pumping seawater. We don't
have oysters in Pleasant Bay now but we have clams and quahaugs.
Although weaker on the pumping scale, could they be used?

These questions, plus a ton more, piqued my interest.

Then I heard a presentation in February 2002 about a program
in Long Island, New York, sponsored by Cornell University

Cooperative Extension. The program is called shellfish gardening. Briefly, the Extension obtains seed shellfish (mostly, if not all, from their own hatchery) that they give (or sell) to individuals. Each gardener gets 500 individuals that they grow in racks or trays, usually under a dock but not always. Half of the eventual adults go to the gardener for personal consumption and half are donated back to the Extension for public stock enhancement. The Extension even sets up plots for non-waterfront property owners so they can be a part of the program. According to the organizers, the program has been a huge success.

The Cornell Extension staff told of other shellfish gardening programs in other parts of the country. I followed up on several of them. There are programs in Virginia, Maryland, North and South Carolina and Louisiana. In Virginia, Sea Grant researchers started the program that is now a recognized independent association called Tidewater Oyster Growing Association. They started with a handful of individuals in the early 1990s and now have over 2000 participants. They have a "Master Gardener" program similar to the Cooperative Extension land-based Master Gardening program. These folks attend a rigorous and comprehensive 4-day training course to learn not only about the basics of growing shellfish and marine animal husbandry, but also learn about biology, diseases, genetics, and a host of more technical subjects.

In many of these programs, the object is not to grow shellfish for personal consumption but to grow shellfish strictly to assist in water quality improvement!

My mind was spinning. I could envision a program, started at the grass-roots level, where the people who are ready, willing and able could lend a hand. There are two community-sponsored hatcheries on the Cape, developed through partnerships. One is located next door in Eastham. The old boathouse Henry Lind first used has been replaced by a new greenhouse. The greenhouse hatchery is owned and operated by the Town of Eastham, but it is a joint program between Barnstable County and Eastham. They have a five-year commitment to serve low and moderate income fishermen and to raise seed for member towns. Barnstable County reimburses the town for labor and supplies, but there is an understanding that any seed raised will be shared by the member towns of Provincetown,

Truro, Wellfleet, Orleans, Brewster and Harwich. The towns support the project by purchasing nets and cages and they are supposed to help defray labor costs as well. The hatchery is producing and it is heavily involved in oyster production, a species in short supply and high demand in some of the member towns.

The second hatchery operates from a joint partnership among Barnstable County Extension, Southeast Massachusetts Aquaculture Center, Massachusetts Maritime Academy and Woods Hole Oceanographic Institution Sea Grant. The hatchery, located at Massachusetts Maritime Academy in Buzzards Bay, will be growing oysters for towns to use in restocking programs. The partners are encouraging towns to participate in a program to re-establish oyster reefs on the Cape. They will provide seed, culch and possibly even nursery bags if towns will do the growing.

These two hatcheries could become important for a citizen shellfish program, endorsed by the towns. With town departments low on time and resources, why not begin citizen shellfish gardens, especially in highly eutrophic ponds where there are already organizations comprised of people who are anxious to help? Sure, there are problems to overcome and the idea needs lots of discussion, but a potentially beneficial program like this needs to focus on the positive, not the naysaying that can get an idea really bogged down.

I think back at what has been accomplished with the water quality monitoring program. Starting with just me, taking samples and bringing them to a lab and then developing and operating a town water quality lab for fecal coliform analysis, to training a few individuals how to take samples, to training individuals in how to analyze samples in the lab, to a full-fledged water quality laboratory and many people involved in several sampling efforts. Look at the results of this program. People like Bob and Peg Wineman took on the responsibility for operating a water quality laboratory and analyzing results as volunteers. They and other volunteers in the water quality program yielded high quality data-gathering that matches certified laboratory results 1:1. It is very gratifying to see something so modest take on a life of its own with such incredible success, thanks to the dedication of the individuals involved.

If the people could do what they have done with water quality, think what they could do with shellfish restoration. A community-based shellfish restoration effort is just what the doctor ordered. It is grass-roots. It takes the burden off the Shellfish Department that is short-staffed. It gets people involved in solving a huge problem. If people get involved in growing shellfish, they will gain an understanding of the complexities involved in shellfish propagation. They will understand aquaculture better, both on the town level and at the private level. They will gain an understanding of estuarine ecology and the interconnectedness of everything within the estuaries. As a bonus, they may get to harvest their "crop" and they may begin to see positive results.

What a great way to get more shellfish in the water, the goal of the Shellfish Department when they hired me in 1974. What a great way to get back to the ideas generated by Dr. Belding at the turn of the 20th century when Massachusetts was among the highest-producing states for shellfish. What a great way to come full circle.

Rowing On

I retired from the town in July 1998, taking advantage of county retirement policies. It was time for me to move on.

For their annual meeting in 1999, the Friends of Pleasant Bay asked me to give a presentation focusing on a retrospective of changes I had observed over the years. I sat down with a few index cards and wrote thirteen phrases or topics that would key my memory as I spoke. My presentation was not exactly well rehearsed but they had given me a time-frame and I seem to recall that I managed to touch on all thirteen subjects within the allotted time. When I was finished, several members said that my comments reflected a perspective not often heard and they said it should be recorded in writing. Shortly after that meeting, the Friends asked me if I would write my comments and expand on them.

I agreed but had no idea when I started the project a couple of years later that it would lead to such an extensive manuscript. The Publications Committee of the Friends worked with me at the beginning to see what I could offer. We mutually agreed it was a project that would be difficult to accomplish by committee and Jeff McLaughlin stepped forward to work with me.

As I continued to receive moral and technical support from Jeff, who volunteered hundreds of hours to take on the job of personal editor for me, gently leading me each step of the way, I began to see the book as he saw it. He called it a "yarn," a personalized narrative covering a period of extraordinary change.

I realized that the quarter-century I spent working for the Town of Orleans were among the most fast-paced, chaotic years of the

20th century. The changes — physical, biological, social, economic and political — made everyone's head spin at times.

I also realized I had been in the vanguard of management issues that defined the period: public shellfish aquaculture on Cape Cod that led to private aquaculture; helping to develop and administer regulations for erosion control structures; recognizing the deficiency of the state law with respect to buffer zones and writing local buffer-zone regulations; developing a water quality program; helping to develop a new paradigm for determining the appropriateness of private docks in sensitive public waters; and helping four towns develop a resource management plan for Pleasant Bay. These were major and diverse management issues, all of which required me to look outside normal channels, to think and act innovatively. In doing so, I was bound to meet resistance, and I did. But I also found a spirit of cooperation that was, and is, immensely gratifying.

All that was a far cry from bullraking in Pleasant Bay, trying to find out why there weren't many quahaugs left.

When anyone asked me how I got the job, my answer was that I was lucky. I was in the right place at the right time. I was lucky and grateful that the town gave me the opportunity to work in a field of my choice in the town I have loved all my life. I was lucky to have Gardy as my first boss — he gave me the wings to fly. I was lucky to get to know the people who have consistently shown me that they too love this place (once they live here for a few years!).

But I am rowing forward. My priorities have changed and although I am still interested in the developments of the town heading into the future, I will work on projects where I can still have fun and enjoy what I am doing. Life is much too short not to, and as anyone who knows me knows, laughter really is the best medicine.

From a bench recently installed at the top of a hill overlooking the Town Cove, I can look across the Cove to Collins Landing where it all began. But now, I look at that water with a tremendous appreciation for all that it is, lucky that opportunities have been presented to me to learn about estuaries, and fortunate to live where I live.

I ran into Gardy shortly before I finished this project and told him that I was writing a book and that he figured prominently in it. I told him I had even included a section on the Clambulance, which made him laugh, and then I told him I wrote about the quahaug out-houses too. He laughed again, his 86-year-old body not as spry as it was almost 30 years ago but his sense of humor and twinkle still intact. He looked me in the eye and said, "Well, it seemed like a good idea at the time."

It sure did, Gardy, it sure did.

References

Beston, Henry, *The Outermost House, A Year on the Great Beach of Cape Cod*, Henry Holt and Co., New York, 1928, Introduction copyright Robert Finch, 1988.

Carson, Rachel, *Silent Spring*, Houghton Mifflin Co., New York, 1962.

Carson, Rachel, *Under the Sea Wind*, Oxford University Press, New York, 1952.

Darling, Warren S., *Quahoging out of Rock Harbor 1890-1930*, Privately printed by the author at Thompson's Printing, Inc., Orleans, MA, 1984.

Dunford, Fred and Greg O'Brien, *Secrets in the Sand*, Parnassus Imprints, Hyannis, MA, 1997.

Eldridge, Dana, *Cape Cod Lucky, In Another Time*, Illustrations by Louise Russell, Cover Illustration by Douglas W. Turner, Stony Brook Publishing and Productions, Inc., Brewster, MA, 2000.

Eldridge, Dana, *Once Upon Cape Cod: From Cockle Cove To the Powder Hole*, Illustrations by Robert LaPointe, Stony Brook Publishing and Productions, Brewster, MA, 1997.

Finch, Robert, Outlands, *Journeys to the Outer Edges of Cape Cod*, David R. Godine, Publisher, Boston, 1986.

Finch, Robert; Photographs by Ralph MacKenzie, *The Cape Itself*, W.W. Norton and Co., New York, 1991.

Hay, John, *The Great Beach*, Ballantine Books, New York, 1963.

Hay, John, *The Sandy Shore*, The Chatham Press, Inc., Chatham, MA, 1968.

Junger, Sebastian, *The Perfect Storm*, Harper Paperbacks, New York, 1997.

Monbleau, Marcia, *Pleasant Bay, Stories from a Cape Cod Place*, Friends of Pleasant Bay, 1999.

Nickerson, Joshua Atkins 2nd, *Days to Remember,* Chatham Historical Society, Chatham, MA, 1988.

Nickerson, W. Sears, *The Bay – as I see it*, Privately printed, 1981; Reprinted 1995 by the Friends of Pleasant Bay, So. Orleans, MA 1981.

Odum, Eugene P. *Fundamentals of Ecology*, Second Edition, W.B. Saunders Co., Philadelphia, 1959.

Oldale, Robert N., *Cape Cod and the Islands, The Geologic Story*, Parnassus Imprints, Orleans, MA, 1992.

Richardson, Wyman, *The House on Nauset Marsh*, Illustrations by Henry Bugbee Kane, The Chatham Press, Riverside, CT, 1947, Reprinted 1972.

Ridgway, John and Hay Blithe, *A Fighting Chance*, J.B. Lippincott Co., Philadelphia, 1967.

Sargent, William, *Shallow Waters, A Year on Cape Cod's Pleasant Bay*, Houghton Mifflin Co., Boston, MA,1981, 134 pp.

Schwind, Phil, *Practical Shellfish Farming*, Illustrated by Coralee Spracht Hays, International Marine Publishing Company, Camden, ME, 1997.

Strahler, Arthur N., *A Geologist's View of Cape Cod*, 1966, Parnassus Imprints, Orleans, MA 1988.

Teal, John and Mildred Teal, *Life and Death of the Salt Marsh*, Drawings by Richard Fish, Little, Brown and Co., Boston, 1969.

Thoreau, Henry David, *The Writings of Henry D. Thoreau, Cape Cod*, Edited by Joseph J. Moldenhauer, Princeton University Press, Princeton, NJ, 1988.

Wood, Donald, *Cape Cod, A Guide*, Little, Brown and Co., Boston, MA, 1973.

Wood, Timothy J., *Breakthrough, The Story of Chatham's North Beach*, Hyora Publications, Chatham, MA. 1988-2002.

Guide Books

Amos, William H. and Stephen H. Amos, *The Audubon Society Nature Guides, Atlantic and Gulf Coasts*, Alfred A. Knopf, New York, 1988.

Bigelow, Henry B. and William C. Schroeder, *Fishes of the Gulf of Maine*, Fishery Bulletin of the Fish and Wildlife Service, Volume 53, United States Government Printing Office, Washington, DC, 1953.

Gosner, Kenneth L., *A Field Guide to the Atlantic Seashore from the Bay of Fundy to Cape Hatteras*, Houghton Mifflin Company, Boston, 1978.

Kingsbury, John M.; Illustrations by Edward and Marcia Norman, *Seaweeds of Cape Cod and the Islands*, Chatham Press, Inc., Chatham, MA, 1969.

Morris, Percy A., *A Field Guide to Shells of the Atlantic and Gulf Coasts and the West Indies*, Houghton Mifflin Company, Boston, 1973.

Robins, Sarah Fraser and Clarice Yentsch, *The Sea is All About Us, A Guide to the Marine Environments of Cape Ann and other Northern New England Waters,* The Peabody Museum of Salem and the Cape Ann Society for Marine Science, Inc., Harcourt Brace Jovanovich, Inc. Publishers. 1973.

Sterling, Dorothy; Illustrations by Winifred Lubell, *The Outer Lands, A Natural History Guide to Cape Cod, Martha's Vineyard, Nantucket, Block Island and Long Island,* The American Museum of Natural History, Natural History Press, Garden City, New York, 1967.

Thorson, Gunnar, *Life in the Sea*, Translated from the Danish by Manon C. Meilgaard and Alec Laurie, World University Library, McGraw-Hill, New York, 1971, reprinted 1978.

Zinn, Donald, *A Handbook for Beach Strollers*, University of Rhode Island Marine Bulletin Number 12, University of Rhode Island, Kingston, RI, Third Printing, 1974.

Zinn, Donald, *Marine Mollusks of Cape Cod*, Cape Cod Museum of Natural History, Natural History Series No. 2, Cape Cod Museum of Natural History, Brewster, MA, 1984.

Reports, Plans, Technical Papers and Statutes

Anderson, D.M., 1979. Toxic dinoflagellate blooms in the Cape Cod region of Massachusetts. Pp. 145-150. In D.L. Taylor and H. Seliger (eds.). Toxic Dinoflagellate Blooms, Developments in Marine Biology, vol. 1. Elsevier/North Holland, New York.

Aubrey, D., G. Voulgaris, W.D. Spencer and S. O'Malley, 1997. Tidal residence time within the Nauset Marsh system. Rep. Submitted to the Town of Orleans, Woods Hole Oceanographic Institution, Department of Geology and Geophysics, Woods Hole, MA.

Bayes, J.C. 1981. Forced upwelling nurseries for oysters and clams using impounded water systems. Pp. 73-83. In: C.Claus, N. DePauw and E. Jaspers (eds.). Nursery Culturing of Bivalve Molluscs. Spec. Publ. 7, European Mariculture Society, Bredene, Belgium.

Belding, D.L., 1910. The scallop fisheries of Massachusetts: Including an account of the natural history of the common scallop. Commonwealth of Massachusetts Commission on Fisheries and Game, Marine Series No. 3, Boston, MA.

Belding, D.L. 1912. A report upon the quahog and oyster fisheries of Massachusetts, including the life history, growth and cultivation of the quahog. Department of Conservation,

Commonwealth of Massachusetts. Wright and Porter Printing Co., Boston, MA.

Belding, D.L. 1930. The Soft-shelled clam fishery of Massachusetts. Massachusetts Department of Fisheries and Game, Boston MA. Originally published in 1907, republished in 1916 with new material and again in 1930.

Buzzards Bay Comprehensive Conservation and Management Plan. 1991. Buzzards Bay Project, Vol. 1. United States Environmental Protection Agency and Massachusetts Executive Office of Environmental Affairs, Boston, MA.

Castagna, M. and J.N. Kraeuter, 1981. Manual for growing the hard clam, Mercenaria. Spec. Rept. 249 in Ocean Engineering and Applied Marine Science, Virginia Institute of Marine Science.

Commonwealth of Massachusetts, Massachusetts General Laws, Chapter 130. Pertaining to Marine Fisheries.

Commonwealth of Massachusetts, Massachusetts General Laws, Chapter 131. Pertaining to Wetlands Protection.

Crawford, R.E., N.E. Stolpe and M.J. Moore. 1998. The Environmental Impacts of Boating. Proceedings of a workshop held at Woods Hole Oceanographic Institution, Woods Hole, MA, December 7-9, 1994. Technical Report WHOI-98-03. Woods Hole Oceanographic Institution, Woods Hole, MA.

Eichner, Edward M., and Thomas C. Cambareri, 1992. Nitrogen loading. Technical Bulletin 91-001, Cape Cod Commission, Barnstable, MA.

Fisk, J.D., C.E. Watson and P.G. Coates, 1967. A study of the marine resources of Pleasant Bay. Commonwealth of Massachusetts Division of Marine Fisheries, Monograph Series 5.

Geist, M.A. (ed.). 1996. The ecology of the Waquoit Bay National Estuarine Research Reserve, Massachusetts Department of Environmental Management, Forests and Parks-Region 1, Waquoit, MA.

Geist, M.A., 1998. Local and Global Effects of Human Induced alterations to the Nitrogen Cycle, Waquoit Bay NERR Science and Policy Bulletin Series No. 6. Waquoit Bay National Estuarine Research Reserve, Waquoit, MA.

Giese, G.S., D.A. Aubrey, and J.T. Liu, 1989. Development, characteristics and effects of the new Chatham Harbor inlet. Technical Report #89-19, Woods Hole Oceanographic Institution, Woods Hole, MA.

Hardin, G. 1968. Tragedy of the Commons, Science 162:1243-1248.

Hidu, H., 1969. Gregarious settling in the American oyster, *Crassostrea virginica*, Gmelin. Chesapeake Science, 10:85-92.

Judson, W.I., R. Macpherson, P. Stewart and W.N. Carver, 1977. Culture of the quahog from hatchery-spawned seed stock. Prince Edward Island Department of Fisheries, Charlottetown, Prince Edward Island, Tech. Rept. Series 185.

Kassner, J. and R.E. Malouf. 1982. An evaluation of "spawner transplants" as a management tool in Long Island's hard-clam fishery. J. Shellfish Res. 2:165-172.

Kraeuter, J.N. and M. Castagna, eds. 2001. Biology of the Hard Clam. Developments in Aquaculture and Fisheries Science, Volume 31. Elsevier, NY.

Loosanoff, V.L. and H.C. Davis 1963. Rearing of bivalve mollusks. Adv. Mar. Biol. 1:1-136.

Lutz, R.A., ed.1980. Mussel Culture and Harvest: A North American Perspective. Developments in Aquaculture and Fisheries Science, Volume 7. Elsevier, NY.

Macfarlane, S.L. 1991. Managing scallops Argopecten irradians irradians (Lamark, 1819) in Pleasant Bay, Massachusetts: large is not always legal. In S.E. Shumway and P.A. Sandifer, (eds.) An International Compendium of Scallop Biology and Culture, World Aquaculture Society, pp. 264-272.

Macfarlane, S.L., 1995. Shellfish as the impetus for embayment management. Estuaries, 19 (2A): 311-319.

Macfarlane, S.L., 1998. The evolution of a municipal quahaug (Hard Clam) *Mercenaria mercenaria* management program: a twenty-year history, 1975-1995. Journal of Shellfish Research, 17(4):1015-1036.

Macfarlane, S.L., 1999. Bay Scallops in Massachusetts Waters: A Review of the Fishery and Prospects for Enhancement/Aquaculture. Report to the Southeast Massachusetts Aquaculture Center and Barnstable County Cooperative Extension, Barnstable, MA. 45 pp.

Macfarlane, S.L., J. Early, T. Balog, T. Henson and A. McClennen, 2000. A resource-based methodology to assess dock and pier impacts in Pleasant Bay, MA. Journal Shellfish Research, 19(1):455-464.

Metcalf and Eddy, Inc. 1993. Stormwater Control Facilities. A report submitted to the Town of Orleans, Orleans, MA.

Pleasant Bay Technical Advisory Committee and Ridley & Associates, Pleasant Bay Resource Management Plan, 1998. Prepared for the Pleasant Bay Steering Committee. 163 pp.

Ramsey, J.S. 1997. Hydrodynamic and Tidal Flushing Study of Pleasant Bay Estuary, MA. Aubrey Consulting, Inc., Cataumet, MA.

Roman, C.T., K.W. Able, K.L. Heck, Jr., J.W. Portnoy, M.P. Fahay, D.G. Aubrey, and M.A. Lazzari, 1989. An ecological analysis of Nauset Marsh, Cape Cod National Seashore, National Park Service Cooperative Research Unit. Wellfleet, MA.

Shumway, S.E., ed. Scallops: Biology, Ecology and Aquaculture. Developments in Aquaculture and Fisheries Science, Volume 21. Elsevier, NY. 1991.

Speer, P.E., D.G. Aubrey, and E. Ruder. 1982. Beach changes at Nauset Inlet, Cape Cod, Massachusetts 1640-1981. Woods Hole Oceanographic Institution technical report WHOI-82-40. Woods Hole, MA.

Teal, John M., 1983. The coastal impact of ground water discharge: an assessment of anthropogenic nitrogen loading in town cove, Orleans, MA. Final Report (WHOI Proposal No. 2778), Woods Hole Oceanographic Institution, Woods Hole, MA.

U.S. Army Corps of Engineers, 1968. Pleasant Bay, Chatham, Orleans, Harwich, Massachusetts. Survey Report. Department of the Army, New England Division, Corps of Engineers, Waltham, MA.

Valiela, I., K. Forman, M. LaMontagne, D. Hersh, J. Costa, P. Peckol, B. DeMeo-Anderson, C. D'Avanzo, M. Babione, C.H. Sham, J. Brawley, and K. Lajtha. 1992. Couplings of watersheds and coastal waters: sources and consequences of nutrient enrichment in Waquoit Bay, Massachusetts. Estuaries 15:443-457.

Valiela, I., G. Collins, J. Kremer, K. Lajtha, M. Geist, B. Seely, J. Brawley, and C. H. Sham, 1997. Nitrogen loading from coastal watersheds to receiving estuaries: New method and application. Ecological Applications 7(2): 358-380.